A Bibliography of Business Ethics, 1976–1980

Publications of the Colgate Darden Graduate School of Business Administration of the University of Virginia available from the University Press of Virginia

Bank Expansion in Virginia, 1962–1966: The Holding Company and the Direct Merger. By Paul Foster.

A Bibliography of Business Ethics, 1971–1975. By Donald G. Jones.

A Financial Planning Model for Private Colleges: A Research Report. By William J. Arthur.

A Selected Bibliography of Applied Ethics in the Professions, 1950–1970: A Working Sourcebook with Annotations and Indexes. By Daniel L. Gothie.

J. P. Morgan, Jr., 1867–1943. By John Douglas Forbes.

A Bibliography of

Business Ethics

1976–1980

Donald G. Jones, *Senior Editor*

and

Helen Troy

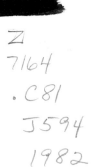
Published for
The Center for the Study of Applied Ethics
The Colgate Darden Graduate School
of Business Administration, University of Virginia

University Press of Virginia
Charlottesville

THE UNIVERSITY PRESS OF VIRGINIA
Copyright © 1982 by the Rector and Visitors
of the University of Virginia

First published 1982

Library of Congress Cataloging in Publication Data
Jones, Donald G.
A bibliography of business ethics, 1976–1980.
(Publications of the Colgate Darden Graduate School of Business
Administration of the University of Virginia)
1. Business ethics—Bibliography. 2. Industry—Social aspects—
Bibliography. I. Troy, Helen. II. Colgate Darden Graduate
School of Business Administration. Center for the Study of Applied
Ethics. III. Title. IV. Series
Z7164.C81J594 [HF5387] 016.174′4 81-16003
ISBN 0-8139-0921-X AACR2

Printed in the United States of America

Contents

Foreword

This reference volume in business ethics is the third in a series of bibliographies issued by the Center for the Study of Applied Ethics at the University of Virginia's Darden Graduate Business School. The first, *A Selected Bibliography of Applied Ethics in the Professions*, covered the period 1950 through 1970. The second, *The Bibliography of Business Ethics*, covered the years 1971 through 1975. This, the third, extends the coverage through the end of 1980.

This volume, like its predecessors, is extensive, with over 2,700 entries being included. The importance of business ethics is continuing to grow apace in both the academic and the business world, and the need for ready reference to useful materials is both essential and encouraging. The Center for the Study of Applied Ethics considers its bibliographical activities to be a major contribution to this important field.

Preparation of this volume has been the joint effort of Professor Donald G. Jones of Drew University and the library staff of the Darden School at the University of Virginia, including librarian Henry W. Wingate and research assistant Helen M. Troy. Their combined efforts have produced a reference book that will serve the interests of both college and business libraries.

The Center for the Study of Applied Ethics is dedicated to stimulating interest in and understanding of the ethical implications that are inherent in the management of organizations. Out of its efforts in research, publications, and conferences, the Center strives to inculcate high standards of business conduct. This bibliography is a major contribution toward that objective.

Louis T. Rader, Director
The Center for the Study
of Applied Ethics

Acknowledgments

This bibliography owes a great deal to Dean C. Stewart Sheppard, whose commitment to the scholarly pursuit and practical implementation of business ethics is without question. Under his encouragement and sponsorship the previous volume, *A Bibliography of Business Ethics, 1971–1975*, and now this five-year update have been published. My greatest debt is to Helen Troy, who as coauthor with me in this project spent many long hours doing both creative bibliographical searches and precise proofing. Her background in library science and graduate business education was an invaluable resource in the preparation of this bibliography.

We are both indebted to staff and academic assistants at Drew University and the University of Virginia. Thanks go to Bruce Grob from the graduate school at Drew University and William P. Beaman and Barry R. Lawrence from the Darden School at the University of Virginia for conscientious and expert editorial guidance. Our gratitude goes to numerous staff and academic assistants, but especially Mary Blair Gibson and Emily Moody of the Darden School and Frances Thompson, Diane Bennett, and Guenter Piehler of Drew.

Finally, thanks are due to Henry Wingate, librarian of the Darden School, for his competent and gracious administrative direction throughout the preparation of this bibliography.

D.G.J.

Madison, New Jersey
Summer 1981

Introduction

Background and Genesis

A project of the Center for the Study of Applied Ethics at the Darden Graduate School of Business Administration, this is the third bibliographic reference guide produced by CSAE in the last decade. The first was the wide-ranging *Selected Bibliography of Applied Ethics in the Professions, 1950–1970*. The second, *A Bibliography of Business Ethics: 1971–1975*, narrowed the focus to business and management ethics. The present volume is a five-year update of most of the categories in the second volume. The years 1976 through 1980 were, however, years of continuing ethical change in business and society. Hence this third bibliography, while updating the second, does contain new and changed categories.

The aim has been to cover the entire field of business and management ethics, selecting pertinent materials that are weighty or that break new ground. The latter criterion has allowed inclusion of nonweighty articles such as a trade journal piece about "A New Code of Ethics for Accountants" and a one-page feature in a magazine on "The Teaching of Ethics in Industry."

Government documents—including hearings, investigative reports, and studies—have been excluded on account of their ready availability and overwhelming numbers. Aside from this sizable exclusion, an effort has been made to be as selective as possible over the entire range of materials, knowing that a selective bibliographer's reach must always exceed his grasp.

Although offered as a comprehensive bibliography, this volume makes that claim only for English-language printed materials published primarily in the United States. Its comprehensiveness includes books, articles, and monographs from a variety of disciplines and perspectives. The cross-disciplinary mix includes management studies, philosophical ethics, economics, policy studies, religious social ethics, sociology, psychology, law, and history. Beyond the academic disciplines, literature cited in this volume includes the perspectives of practicing business managers—from middle to top.

At the outset, the intention was to cross-reference and annotate most, if not all, items. It soon became clear, as the quantity of entries grew, that this high-minded goal was impractical. The volume would have been more than twice its present size. The cost would have been formidable for most purchasers, and the publication date would have been pushed back so far as to erode timely usefulness. Choosing to go without annotations and cross-referencing was one of those critical trade-off decisions characteristic of the many quandaries represented in the citations of this bibliography.

Preparation involved several search methods. Relevant computer services at university and business libraries were employed. Periodical indexes, book indexes, guides, abstracts, and digests were consulted, both for primary data and in order to cross-check computer information. Besides these routine ways of gathering and cross-checking bibliographical citations, there were also more direct methods. Book reviews and notes were read in appropriate journals. Data were gleaned, too, from major books on business ethics by examining their footnotes and bibliographies.

This multiple methodology functioned as a quality control system, undergirded by the practice of verifying citations. More than 90 percent of the citations were verified by going directly to primary sources to see if the material existed and to be assured of its relevance.

The mixture of search methods and quality checks yielded a total of 649 book entries and 2,092 article and monograph entries for the years 1976–1980. The numbers are considerably larger than those for the 1971–1975 bibliography, which cited 501 books and 1,087 articles.

Scope and Organization

Five major categories structure this bibliography:
    Business Ethics: General Works
    Business Ethics and Management Issues
    Business and Social Responsibility
    Business and Society: Particular Issues
    Theoretical and Applied Ethics
The first category includes basic studies and texts with general overviews, comments, practical guidance, and theoretical and advocacy contributions. Here the researcher will find a number of introductory texts for the teaching of business ethics, such as *Ethical Theory and Business*, edited by Tom L. Beauchamp and Norman E. Bowie, and *Ethical Issues in Business: A Philosophical Approach*, edited by Thomas Donaldson and Patricia H. Werhane. The section also functions as a miscellaneous bin. If an item would not fit elsewhere, it was tossed into this more general category.

In contrast, the second category focuses on particular questions arising within functional areas of corporate management. Thirteen areas are arranged alphabetically, from "Accounting" to "Research and Development."

The third category, "Business and Social Responsibility," centers on the continuing debate over the meaning, limits, and extent of the social responsibility of business. The section also includes materials on the social control of business—for example, the book *Where the Law Ends* by Christopher Stone.

The fourth category, "Business and Society: Particular Issues," attempts to identify wider issues. The subject matter tends to fall outside of traditional management roles and a self-contained market system. Indeed, the section focuses on issues that fall in the cracks between the market and the macroenvironment of business. Most of the citations reflect a new interface between business and external publics, new environments, changing societal values, and the new era of business accountability.

The final category, "Theoretical and Applied Ethics," cites books and articles that explore the meaning of ethics and justice or that offer metaethical reflections on the principles of the market economy. It also includes, on the applied side, descriptive and normative works on codes of conduct and self-regulation and materials pertaining to the burgeoning literature on teaching business ethics. In its final subsection, "Religion and Business," the category documents both theological reflections on business enterprise and the sociological dynamics of the current confrontation between religion and business.

The Field of Business Ethics

What Is Ethics?

At rock bottom, ethics looks at who is getting hurt and how much, and at who is being helped and how much. Concerned with actions and social arrangements that inflict harm or promote human welfare, ethics aims to minimize the former and maximize the latter. The task of ethics, then, is the systematic study of the ethical values that ought to guide human conduct; the study of what constitutes the obligations and responsibilities of agents and institutions; the examination of predictable outcomes in human costs and benefits; the study of character traits or dispositions—all in the interest of promoting human welfare.

The four points of entry into ethical study—values, obligations, costs and benefits, character—apply to institutional arrangements as well as individuals. Ethics is just as concerned with policies, planning, and organization as it is with individual behavior. Unfair policies, short-sighted planning, and ill-conceived organizational structures can maim humans and inflict social injury to a far greater degree than individual malfeasance. For the same reason, ethics is just as concerned with the character of organizational life as with individual character formation.

In sum, ethics is orderly, rational reflection on spheres of life where there is actual or potential human harm or benefit. Hence, the field of social ethics has traditionally included political ethics, medical ethics, military ethics, legal ethics, the ethics of human sexuality, marriage and family ethics, and the ethics of the economic order.

The New Concern with Business Ethics

In recent years professional ethicists, management theorists, policy experts, sociologists, and culture critics have combined to develop the emerging discipline of business ethics. Classroom courses in business ethics have increased exponentially. Several executive development and management training programs and numerous forums, symposia, and workshops have been offered. The books, articles, and monographs published in the field in the past few years represent an explosion. Business ethics has become a growth market.

Interest in the subject is widespread but comes primarily from two groups: academicians and business people. It has gradually occurred to a number of professional ethicists that the weakest part of their discipline has been the application of ethical theory to business. Professional business managers and training specialists have become aware that what has been missing from their pragmatic, scientific, and technologically oriented learning is an ethical and humanistic dimension.

The emergence of business ethics as a new interest owes much to a simple but profound fact. National and multinational corporations are the most characteristic feature of contemporary democratic society. They impinge on the life of people in North America, Japan, and most of Western Europe, much in the way that the Roman Catholic Church impinged on the lives of people in medieval Europe.

Academicians and business managers have gradually come to understand the dominance of business in our culture. The understanding has engendered a sense of obligation to accommodate the power and pervasiveness of corporate organization and management conduct to ethical theory.

The need for a more refined, intellectually rigorous, and, at the same time, practical application of ethics to business has been felt for a variety of reasons. One of the most compelling is the discovery that traditional means of ethical governance, the market and the law, no longer work well enough to guide business decision making in a large number of new and complex areas. The old "market ethics" and the new "regulation and litigious ethics" need supplementation.

Business ethics provides this supplementation by applying ethical theory and relevant knowledge from other disciplines to areas of business not adequately, or perhaps wrongly, covered by the market and the law. The focal point of business ethics is the intersection of normal business goals and strategies with the specifically human ends. Issues of personal and social injury and of human welfare are touchstones of the field.

Among business issues currently under ethical scrutiny are product quality and safety; fairness in hiring, promoting, and firing; just prices and profits; disclosure and client loyalty in accounting; workplace quality and safety; truthfulness in advertising; bribery; whistle-blowing; the impact of multinational firms on host countries; the complex set of trade-offs involving environment, energy, employment, and inflation; and the larger issues of wealth production and distribution in a market economy.

This list of issues suggests the cross-disciplinary nature of business ethics. Among the fields obviously involved are applied social ethics, management science, policy studies, economics, sociology, psychology, history, and law. Business management, too, is a necessary component. Just as physicians have been primary participants in the development of medical ethics, so business managers have become essential contributors to the emergence of business ethics.

While ethics is not new, business ethics, with its focus on management, is. Despite the inevitable disarray of a nascent discipline, it is already clear that business ethics is no fad. Rather, it is a serious, long-term effort to apply ethical theory systematically to a profoundly significant sector of national and global life.

Intended to clarify the subject and help readers identify specific issues through orderly categorization, this bibliography documents the rapid development of a new field with the expectation of playing a role in the development of a consensus as to its meaning and worth.

Donald G. Jones

Business Ethics: General Works

Business Ethics: General Works

Books

Armerding, George D., and Phil Landrum. *The Dollars and Sense of Honesty: Stories from the Business World*. New York: Harper & Row, 1979.

Barry, Vincent. *Moral Issues in Business*. Belmont, Calif.: Wadsworth Publishing Co., 1979.

Baum, Robert. *Ethical Arguments for Analysis*. New York: Holt, Rinehart, and Winston, 1976.

Beauchamp, Tom L., and Norman E. Bowie, eds. *Ethical Theory and Business*. Englewood Cliffs, N.J.: Prentice-Hall, 1979.

Bergier, Jacques. *Secret Armies: The Growth of Corporate Industrial Espionage*. Indianapolis: Bobbs-Merrill Co., 1976.

Brown, Courtney C. *Beyond the Bottom Line*. New York: Macmillan, 1979.

Callis, Robert, ed. *Ethical Standards Casebook*. Falls Church, Va.: American Personnel and Guidance Association, 1976.

Clinard, Marshall B., and Peter C. Yeager. *Corporate Crime*. New York: Free Press, 1980.

Dam, Cees van, and Laud M. Stallaert, eds. *Trends in Business Ethics: Implications for Decision Making*. Boston: Kluwer, 1978.

Danner, Peter L. *An Ethics for the Affluent*. Washington, D.C.: University Press of America, 1980.

D'Aprix, Roger M. *In Search of a Corporate Soul*. New York: American Management Association, 1976.

Davids, Lewis E. *What Every Director Should Know about Corporate Ethics*. St. Louis: Director Publications, 1978.

DeGeorge, Richard T., and Joseph A. Pichler, eds. *Ethics, Free Enterprise, and Public Policy: Original Essays on Moral Issues in Business*. New York: Oxford University Press, 1978.

DeMente, Boye. *Japanese Manners and Ethics in Business*. Paradise Valley, Ariz.: Phoenix Books, 1976.

Donaldson, Thomas, and Patricia Werhane, eds. *Ethical Issues in Business: A Philosophical Approach*. Englewood Cliffs, N.J.: Prentice-Hall, 1979.

Dworkin, Gerald, Gordon Beemanto, and Peter G. Brown, eds. *Markets and Morals*. Washington, D.C.: Hemisphere Publishing Corp., 1977.

Engelbourg, Saul. *Power and Morality: American Business Ethics, 1840–1914.* Westport, Conn.: Greenwood Press, 1980.

Epstein, Edwin M., and Dow Votaw, eds. *Legitimacy, Responsibility, and Rationality.* Santa Monica, Calif.: Goodyear, 1978.

Evans, William A. *Management Ethics: An Intercultural Perspective.* Boston: Martinus Nijhoff, 1981.

Geis, Gilbert, and Robert S. Meier. *White Collar Crime: Offenses in Business, Politics, and Professions.* New York: Free Press, 1977.

Gelinier, Octave. *The Enterprise Ethic.* Central Islip, N.Y.: Transatlantic, 1980.

Hess, J. Daniel. *Ethics in Business and Labor.* Scottsdale, Pa: Herald Press, 1977.

Hill, Ivan, ed. *The Ethical Basis of Economic Freedom.* Chapel Hill, N.C.: American Viewpoint, 1976.

Hoffman, W. Michael, ed. *Proceedings of the First National Conference on Business Ethics.* Waltham, Mass.: Center for Business Ethics at Bentley College, 1977.

Hoffman, W. Michael, ed. *Proceedings of the 2nd National Conference on Business Ethics.* Wolfe City, Tex.: University Press of America, 1979.

Jones, Donald G. *A Bibliography of Business Ethics, 1971–1975.* Charlottesville: University Press of Virginia, 1977.

Kaufman, Andrew L. *Problems in Professional Responsibility.* Boston: Little, Brown and Co., 1976.

Kintner, Earl W. *A Primer on the Law of Deceptive Practices: A Guide for Business.* New York: Macmillan, 1978.

Kranzberg, Melvin, ed. *Ethics in an Age of Pervasive Technology.* Boulder, Colo.: Westview 1980.

Kugel, Yerachmiel, and Gladys W. Gruenberg, eds. *Ethical Perspectives on Business and Society.* Lexington, Mass.: D. C. Heath and Co., 1977.

LaCroiz, W. L. *Principles for Ethics in Business.* Washington, D.C.: University Press of America, 1979.

Litschert, Robert J., et al. *The Corporate Role and Ethical Behavior: Concepts and Cases.* New York: Van Nostrand Reinhold Co., 1977.

Moffitt, Donald, ed. *Swindled! Classic Business Frauds of the Seventies.* Princeton: Dow Jones Books, 1976.

Moskowitz, Milton R., Michael Katz, and Robert Levering, eds. *Everybody's Business: An Almanac.* San Francisco: Harper and Row, 1980.

Parker, Donn B., ed. *Ethical Conflicts in Computer Science and Technology.* Menlo Park, Calif.: Stanford Research Institute, 1978.

Purcell, Theodore V., and James Weber, S.J. *Institutionalizing Corporate Ethics: A Case History.* New York: The Presidents Association, 1979.

Robinson, Henry Mauris. *Relativity in Business Morals.* New York: Houghton Mifflin Co., 1978.

Rohr, John A. *Ethics for Bureaucrats: An Essay on Law and Values.* Park Forest South, Ill.: Governors State University, 1978.

Selekman, Sylvia Kopald, and Benjamin M. Selekman. *Power and Morality in a Business Society.* Westport, Conn.: Greenwood Press, 1978.

Simon, William E. *A Time for Truth.* New York: McGraw-Hill, 1978.

Sobel, Lester A., ed. *Corruption in Business.* New York: Facts on File, 1977.

Southard, Samuel. *Ethics for Executives.* New York: Cornerstone, 1977.

Stevens, Edward. *Business Ethics.* New York: Paulist Press, 1979.

Sufrin, Sidney C. *Management of Business Ethics.* Port Washington, N.Y.: Kennikat Press, 1980.

Twentieth Air Force Academy Assembly. *The Ethics of Corporate Conduct.* Englewood Cliffs, N.J.: Prentice-Hall, 1978.

Uris, Auren. *The Blue Book of Broadminded Business Behavior.* New York: Harper and Row, 1977.

Veri, Anthony. *The New Moral Code of Action for the Large Corporation's Executive.* Albuquerque, N.M.: American Classical Collegiate Press, 1977.

Walton, Clarence C., ed. *The Ethics of Corporate Conduct.* Englewood Cliffs, N.J.: Prentice-Hall, 1977.

Wheatley, Edward W. *Values in Conflict.* Miami: Banyan Books, 1976.

Whiteside, Thomas. *Computer Capers: Tales of Electronic Thievery, Embezzlement, and Fraud.* New York: Thomas Y. Crowell Co., 1978.

Articles

Agee, William M. "The Moral and Ethical Climate in Today's Business World." *MSU Business Topics* 26 (Winter 1978), 16–19.

Allen, Fred T. "Corporate Morality: Executive Responsibility." *Atlanta Economic Review* 26 (May–June 1976), 8–11.

Allen, Fred T. "Should Corporate Ethics Be Regulated?" *Management Review* 66 (May 1977), 16–17.

Andrews, Frederick. "Corporate Ethics: A Report and Talks Held off the Record." *New York Times* (April 18, 1977), 49–52.

Arlow, Peter, and Thomas A. Ulrich. "Auditing Your Organization's Ethics." *Internal Auditor* 37 (August 1980), 26–31.

Arras, John D. "Medicine Men, Businessmen." *The Hastings Center Report* 10 (June 1980), 41–43.

Ashe, T. Michael. "Insider Dialing—What Can and Should Be Done?" *Accountancy* 87 (June 1976), 50–52.

Beran, Walter F. "How to Be Ethical in an Unethical World: Ten Commandments, a Fundamental Guide for Business." *Vital Speeches of the Day* 42 (July 15, 1976), 602–608.

Berkman, Harold W. "Corporate Ethics: Who Cares?" *Journal of the Academy of Marketing Sciences* 5 (Summer 1977), 154–167.

Bizzell, E. Guy. "Ethics: A Sense of Fairness." *Vital Speeches of the Day* 45 (July 15, 1979), 606–608.

Blott, Richard L. "FF Industry Must Still Face Ethics after All Legality Has Been Met." *Quick Frozen Foods* 41 (September 1978), 26–33.

Blumenthal, W. Michael. "Business Ethics: A Call for a Moral Approach." *Financial Executive* 44 (January 1976), 32–34.

Blumenthal, W. Michael. "Rx for Reducing the Occasion of 'Corporate Sin.'" *SAM Advanced Management Journal* 42 (Winter 1977), 4–13.

Bock, Robert H. "Introduction: Modern Values in Business and Management." *AACSB Bulletin, Proceedings, Annual Meeting 1979*, 1–19.

Bowman, James S. "Managerial Ethics in Business and Government." *Business Horizons* 19 (October 1976), 48–54.

Bremner, E. D. "Professional Ethics in Industry." *Accountants Magazine* 83 (August 1979), 328–332.

Brenner, Steven N., and Earl A. Molander. "Is the Ethics of Business Changing?" *Harvard Business Review* 55 (January–February 1977), 57–71.

Bunke, Harvey C. "The Editor's Chair." *Business Horizons* 22 (June 1979), 2+.

Bureau of National Affairs. "Special Report on White Collar Crime." *Securities Regulation and Law Report.* Washington, D.C. (April 14, 1976), Part II.

Burgen, Carl. "How Companies React to the Ethics 'Crisis.' " *Business Week* (February 9, 1976), 78–79.

Burr, Pat L. "A Test for Morals." *Business and Society Review* (Fall 1976), 77.

Bush, Sherida. "Profits before Ethics." *Psychology Today* 11 (July 1977), 30.

"Business Ethics." *Dun's Review* 107 (April 1976), 100.

Byron, William J. "The Meaning of Ethics in Business." *Business Horizons* 20 (December 1977), 31–34.

Calian, Samuel Carnegie. "Ethics or Profits: Which Wins in the End?" *New Catholic World* (May–June 1979), 131–135.

Carmichael, D. R. "Corporate Accountability and Illegal Acts." *Journal of Accountancy* 143 (January 1977), 77–81.

Carnahan, George R. "The Businessman and Ethics." *Management World* 5 (May 1976), 14–16.

Carnahan, George R. "The Ethics Question: Every Manager Must Face It." *Management World* (March 1976), 9–11.

Carroll, Archie B. "A Three-Dimensional Conceptual Model of Corporate Performance." *Academy of Management Review* 4 (October 1979), 497–505.

Carroll, Archie B. "Business Ethics and the Management Hierarchy." *National Forum* 58 (Summer 1978), 37–40.

Carter, John Mack. "You Can't Fool *Any* of the People *Any* of the Time *Any* More: Only the Truth Will Set Our Enterprise Free." *Vital Speeches of the Day* 44 (August 1, 1978), 629–632.

"A Case for Institutionalizing Corporate Ethics," *Management Review* 68 (November 1979), 36.

Cebik, L. B. "Who Do You Work For? Thoughts on the State of Business Ethics." *Management World* 7 (March 1978), 36–38.

"The Chicken or the Egg: Which Comes First in Ethics?" *Management Review* (December 1977), 56.

Clausen, A. W. "Voluntary Disclosure: Someone Has to Jump into the Icy Water First." *Financial Executive* 44 (June 1976), 20–26.

Collier, Abram T. "The Co-Corp: Big Business Can Re-form Itself." *Harvard Business Review* 57 (November-December 1979), 121+.

Comarow, Avery. "When Conscience and Career Collide." *Money* 5 (September 1976), 48–50+.

Cook, James A., Jr. "It's Ethical, But Is It Fair?" *Forbes* 118 (September 15, 1976), 107–108.

Cooper, Terry L. "Ethics, Values, and Systems." *Journal of Systems Management* 30 (September 1979), 6–12.

"Corporate Ethics." *CPA Journal* 46 (November 1979), 77–78.

"The Corporate Rush to Confess All." *Business Week* (February 23, 1976), 22–24.

Cressy, Donald R. "The Roots of Management Fraud: A Case of Multiple Moralities." *World* 14 (Spring 1980), 44–46.

Currie, Brian. "Ethics—Are We Going Fast Enough?" *Accountancy* 88 (June 1977), 91–92+.

Cushman, Robert. "Let's Put Our House in Order: A Businessman's Plea." *Business and Society Review* 16 (Winter 1975–76), 49–52.

Dagher, Samir P., and Peter H. Spader. "Improving Business Ethics: Poll of Top Managers Stresses Education and Leadership-by-Example as Strong Forces for Higher Standards." *Management Review* 69 (March 1980), 54–57.

Day, Ralph L. "Prescription for the Marketplace—Everyone Listen Better!" *Business Horizons* 19 (December 1976), 57–64.

DeHaven, Donald L., and Carol S. DeHaven. "Change in Moral Awareness: A Positive Approach to Social Responsibility." *Woman CPA* 40 (January 1978), 7–8.

Drucker, Peter F. "The Ethics of Responsibility." *Modern Office Procedures* 24 (June 1979), 12–16.

Drucker, Peter F. "What Is 'Business Ethics?'" *The Public Interest* 63 (Spring 1981), 18–36.

Dunstan, G. R. "Moral Reasoning in Management." *Management Decision* 61 (1978), 75–92.

Englebert, Renny. "Morality and Management." *Accountant* 117 (August 4, 1977), 134–135.

"Ethics Panel Limits Computer Business." *Legal Times Washington* 3 (November 24, 1980), 4.

Faber, Eberhard. "How I Lost Our Great Debate about Corporate Ethics." (Board of Directors Meeting at Eberhard Faber Inc.) *Fortune* 94 (November 1976), 180–182+.

Fenderson, Kendrick E. "Roots of Controversial Business Behavior." *Public Relations Journal* 34 (April 1978), 50–52.

Ferrel, O. C., and K. Mark Weaver. "Ethical Beliefs of Marketing Managers." *Journal of Marketing* 42 (July 1978), 69–73.

Finn, David. "Truth or Consequences." *Saturday Review* 5 (January 21, 1978), 26–27.

Flieger, Howard. "The Boom in Ethics." *U.S. News and World Report* 8 (August 16, 1976), 72.

Friedman, Milton. "Standards of Morality." *Newsweek* 92 (December 18, 1978), 70.

Friedman, Milton. "The Uses of Corruption." *Newsweek* 87 (March 22, 1976), 73.

Frye, Alexandra, and Elaine Shimberg. "Little Fibs to Big Whoppers: Are They a Business Fact of Life? *Glamour* 77 (March 1978), 86+.

George, James. "Ethics or Expediency: The Personnel Dilemma." *Personnel Management* 12 (November 1980), 28–32.

Getlein, Frank. "Sweet Land O'Goshen: Aren't Corporations Sinners Too?" *Commonwealth* 105 (October 27, 1978), 679+.

Goldman, Alan H. "Business Ethics: Profits, Utilities, and Moral Rights." *Philosophy and Public Affairs* 9 (Spring 1980), 280–286.

Goodpaster, Kenneth E., and Kenneth M. Sayre. "An Ethical Analysis of Power Company Decision-Making." *Values in the Electric Power Industry*. Ed. Kenneth M. Sayre. University of Notre Dame Press, 1977.

Gore, George J. "Ethics: Another Kind of Oil Shortage: Individual Responsibility." *Vital Speeches of the Day* 43 (March 1, 1977), 292–294.

Graber, Dean E. "Ethics Enforcement—How Effective?" *CPA Journal* 49 (September 1979), 11–14+.

Greenleaf, Robert K. "Business Ethics—Everybody's Problem." *New Catholic World* 223 (November–December 1980), 275+.

Griffith, Harold M. "Business Ethics in the Private Enterprise System." *RIA Cost and Management* 51 (May–June 1977), 18–21.

Haas, Paul F. "The Conflict between Private and Social Responsibility." *Akron Business and Economic Review* 10 (Summer 1979), 33–36.

Hailwood, Ed. "Cops and Corporate Robbers." *Canadian Business Magazine* 50 (December 1977), 62–73+.

Hayes, James L. "Ethics: To See Ourselves As Others Do." *Management Review* 69 (December 1980), 2–3.

Hayes, James L. "Modern Values or Just Values?" *AACSB Bulletin, Proceedings, Annual Meeting 1979*, 21–29.

Heckert, Richard E. "Corporate Ethics." *Chemical and Engineering News* 56 (April 3, 1978), 5.

Helco, Hugh, Fred R. Brown, and Conley Dillon. "Watergate in Retrospect: The Forgotten Agenda." *Public Administration Review* 36 (May–June 196), 306–310.

Hennessey, J. W., Jr. "The Business Corporation in an Age of Accountability." *AACSB Bulletin, Proceedings, Annual Meeting 1979*, 75–85.

Hill, Ivan. "Ethics and Business." *Enterprise* 1 (November 1977), 6–7.

Hill, Ivan. "Honesty, Freedom, and Business Ethics: Shall We Be Honest and Free or Dishonest and Policed?" *Vital Speeches of the Day* 45 (July 15, 1979), 581–585.

Hill, Robert L. "Considering Corporate Morality." *Public Utilities Fortnightly* 98 (July 15, 1976), 11–13.

Hipp, Hayne. "Business Ethics—And Society's Future." *National Underwriter* 83 (September 8, 1979), 2.

Hipp, Hayne. "Business Ethics—And Society's Future." *National Underwriter* 83 (September 14, 1979), 36–37.

"How to Make Business Behave Better." *The Economist* 265 (October 8, 1977), 89–90.

Hutchinson, Charles T. "Serenade to the U.S. Corporation." (Unpublished paper. 71 South Turkey Hill Road, Westport, Conn. 06880).

"The Industrial Ethic: Two Buildings by James Stewart Polshek and Associates." *Architectural Record* 163 (February 1978), 95+.

Jaspan, Norman. "Motivations Lurking behind White Collar Fraud." *Security Management* 22 (December 1978), 28–31.

Johnson, Deborah G. "Ethics and Computing in Business and the Professions." *Business and Professional Ethics* 2 (Winter 1979).

Jonas, Hans. "Responsibility Today: The Ethics of an Endangered Future." *Social Research* 43 (Spring 1976), 77–97.

Jones, Donald G. "What Is Ethics?" *The Secretary* 38 (May 1978), 6–7.

Jurgen, R. J. "Business of Business Ethics." *Intellect* 105 (December 1976), 177–178.

Kirby, Robert E., Ramsey Clark, William M. Agee, et al. "Is Dishonesty Good for Business?" *Business and Society Review* 30 (Summer 1979), 4–19.

Klein, Joan D. "Personal Dilemma: Situational Ethics and Flexible Morality in America." *Public Relations Journal* 32 (August 1976), 10–13.

Kristol, Irving. "Business Ethics and Economic Man." *Wall Street Journal* (March 20, 1979), 22.

Lawrence, Floyd G. "Whose Ethics Guide Business?" *Management Review* 65 (April 1976), 44–48.

Lerner, Max. "Business Ethics at Home and Abroad." *Personnel Administrator* 22 (August 1977), 13–16+.

Levy, Robert. "Business' Big Morality Play." *Dun's Review* 116 (August 1980), 56–61.

Linowes, David F. "International Business and Morality: Integrity and Ethics." *Vital Speeches of the Day* 43 (May 15, 1977), 475–478.

Lowe, Kenneth E. "Ethics in the Workplace—Where to Draw the Line." *Pulp and Paper* 50 (October 1976), 220.

Lusch, Robert F., Gene R. Laczniak, and Patrick E. Murphy. "The 'Ethics of Social Ideas' versus the 'Ethics of Marketing Social Ideas.'" *Journal of Consumer Affairs* 14 (Summer 1980), 156–164.

McAdams, Tony. "Speaking Out in the Corporate Community." *Academy of Management Review* 2 (April 1977), 198–205.

McAdams, Tony, and C. Burk Tower. "Personal Accountability in the Corporate Sector." *American Business Law Journal* (Spring 1978), 67–82.

McCormick, Brooks. "Resources, Results, and the Seven Deadly Sins: A Sense of Excellence." *Vital Speeches of the Day* 45 (May 1, 1979), 446–448.

McGuire, Joseph W. "The Business of Business Ethics." *National Forum* 58 (Summer 1978), 32.

MacIntyre, Alasdair. "Power Industry Morality." *Harpers* 259 (October 1979), 59–61.

McQuaid, Kim. "Competition, Cartellization, and the Corporate Ethic: General Electric's Leadership during the New Deal Era, 1933–40." *American Journal of Economics and Sociology* 36 (October 1977), 417–428.

Madsen, Edgar B., and Glenn V. Rufrano, "Antidote for Corruption." *Appraisal Journal* 47 (July 1979), 332–339.

Mahon, Gigi. "Moaning at the Bar—Conflict of Interest Is Suddenly a Hot Issue." *Barron's* 56 (August 9, 1976), 3.

Mallor, Jane. "The Insurer's Duty to Cancel in Good Faith." *Business Horizons* 20 (October 1977), 72–74.

Mandelman, Avner. "The Invisible Hand, or: The Corporate Acquisition as an Ethical Catalyst." *Business Quarterly* 42 (Winter 1977), 30–35.

Mann, Bruce Alan. "Moral and Ethical Problems; Loans to Management and Compensation Problems." *Business Lawyer* 31 (March 1976), 1305–1312.

Margolis, Richard J. "Steps toward Ethical Maturity." *Change* 9 (January 1977), 50–53.

Mechling, Thomas B. "The Mythical Ethics of Law, PR, and Accounting." *Business and Society Review* 20 (Winter 1976–1977), 6–10.

Meyer, G. Dale. "Ethical Business Behavior: Have We Lost It?" *Colorado Business* 5 (October 1978), 82.

Migliore, R. Henry. "Integrity and Business." *Business and Society Review* 31 (Fall 1979), 65.

"More Pressure to Prosecute Executive Crime." *Business Week* (December 18, 1978), 104.

Morgan, Lee L. "Business Ethics Start with the Individual." *Management Accounting* 58 (March 1977), 11–14+.

Moser, S. Thomas. "Meeting the Challenge of the 'Corporate Watergate' Phenomenon." *Internal Auditor* 35 (April 1978), 19–25.

Moskal, Brian S. "Sleuthing the Opposition—Does Anything Go?" *Industry Week* 195 (November 21, 1977), 52–57.

"Most Firms in Study Say They Practice U.S. Ethics Abroad." *Wall Street Journal* (May 5, 1977), 44.

Mukhopadhyay, Sampat. "Ethics in Business and Economics." *Chartered Accountant* 26 (October 1977), 196–198.

Murphy, Thomas A. "Two Vital Issues: Business Ethics and National

Planning." *University of Michigan Business Review* 28 (July 1976), 1–6.

Murphy, Thomas P. "Survival Notes." *Forbes* 124 (November 26, 1979), 202+.

Newstrom, John W., and William A. Ruch. "The Ethics of Business Students: Preparation for a Career." *AACSB Bulletin* 12 (April 1976), 21–29.

Nielsen, Richard P. "Criminal Executives." *Business and Society Review* 20 (Winter 1976–77), 73.

"On Business Ethics." *Wall Street Journal* (March 31, 1977), 16.

Owens, James. "Business Ethics: Age-Old Ideal, Now Real." *Business Horizons* 21 (February 1978), 26–30.

Payne, Phillis. "The Reach of Corporate Corruption." *American Federationist* 85 (October 1978), 17–25.

Phelps, Thomas W. "Can We Afford to Be Honest?" *Vital Speeches of the Day* 43 (October 15, 1976), 2–4.

Pomeranz, Felix. "Business Ethics—Can We Stem the Decline?" *Journal of Accounting, Auditing, and Finance.* 1 (Spring 1978), 257–263.

"The Pressure to Compromise Personal Ethics." *Business Week* (January 31, 1977), 107.

Purcell, Theodore V. "Institutionalizing Ethics into Top Management Decisions." *Public Relations Quarterly* 22 (Summer 1977), 15–20.

Radest, Howard B. "Innocence in the Marketplace: A Note on Ethics in the Business Society." *Humanist* 38 (November–December 1978), 54+.

Reichardt, Care E. "Good Ethics Is Good Business." *Journal of Commercial Bank Lending* 60 (August 1978), 2–9.

Rein, Lowell G. "Is Your (Ethical) Slippage Showing?" *Personnel Journal* 59 (September 1980), 740–743.

Reynolds, John I. "Improving Business Ethics: The President's Lonely Task." *Business and Society* 19 (Fall 1978), 10–16.

Robinson, Joan. "Morality and Economics." *Challenge* 21 (March–April 1978), 62–64.

Rockefeller, David. "Shaping a Corporate Ethic." *Dallas Magazine* 56 (December 1977), 20+.

Rohr, John A. "The Study of Ethics in the P.A. Curriculum." *Public Administrative Review* 36 (July–August 1976), 398–406.

Ross, Irwin. "How Lawless Are Big Companies?" *Fortune* 102 (December 1, 1980), 57–64.

Savoie, Leonard M. "Business Ethics." *Price Waterhouse Review* 22 (November 3, 1977), 10–17.

Schlender, William E. "Countervailing Values in Business Decision-Making." *The Cresset* (March 1980), 7–12.

Schlesinger, Arthur, Jr. "Government, Business, and Morality." *Wall Street Journal* (June 1, 1976), 16.

Schollhammer, Hans. "Ethics in an International Business Context." *MSU Business Topics* 25 (Spring 1977), 54–63.

Seligmann, Jean, and Phyllis Malamud. "The Game of Lying?" *Newsweek* 93 (February 26, 1979), 57.

Silva, Macel L. "Business Ethics: What's Right? What's Wrong?" *Management World* 9 (August 1980), 12–14.

Sneath, William S. "Framework for a Business Ethic: Whose Responsibility, Business or Government?" *Vital Speeches of the Day* 44 (March 1, 1978), 301–304.

Sommers, Albert T. "Ends and Means in the 1980's." *Across the Board* 16 (September 1979), 20–27.

Stackhouse, Max L. "Business and Ethics." *Hastings Center Report Supplement* (December 1977), 10–12.

Steiner, John F. "The Prospect of Ethical Advisors for Business Corporations." *Business and Society* 16 (Spring 1976), 5–10.

Stone, Christopher D. "Controlling Corporate Misconduct." *Public Interest* 48 (Summer 1977), 55–71.

Stone, Marvin. "Are Ethics on the Way Back?" *U.S. News and World Report* 86 (January 22, 1979), 80.

Sufrin, Sidney C. "Men, Models, and Morality." *Rivista Internazionale di Scienze Economiche e Commerciali* 25, no. 5 (1978), 385–396.

Toros, Vita. "Who's Afraid of Transparency?" *Public Relations Journal* 33 (July 1977), 14–17.

Unger, Harlow. "A Matter of Ethics, Not Profit." *Canadian Business Magazine* 50 (June 1977), 8.

Varner, Iris I. "Business Ethics—Intuition or Logic?" *Journal of Business Communication* 16 (Winter 1979), 27–32.

Velocci, Tony. "Can Business Collar White-Collar Crime?" *Nation's Business* 66 (November 1978), 35–36+.

Wakefield, Susan. "Ethics and the Public Service: A Case of Individual Responsibility." *Public Administration Review* 36 (November-December 1976), 661–666.

Walker, H. E. "Business Ethics, and Society: Shell Oil." *Intellect* 104 (April 1976), 525–526.

Walton, Clarence C. "Business Ethics—The Present and the Future—A Review of Recent Literature." *Hastings Center Report* 10, no. 5 (1980), 16–20.

Walton, Richard. E. "Some Neglected Aspects of Information Processing Ethics." *Business and Professional Ethics* 2 (Winter 1979), 2–4.

"The War on White Collar Crime." *Business Week* (June 13, 1977), 66–71.

Warden, Robert A. "Civil Fraud by a Corporation: The Implications for Corporation, Stockholder." *Journal of Taxation* 47 (October 1977), 234–236.

"When Businessmen Confess Their Social Sins." *Business Week* (November 6, 1978), 175.

"Why Companies Leave the Straight and Narrow." *Management Review* 68 (February 1979), 59–60.

Will, George F. "Morality and the 'Martini Lunch.'" *Newsweek* 90 (October 17, 1977), 120.

Winthrop, Henry. "The Effects of Scale of Accuracy and Morality in Decision-Making." *Darshana International* 17 (July 1977), 62–67.

Zullinger, David. "Focusing on Management Responsibility." *Perspective* 5 (Fall-Winter 1979), 27–29.

Business Ethics and Management Issues

Business Ethics and Management Issues

Accounting

Books

Briloff, Abraham J. *The Truth about Corporate Accounting.* New York: Harper and Row, 1981.

Briloff, Abraham J. *More Debits than Credits.* New York: Harper and Row, 1976.

Burns, Joseph M. *Accounting Standards and International Finance: With Special Reference to Multinationals.* Washington, D.C.: American Enterprise Institute for Public Policy Research, 1976.

Carmichael, D. R., and Ben Makela, eds. *Corporate Financial Reporting: Benefits and Problems of Disclosure: A Symposium.* New York: American Institute of Certified Public Accountants, 1976.

Causey, Denzil Y., Jr. *Duties and Liabilities of the CPA.* Austin: Bureau of Business Research, University of Texas, 1976.

Gambling, Trevor. *Beyond the Conventions of Accounting.* London: Macmillan Press, 1978.

Levy, Morton. *Accounting Goes Public.* Philadelphia: University of Pennsylvania Press, 1977.

Lillie, Richard E., and John R. Simon. *Accounting Has Principles.* Prospect Heights, Ill.: Waveland Press, 1979.

Loeb, Stephen E. *Ethics in the Accounting Profession.* New York: Wiley, 1978.

Russell, Harold F. *Foozles and Fraud.* Altamonte Springs, Fla.: Institute of Internal Auditors, 1977.

Soble, Ronald, and Robert E. Dallas. *Impossible Dream, the Equity Funding Story: The Fraud of the Century.* New York: G. P. Putnam & Sons, 1975.

Windal, Floyd, and Robert Corley. *The Accounting Professional: Ethics, Responsibility, and Liability.* Englewood Cliffs, N.J.: Prentice-Hall, 1980.

Articles

"Accountable Accountants, to Abe Briloff, That's the Professional Ideal." *Barron's* 56 (April 26, 1976), 9+.

"AICPA Ethics Rulings." *Journal of Accountancy* 141 (March 1976), 71–72.

"AICPA Ethics Rulings: Official Releases." *Journal of Accountancy* 142 (July 1976), 90–96.

Allen, Brandt. "The Biggest Computer Frauds: Lessons for CPA's." *Journal of Accountancy* 143 (May 1977), 52–62.

"Amendments to the Ethical Guide." *Accountancy* 89 (December 1978), 122.

"The Annual Report 1978: Thick and Innovative." *Business Week* (April 16, 1979), 114+.

Anthony, Robert N. "Nonbusiness Financial Reporting: Is There Enough Guidance?" *Journal of Accountancy* 150 (August 1980), 48–54.

Armstrong, M. B. "Disclosure: Considering Other Views." *Financial Executive* 44 (May 1976), 36–40.

Arndt, Terry L., and George F. Hanks. "Ethical Considerations for Non-Public CPA's." *Ohio CPA* 37 (Summer 1978), 69–72.

Arreder, Steven S. "No Last Trumpet; Abe Briloff Still Leads the Crusade for Honest Accounting." *Barron's* 56 (April 12, 1976), 3+.

Arthur, David. "Independence, Yes, but Where Do We Draw the Line?" *Accountancy* 89 (December 1978), 90.

Bailey, Jim. "What Is the Internal Auditor's Role? Fraud Investigation." *Internal Auditor* 35 (April 1978), 26–32.

Baker, C. Richard. "An Investigation of Differences in Values: Accounting Majors vs. Nonaccounting Majors." *Accounting Review* 51 (October 1976), 886–893.

Banks, Warren E., and Jackson A. White. "Accountants' Malpractice: Ernst and Ernst v. Hochfelder." *American Business Law Journal* 14 (Winter 1977), 411–415.

Baron, C. David, Douglas A. Johnson, D. Gerald Bearfoss, and Charles H. Smith. "Uncovering Corporate Irregularities: Are We Closing the Expectation Gap? To What Extent Do New Auditing Standards Satisfy the Need for Increased Auditor Responsibility?" *Journal of Accountancy* 144 (October 1977), 56–66.

Beacham, R. H. S. "Professional Ethics and the Employed Accountant." *The Accountant* 181 (October 4, 1979), 476–477.

Benjamin, James J. "Corporate Social Responsibility: The Viewpoints of CPA's." *National Public Accountant* 22 (March 1977), 18–22.

Benson, Henry, Sir. "The Story of International Accounting Standards." *Accountancy* 87 (July 1976), 34–36+.

Beyer, Harmon W. "Accountants—Policemen for Business Ethics?" *Ohio CPA* 38 (Winter 1979), 11–15.

Blazouske, J. D. "The Accounting Profession and Social Responsibilities." *RIA Cost and Management* 51 (May–June 1977), 4–8.

Bleiberg, Robert M. "FASB-8-Catch-22: In the Foreign Money Game, Nearly Everyone Loses." *Barron's* 56 (November 1, 1976), 7.

Bowen, Linda C. "Social Responsiveness of the Accounting Profession." *CPA Journal* 48 (June 1978), 29–35.

Briloff, Abraham J. "New Accountants Can Recover Their Balance." *Business and Society Review* 24 (Winter 1977–78), 64–68.

Briloff, Abraham J. "Quis Custodiet Ipsos Custodes? Accountants and the Public Good." *National Forum* 58 (Summer 1978), 27–31.

Briston, Richard, and Robert Parks. "The External Auditor—His Role and Cost to Society." *Accountancy* 88 (November 1977), 48–50+.

Bunker, G. B. "The Ethics of Artificial Tax Avoidance." *Accountancy* 89 (October 1978), 144.

Burns, David C., and William J. Haga. "Much Ado about Professionalism: A Second Look at Accounting." *Accounting Review* 52 (July 1977), 705–715.

Burton, John C. "A Critical Look at Professionalism and Scope of Services." *Journal of Accountancy* 149 (April 1980), 48–56.

"Can Accountants Uncover Management Fraud?" *Business Week* (July 10, 1978), 92+.

Causey, Denzil Y., Jr. "Newly Emerging Standards of Auditor Responsibility." *Accounting Review* 51 (January 1976), 19–30.

Cauthon, L. Terry. "Whatever Happened to Social Accountants?" *Management Accounting* 58 (April 1977), 32–34.

Chambers, R. U. "The Possibility of a Normative Accounting Standard." *Accounting Review* 51 (July 1976), 646–652.

Chau, Tran Thi Minh. "Accounting with Integrity." *CA Magazine* 111 (February 1978), 34–37.

Chen, Kung H., and B. J. Lambert. "A Study of the Consensus on Disclosure among Public Accountants and Security Analysts: An Alternative Interpretation." *Accounting Review* 52 (April 1977), 508–512.

Colegrove, Reed L. "The Functions and Responsibilities of the Corporate Audit Committee." *Management Review* 65 (September 1976), 41–43.

Corless, John C. "Internal Auditors: The Conscience of Top Management?" *Internal Auditor* 35 (August 1978), 12–16.

Davison, Ian Hay. "Standards—Where Do We Go from Here?" *Accountancy* 87 (April 1976), 26–28.

DeMarco, Victor F. "How Internal Auditors Can Help CPA's Stamp Out Illegal Acts." *Internal Auditor* 35 (February 1978), 60–65.

Diamond, Sidney A. "Beware of Naming the Competitor." *Advertising Age* 49 (October 23, 1978), 66.

Emmanuel, C. R., and S. J. Gray. "Segmental Disclosures and the Segment Identification Problem." *Accounting and Business Research* (Winter 1977), 37–50.

Emmanuel, C. R., and S. J. Gray. "Segmental Disclosures by Multi-business Multinational Companies: A Proposal." *Accounting and Business Research* (Summer 1978), 169–177.

Englebert, Renny. "Accounting and Social Responsibility." *The Accountant* 175 (August 12, 1976), 183–184.

"Ethics Interpretation No. 101–8—Effect on Independence of Financial Interests in Non-Clients Having Investor or Investee Relationships with a Member's Client." *Journal of Accountancy* 148 (August 1979), 100–102.

Field, Robert E. "Accountants Are Not Perfect." *Price Waterhouse Review* 21, no. 3 (1976), 10–15.

Firth, Michael. "Perceptions of Auditor Independence and Official Ethical Guidelines." *Accounting Review* 55 (July 1980), 451–466.

Frank, Walter C. "Your Responsibilities in Tax Practice—A Review of the Nine AICPA Statements." *Practical Accountant* 9 (March–April 1976), 22–25.

"Fuller Disclosure for Banks—At Last." *Business Week* (April 19, 1976), 74+.

Garbis, M. J., and L. P. Marvel. "Supreme Court's Decision in Fisher Requires Greater Alertness in Handling Tax Fraud Cases." *The Practical Accountant* 9 (July 1976), 35–38.

Giacoleth, R. R. "Auditor's Liability for Fraud." *Management Accounting* 59 (July 1977), 29–32.

Gillis, John G. "Disclosure of Questionable Foreign Payments." *Financial Analysts Journal* 32 (September–October 1976), 12–14+.

Gran, Bradford H. "Evaluating Controls: Primary Responsibility of the Internal Auditor." *Internal Auditor* 34 (June 1977), 48–53.

Green, Donald E. F. "Changing Auditors: Why Directors Should Not Vote." *The Accountant* 180 (February 15, 1979), 191–192.

Griffin, Carleton H. "Beleaguered Accountants: A Defendant's Viewpoint." *American Bar Association Journal* 62 (June 1976), 759–763.

Grosman, Norman C. "How to Audit a Known Fraud." *Touche Ross Tempo* 22 (1976), 12–18.

Hanson, Walter E. "Focus on Peer Review, Illegal Payments, and Lawyers' Letters." *Journal of Accountancy* 141 (May 1976), 90–93.

Hanson, Walter E. "The Role of the Internal Auditor Is Changing." *Internal Auditor* 34 (October 1977), 19–24.

Hartley, Philip B. "The Credibility of Financial Statements." *Bankers Magazine* 159 (Winter 1976), 78–84.

Hatherly, David. "How Much Can You Rely on the Internal Auditor?" *Accountancy* 90 (August 1979), 110–111.

Herzog, R. H. "The Numbers Game: What Industry Accountants Can Do for Society." *Management Accounting* 58 (May 1977), 17–19.

Holmes, Bryan. "Geometry of Price Discrimination." *The Accountant* 178 (January 5, 1978), 29–30.

Hull, Rita P., and John Everett. "Unanswered Questions concerning the SEC's Recent Dismissal of Additional Social Disclosure." *Akron Business and Economics Review* 11 (Fall 1980), 48–52.

"In the Public Interest." *The Accountant* 177 (November 10, 1977), 589–590.

Ingraham, John W. "The Financial Reporting Environment." *Commercial Bank Lending* 58 (January 1976), 15–34.

"The Institute Proposes Tighter Ethical Guidelines on Professional Independence." *Accountancy* 89 (January 1978), 10.

"International Accounting Standards No. 3: 'Consolidated Financial Statements.'" *Accountancy* 87 (September 1976), 100–102+.

Johnson, Johnny R., Robert R. Rice, and Roger A. Roemmich. "Pictures That Lie: The Abuse of Graphs in Annual Reports." *Management Accounting* 62 (October 1980), 50–56.

Johnstone, Andrew G. "Fraud Detection and the Auditor's Role." *Accountancy* 90 (December 1979), 67–68.

Jubb, Guy. "Objectives and Advantages of Audit Committees." *Accountancy* 90 (February 1979), 103+.

Kapnick, Harvey E. "Responsibility and Detection in Management Fraud." *CPA Journal* 46 (May 1976), 19–23.

Keister, Orville R. "A Time for Change in Governmental Accounting." *Akron Business and Economic Review* 9 (Fall 1978), 28–32.

Kelley, Eleanor M. "Financial Accounting and Reporting: From Simple Bookkeeping to Being Awash in a Sea of Disclosure." *Financial Executive* 44 (July 1976), 12–22.

Kirkman, Patrick. "The Industrial Accountant and His Ethics." *Accountancy* 89 (October 1978), 52–53.

Klock, David, and Carl Bellas. "Director Liability Committee and the Audit." *California Management Review* 19 (Winter 1976), 34–43.

Knoll, M. "Auditor's Report—Society's Expectations v. Realities." *Accounting and Business Research* (Summer 1976), 182–200.

Kopcke, Richard W. "Current Accounting Practices and Proposals for Reform." *New England Economic Review* (September–October 1976), 3–29.

Loeb, Stephen E., and Gordon S. May. "Confidentiality, Privilege, and Public Responsibility under the Altest Function." *Journal of Accountancy* 142 (September 1976), 52+.

Loeb, Stephen E., Roger H. Hermanson, and Martin E. Taylor. "Ethical Standards: The Industrial Accountant." *Atlanta Economic Review* 27 (September–October 1977), 11–16.

MacFarlane, Ian. "Auditing Standards—Let's Not Denigrate Ourselves Too Much." *Accountancy* 88 (February 1977), 78+.

Marshall, Juanita. "The Full Disclosure Problem." *Management Accounting* 58 (February 1977), 24–26.

Maust, John. "Voluntary Disclosure: So Far So Credible." *Christianity Today* 23 (October 5, 1979), 57+.

Mayer, Caroline E. "Accountants—Cleaning Up America's Mystery Profession." *U.S. News and World Report* 83 (December 19, 1977), 39–42.

"Member Providing Actuarial Services: AICPA Ethics Rulings." *Journal of Accountancy* 141 (March 1976), 72.

Merjos, Anna. "Lost in Translation: The Effects of FASB-8 Are Rippling Far and Wide." *Barron's* 56 (December 6, 1976), 11+.

Morse, Ellsworth H., Jr. "Professional Accountants in Government: Roles and Dilemmas." *Public Administration Review* 38 (March–April 1978), 120–125.

Moscove, Stephen A. "Should Nonfinancial Information Be Included in the Auditor's Attestation?" *National Public Accountant* 22 (June 1977), 27–33.

Moxley, David. "Audit Committees: What They Should Not Do." *Journal of Contemporary Business* 8, no. 1 (1979), 43–55.

Nelligan, James L. "Regulating the Accounting Profession." *Government Accountants Journal* 27 (Fall 1978), 10–16.

"Nervous Bank Awaits New Accounting Rules." *Business Week* (November 8, 1976), 69–70.

Nichols, Donald R., and Kenneth H. Price. "The Auditor-Firm Conflict: An Analysis Using Concepts of Exchange Theory." *Accounting Review* 51 (April 1976), 335–346.

O'Reilly, Donald J. "Accounting Standards, Provisions of the Foreign Corrupt Practices Act of 1977." *The Magazine of Bank Administration* 55 (March 1979), 24–27.

Pearson, Michael A. "The Commission on Auditor's Responsibilities: Recommendations on CPA Independence." *Baylor Business Studies* 11 (February-March 1980), 25–38.

Plaistowe, Ian. "Do the Ethical Guide Proposals Go Far Enough?" *Accountancy* 89 (August 1978), 75–76.

"Price Waterhouse and a Question of Ethics." *Accountancy* 88 (March 1977), 4.

"Profession Negligence Affecting Accountants." *The Accountant* 175 (July 8, 1976), 50–51.

"Professional Ethics for the Accountancy Profession." *Accountancy* 90 (August 1979), 78+.

"Professional Independence." *The Accountant.* 178 (January 5, 1978), 17–20.

"Proposed MAS Ethics Rulings." *CPA Journal* 46 (November 1976), 82–85.

Rabarts, Alec. "What Auditors Need to Know about Fraud." *Accountancy* 89 (December 1978), 46–48.

Rachlin, Norman S. "How to Tell Your Clients That Fraud Is Their Responsibility." *Practical Accountant* 10 (May–June 1977), 35–36.

Randall, R. "Computer Fraud: A Growing Problem." *Management Accounting* 60 (April 1978), 61–64.

Reckers, Philip M., and Stephen E. Loeb. "Making Ethical Decisions:

Some Guidance to Auditors, Accountants, and Financial Managers." *Government Accountants Journal* 29 (Spring 1980), 51–53.

Reed, Joel L. "Are Auditors Sentinels for Society?" *The CPA Journal* 46 (June 1976), 15–18.

Ricchiute, David N. "The CPA's Responsibility for Detecting Irregularities." *CPA Journal* 48 (March 1978), 15–18.

Robinson, Chris. "Efficient Markets and the Social Role of Accounting." *CA Magazine* 113 (March 1980), 67+.

"The SEC and Corporate Disclosure." *Business Lawyer* 36 (November 1980), 119–157.

Samuels, Alec. "Accountants and Auditors—Some Thoughts on Legal Liabilities and Professional Duties." *Accountancy* 89 (July 1978), 105–106.

Sawyer, Lawrence B. "Janus or the Internal Auditor's Dilemma." *Internal Auditor* 37 (December 1980), 19–27.

Schlesinger, M. "Hochfelder Decision: How It Will Affect Future Malpractice Suits against Accountants." *The Practical Accountant* 9 (September 1976), 77–81.

Sheldahl, Terry K. "Toward a Code of Professional Ethics for Management Accountants." *Management Accounting* 62 (August 1980), 36–40.

Simonetti, Gilbert, Jr. "The Corporate Accountability System under Fire." *Price Waterhouse Review* 22, no.3 (1977), 2–9.

Slavin, Nathan S. "The Elimination of 'Scienter' in Determining the Auditor's Statutory Liability." *Accounting Review* 52 (April 1977), 360–368.

"Standards of Conduct." *The Accountant* 175 (July 29, 1976), 117–118.

Standish, Peter E. M. "Can Auditing Survive Sandilands?" *Accountancy* 87 (November 1976), 44+.

"Statement 1 of the Ethical Guide—Proposed Revision." *Accountancy* 89 (January 1978), 78–80.

"Statement 1—Professional Independence." *Accountancy* 90 (May 1979), 45–47.

Steeds, David. "Changes in Social Values and the Role of the Profession." *Accountancy* 87 (August 1976), 76–79.

Stettler, Howard F. "Two Proposals for Strengthening Auditor Independence." *MSU Business Topics* 28 (Winter 1980), 37–41.

Talbert, William L. "Who Should Set Accounting Standards?" *Atlanta Economic Review* 28 (October 1978), 12–17.

Tipgos, Manuel A. "The Case for Offensive Auditing." *CPA Journal* 46 (September 1976), 19–23.

Urbancic, F. R. "Illegal Acts by Clients." *Journal of Accountancy* 146 (December 1978), 48–53.

Vanatta, Chester B. "Accounting—Business Ruler or Social Yardstick." *Journal of Accountancy* 149 (January 1980), 68–71.

"Vital Nations: What Chance of International Standards?" *The Accountant* 175 (November 25, 1976), 622–623.

Watts, Ross L., and Jerold L. Zimmerman. "Towards a Positive Theory of the Determination of Accounting Standards." *Accounting Review* 53 (January 1978), 112–134.

Waymire, Gregory, and Richard Baker. "New Pressures for Financial Disclosure: A Changing Concept of the Audit." *Business Horizons* 21 (April 1978), 81–86.

Whitehand, Frank. "Management Fraud: What to Look for and What to Do about It." *Practical Accountant* 11 (October–November 1978), 59–65.

Whitehurst, Frederick D. "The Impact on Professional Ethics of Theoretical Difficulties in Periodic Income Measurement." *Woman CPA* 40 (July 1978), 4–7.

Williams, Harold M. "The Emerging Responsibility of the Internal Auditor." *Internal Auditor* 35 (October 1978), 45–52.

Woolf, Emile. "Auditors Must Measure Up to Independence." *Accountancy* 88 (March 1977), 18.

Yaude, Alfred F. "Professional Advertising and the Public Interest." *National Public Accountant* 22 (August 1977), 12–13.

Zeisel, Gerald, and Ralph Estes. "Accounting and Public Service." *Accounting Review* 54 (April 1979), 402–408.

Advertising

Books

Barnes, Michael, ed. *The 3 Faces of Advertising.* London: The Advertising Association, 1975.

Bloom, Paul N. *Advertising, Competition, and Public Policy.* Cambridge, Mass.: Ballinger Publications, 1976.

Ewen, Stuart. *Captains of Consciousness: Advertising and the Social Roots of the Consumer Culture.* New York: McGraw, 1977.

Goffman, Erving. *Gender Advertisements.* Cambridge: Harvard University Press, 1979.

Legal and Business Problems of the Advertising Industry 1978 Course Handbook. New York: Practicing Law Institute, 1978.

Preston, Ivan L. *The Great American Blow-Up: Puffery in Advertising and Selling.* Madison: University of Wisconsin Press, 1975.

Sethi, S. Prakash. *Advocacy Advertising and Large Corporations: Social Conflict, Big Business Image, the News Media, and Public Policy.* Lexington, Mass.: Lexington Books, 1976.

Articles

Armstrong, Gary M., Metin N. Gurol, and Frederick A. Russ. "Detecting and Correcting Deceptive Advertising." *Journal of Consumer Research* 6 (December 1979), 237–246.

"Back on the Warpath against Deceptive Ads." *Business Week* (April 19, 1976), 148+.

"Bad Aftertastes: The Benefits of Honest Advertising." *Human Behavior* 7 (September 1978), 60.

Baker, C. Edwin. "Commercial Speech: A Problem in the Theory of Freedom." *Iowa Law Review* 62 (October 1976), 1–56.

"Basic Principles to Ensure Truth in Your Advertising." *Professional Report* 7 (March 1977), 15–17.

Bauman, Larry. "Social Responsibility in Advertising." *Best's Review* (Life/Health Insurance Edition) 78 (May 1977), 91–92.

Becker, Helmut. "Advertising Image and Impact: A Multi-Faceted Approach to Advertising Policy Should Include Protection, Information, and Education." *Journal of Contemporary Business* 7, no. 4 (1978), 77–93.

Bernacchi, M. D. "Expanding Jurisdiction of Deceptive, Misleading and False Advertising by the FTC." *Journal of Advertising* 6 (1977), 30+.

Bernacchi, M. D. "Substantive False Advertising Standards: Discretion and Misinformation by the FTC." *Marquette Business Review* 21 (Summer 1977), 89–95.

Bernstein, Sid. "The Kids Are Checking You Out." *Advertising Age* 49 (February 20, 1978), 12+.

Bloom, Paul N. "Advertising in the Professions: The Critical Issues." *Journal of Marketing* 41 (July 1977), 103–110.

Blumenthal, John. "Is Truth Bar to Creativity?" *Advertising Age* 49 (October 9, 1978), 75.

Brack, Reginald, Jr. "In Defense of Advertising." *Public Relations Journal* 32 (March 1976), 17.

Brandt, Michael T., and Ivan L. Preston. "The Federal Trade Commission's Use of Evidence to Determine Deception." *Journal of Marketing* 41 (January 1977), 54–62.

Burr, Pat L., and Richard M. Burr. "Television Advertising to Children—What Parents Are Saying about Government Control." *Journal of Advertising* 5 (Fall 1976), 37–41.

Carvell, Frank. "Kid's T.V.—Does Mikey Really Like the Cereal?" *Media Decisions* 13 (August 1978), 98–100.

Charren, Peggy. "Children's TV: Sugar and Vice and Nothing Nice." *Business and Society Review* 22 (Summer 1977), 65–70.

Charren, Peggy. "Should We Ban TV Advertising to Children? Yes." *National Forum* 69 (Fall 1979), 13–16.

Cohen, Dorothy. "Advertising and the First Amendment." *Journal of Marketing* 42 (July 1978), 59–68.

Cohen, Stanley E. "Truth in Ads Self-Regulation in No Danger: FTC's Nye." *Advertising Age* 47 (March 1, 1976), 1+.

Cohen, Stanley E. "What Triggered FTC Investigation of Ad Industry Self-Regulation." *Advertising Age* 47 (February 3, 1976), 4.

Cohen, Stanley E. "Widespread FTC Probe Will Seek Codes That Hinder Comparative Ads." *Advertising Age* 47 (February 23, 1976), 1+.

Cornfeld, Richard S. "A New Approach to an Old Remedy: Corrective Advertising and the Federal Trade Commission." *Iowa Law Review* 61 (February 1976), 693–721.

Cox, Steven M., and Robert J. Zimmer. "Corporate Responsiveness to Consumer Requests for Substantiation of Advertised Claims." *Akron Business and Economic Review* 9 (Winter 1979), 33–36.

Dam, Andre van. "Can Advertising Change Lifestyles?" *Business Quarterly* 41 (Winter 1976), 35–38.

Darling, Harry L. "Marketing Regs: Tough Today, Tougher Tomorrow." *Marketing Times* 25 (March–April 1978), 26–27.

DeMuth, Christopher C. "The FTC Tantrum against Children's Television." *American Spectator* 12 (April 1979), 18–21+.

Dunn, Donald. "If the Product Is the Problem, Do You Censor the Ads?" *Business Week* (April 3, 1978), 90.

Dyer, Robert F., and Phillip G. Kuehl. "A Longitudinal Study of Corrective Advertising." *Journal of Marketing Research* (February 1978), 39–48.

Elman, Philip. "The New Constitutional Right to Advertise." *American Bar Association Journal* 64 (February 1978), 207–210.

"Fairness and Unfairness in Television Product Advertising." *Michigan Law Review* 76 (January 1978), 498–550.

"A Financial Advertising Guide for Banks." *Banking* 69 (August 1977), 95.

Flood, Robert. "Out-of-Home-Self-Regulation." *Media Decisions* 11 (May 1976), 78.

Frazer, Charles F. "Advertising Ethics: The Role of the Educator." *Journal of Advertising* 8 (Winter 1979), 43–46.

"FTC Easing Ad Disclosure Push." *Advertising Age 49* (December 18, 1978), 1+.

"FTC Moves In on Deceptive Ad Techniques; First Proposal Hits 'Personal Endorsements.' " *Product Marketing* 7 (May 1978), 10–13.

"The FTC's Injunctive Authority against False Advertising of Food and Drugs." *Michigan Law Review* 75 (March 1977), 745–767.

Furth, Joseph. "Is FTC Action in Listerine Case Legal?" *Advertising Age* 49 (June 5, 1978), 56+.

Gardner, David M. "Deception in Advertising: A Receiver Oriented Approach to Understanding." *Journal of Advertising* 5 (Fall 1976), 5-11+.

Ginter, Peter M., and Jack M. Starling. "Issues in Comparative Advertising." *Atlanta Economic Review* 27 (September–October 1977), 23–28.

"Giving Advertisers a Right to Free Speech." *Business Week* (February 2, 1976), 21–22.

Goldoff, A. C. "TV Advertising Is Injurious to Your . . ." *Social Policy* 7 (May 1976), 26–31.

Gordon, Richard L. "FTC Judge Gives Anacin $24,000,000 Headache." *Advertising Age* 49 (September 18, 1978), 1+.

Gordon, Richard L. "Industry Objections Fail to Halt Action on Kids' TV Code." *Advertising Age* 50 (May 7, 1979), 1+.

"Guidelines for Print Ads Set by Ethics Committee." *Direct Marketing* 39 (February 1977), 28–30.

Holt, Robert B., Jr. "Corporate Advocacy Advertising: When Business' Right to Speak Threatens the Administration of Justice." *Detroit College of Law Review* (Winter 1979), 623–675.

Hunt, H. K. "Decision Points in FTC Deceptive Advertising Matters." *Journal of Advertising* 6 (Spring 1977), 28–31.

"The Impact of Advertising on Children's Nutrition." *Corporate Information Center Brief* (October 1978), 3A–3D.

"Industry Stonewalled over Kids' Rule." *Advertising Age* 49 (November 20, 1978), 1+.

Johnson, Donald E. L. "Court Rulings Unleash Health Care Advertising." *Advertising Age* 50 (April 2, 1979), 12–13.

Jordan, Robert. "Sending Out Advertising Mail Is Not Invasion of Privacy." *Direct Marketing* 38 (March 1976), 24–26.

Kelly, J. Steven. "Subliminal Embeds in Print Advertising: A Challenge to Advertising Ethics." *Journal of Advertising* 8 (Summer 1979), 20–24.

Kershaw, Andrew G. "For and Against Comparative Advertising: Against." *Advertising Age* 47 (July 5, 1976), 25–26+.

Kliment, Stephen A. "Advertising the Architect's Services: Moving from Legal and Ethical Controversy to Marketing Strategy." *Architectural Record* 163 (January 1978), 55+.

Koskoff, Theodore I. "Ethics, Advertising, and Specialization." *Trial* 16 (June 1980), 4+.

Kuehl, P. G. "Applications of the 'Normative Belief' Technique for Measuring the Effectiveness of Deceptive and Corrective Advertisements." *Advances in Consumer Research* 4 (1977), 204–212.

LaBarbera, Priscilla A. "Advertising Self-Regulation: An Evaluation." *MSU Business Topics* 28 (Summer 1980), 55–63.

LaBarbera, Priscilla A. "Analyzing and Advancing the State of the Art of Advertising Self-Regulation." *Journal of Advertising* 9, no. 4 (1980), 27–38.

Laric, Michael V., and Lewis R. Tucker, Jr. "Toward Socially Responsible Advertising: The Concept Testing Panel Approach." *Business and Society* 17 (Spring 1977), 27–34.

Lee, Gail Ellen. "Unsafe for Little Ears? The Regulation of Broadcast Advertising to Children." *UCLA Law Review* 25 (June 1978), 1131–1186.

Lieberman, Jethro K. "Advertisers Win a Free Speech Case." *Business Week* (June 7, 1976), 26.

Lourie, Roger. "Ethics Committee Relies on Liaison Contact for Action." *Direct Marketing* 41 (November 1978), 128+.

McKie, James W. "Advertising and Social Responsibility." *Society* 16 (March–April 1979), 39–43.

Marshall, Christy. "Lawyers Struggle to Devise Workable Ad Code." *Advertising Age* 49 (July 24, 1978), 10+.

Mason, J. Barry, and J. B. Wilkinson. "Are Supermarket Advertisements Designed to Deceive Consumers?" *Journal of Advertising* 7 (1978), 56–59.

Mason, Kenneth. "Responsibility for What's on the Tube: Corporations That Sponsor Programs for Children Cannot Evade the Fact That the Quality of Television for the Young Must Be Upgraded." *Business Week* (August 13, 1979), 14.

Miaoulis, George, and Nancy Damato. "Consumer Confusion and Trademark Infringement." *Journal of Marketing* 42 (April 1978), 48–55.

Michalos, Alex C. "Advertising: Its Logic, Ethics, and Economics." (A paper written for the Logic Conference at the University of Windsor, Windsor, Ontario, 26–28 June 1978.)

Milmo, Sean, and William Carnahan. "Comparative Advertising Attracts Divergent Views." *Advertising Age* 48 (November 21, 1977), 84.

O'Connor, Neal W. "To Tell the Truth: Credibility in Advertising." *Vital Speeches of the Day* 42 (July 1, 1976), 567-570.

Oliver, Richard L. "An Interpretation of the Attitudinal and Behavioral Effects of Puffery." *Journal of Consumer Affairs* 13 (Summer 1979), 8–27.

Olson, Jerry C., and Philip A. Dover. "Cognitive Effects of Deceptive Advertising." *Journal of Marketing Research* 15 (February 1978), 29–38.

Peebles, Dean M., and John K. Ryans, Jr. "Advertising as a Positive Force." *Journal of Advertising* 7 (Spring 1978), 48–52.

Peterson, Robin T., and Charles W. Gross. "Social Responsibility in Magazine Advertisements." *Atlanta Economic Review* 28 (March–April 1978), 35–38.

Pitofsky, Robert. "Beyond Nader: Consumer Protection and the Regulation of Advertising." *Harvard Law Review* 90 (February 1977), 661–701.

Preston, Ivan L. "A Comment on 'Defining Misleading Advertising' and 'Deception in Advertising.' " *Journal of Marketing* 40 (July 1976), 54–60.

Preston, Ivan L. "The FTC's Handling of Puffery and Other Selling Claims Made 'By Implication.' " *Journal of Business Research* 5 (June 1977), 155–181.

"PUSH Asks Ad Industry Aid in Media Ethics Drive." *Advertising Age* 48 (January 24, 1977), 79.

"Reports by FTC's Staff Recommends Major Strictures on Children's TV Ads." *Advertising Age* 49 (February 27, 1978), 1+.

Rijkens, Rein. "Marketers and Admen Challenge EEC Directive." *Advertising Age* 49 (September 11, 1978), 113.

Roberts, Eirlys. "Persuade or Legislate—The Debate Continued." *Advertising Quarterly* 49 (Autumn 1976), 14–16.

Rodriguez, Bonnie. "Six Major Areas in Which Ethics Committee Deals." *Direct Marketing* 41 (November 1978), 124+.

Rollins, O. Randolph. "Comparative Price Advertising." *Business Lawyer* 33 (April 1978), 1771–1797.

Rotenberg, Ronald H., Pierre R. Poirier, and Jean A. C. Tremblay. "A Decade after 'the Permissible Lie': Have Things in the Ad Business Really Changed?" *Journal of Consumer Affairs* 12 (Summer 1978), 170–175.

Rotfeld, Herbert J., and Leonard N. Reid. "Advertiser Supplied Message Research: Extending the Advertising Substantiation Program." *Journal of Consumer Affairs* 11 (Summer 1977), 128–134.

Rotfeld, Herbert J., and Leonard N. Reid. "Potential Secondary Effects of Regulating Children's Television Advertising." *Journal of Advertising* 8 (Winter 1979), 9–14.

Rotzoll, Kim B., and Clifford G. Christians. "Advertising Agency Practitioners' Perceptions of Ethical Decisions." *Journalism Quarterly* 57 (Autumn 1980), 425–431.

Scheibla, Shirley Hobbs. "Stand Up and Be Counted: Corporations Fight Efforts in Congress to Muzzle Them." *Barron's* (May 22, 1978), 9–10.

Shimp, Terence A., Robert F. Dyer, and Salvatore F. Divita. "An Experimental Test of the Harmful Effects of Premium-Oriented

Commercials on Children." *Journal of Consumer Research* 3 (June 1976), 1–11.

Shimp, Terence A. "Do Incomplete Comparisons Mislead?" *Journal of Advertising Research* 18 (December 1978), 21–27.

"Shouldn't Turn Ad Regulation Over to NARB, FTC Argues." *Advertising Age* 47 (November 15, 1976), 2+.

Sklar, William. "Ads Are Finally Getting Bleeped at the FTC." *Business and Society Review* 26 (Summer 1978), 38–46.

"Social Psychological (Mis)Representations in Television Advertising." *Journal of Consumer Affairs* 13 (Summer 1979), 28–40.

"State Seeking Cleanup of Auto Ads in Boston." *Automotive News* (October 18, 1976), 19.

Surlin, Stuart H. "Sex Differences in Socially Responsible Advertising Decisions." *Journal of Advertising* 7 (Summer 1978), 36–39.

Sweeney, Terrance. "Advertising in the Context of the Combines Investigation Act." *Business Quarterly* 42 (Spring 1977), 4–5+.

Thain, Gerald. "Suffer the Hucksters to Come unto the Little Children? Possible Restrictions of Television Advertising to Children under Section 5 of the Federal Trade Commission Act." *Boston University Law Review* 56 (July 1976), 651–684.

Thompson, Mayo J. "Government Regulation of Advertising: Killing the Consumer in Order to 'Save' Him." *Antitrust Law and Economics Review* 8 (1976), 81–92.

Tribe, Laurence H. "Should We Ban TV Advertising to Children? No." *National Forum* 69 (Fall 1979), 17–20.

Turk, Peter. "Children's Advertising: An Ethical Morass for Business and Government." *Journal of Advertising* 8 (Winter 1979), 4–8.

Ward, Scott. "Compromise in Commercials for Children (Some Proposals)." *Harvard Business Review* 56 (November–December 1978), 128–136.

Whitman, Douglas. "Advertising by Professionals." *American Business Law Journal* (Spring 1978), 39–59+.

Wilkinson, J. B., and J. Barry Mason. "Unavailability and Mispricing of Advertised Specials: The Food Shipper's Knowledge, Experience, and Response." *Journal of Consumer Affairs* 12 (Winter 1978), 355–363.

Woodside, Arch G. "Advertisers' Willingness to Substantiate Their Claims." *Journal of Consumer Affairs* 11 (Summer 1977), 135–144.

Business Policy and Planning

Books

Burgher, Peter H., ed. *Changement: Understanding and Managing Business Change*. Lexington, Mass.: Lexington Books, 1979.

Dunlop, John T. *Business and Public Policy*. Cambridge: Harvard Business School, 1980.

Eldredge, David L., and Donald L. Bates. *Business Strategy and Policy Games*. Dubuque, Iowa: William C. Brown, 1980.

Finnin, Williams M., Jr., and Gerald Alonzo Smith, eds. *The Morality of Scarcity: Limited Resources and Social Policy*. Baton Rouge: Louisiana State University Press, 1979.

Foy, Nancy. *The Yin and Yang of Organizations*. New York: Morrow, William, and Co., 1980.

Geer, Douglas F. *Industrial Organization and Public Policy*. New York: Macmillan Publishing Co., 1979.

Goolrick, Robert M. *Public Policy toward Corporate Growth: The ITT Merger Cases*. Port Washington, N.Y.: Kennikat Press, 1978.

Gray, Edmund R., ed. *Business Policy and Strategy: Selected Readings*. Austin, Tex.: Austin Press, 1979.

Haner, F. T. *Business Policy, Planning, and Strategy*. Englewood Cliffs, N.J.: Winthrop, 1976.

Keith, David, William C. Frederick, and Robert L. Blumstrom. *Business and Society: Concepts and Policy Issues*. 4th ed. New York: McGraw-Hill, 1980.

Preston, Lee E., ed. *Research in Corporate Social Performance and Policy: An Annual Compilation of Research*. Vol. I, 1978. Greenwich, Conn.: JAI Press, 1979.

Articles

"Assessing Public Policies and Programs: Equity Considerations." *American Journal of Agricultural Economics* 59 (December 1977), 1001–1021.

Bailey, Richard. "Still Waiting for an Industrial Policy." *The Accountant* 178 (March 30, 1978), 425–426.

Bleiberg, Robert M. "Chosen Instrument? Competition Is Rarely Fostered through Creating a Monopoly." *Barron's* 57 (September 12, 1977), 7.

Bock, Betty. "The Lizzie Borden Solution: Breaking Up the Major Oil Companies Would Be a Drastic, Highly Specialized, and Irreversible Action. And the Problem Is Not Too Little Competition but Too Little Energy." *Across the Board* 14 (April 1977), 46–53.

Bond, Ronald S., and Warren Greenberg. "Industry Structure, Market Rivalry, and Public Policy: A Comment." *Journal of Law and Economics* 19 (April 1976), 201–204.

Brenner, Steven N. "Business and Politics—An Update." *Harvard Business Review* 57 (November–December 1979), 149–163.

Cox, James C., and Arthur W. Wright. "The Determinants of Investment in Petroleum Reserves and Their Implications for Public Policy." *American Economic Review* 66 (March 1976), 153–167.

Dunlop, John T., Alfred D. Chandler, Jr., George P. Schultz, and Irving S. Shapiro. "Business and Public Policy: Four Noted Americans Discuss the Growing Complexity of Public-Private Relationships in Achieving Social Purposes." *Harvard Business Review* 57 (November–December 1979), 85–102.

Heilbroner, Robert L. "Missing Link(s)." *Challenge* 21 (March–April 1978), 16–17.

Higgins, J. C., and D. Romano. "Social Forecasting: An Integral Part of Corporate Planning?" *Long Range Planning* 13 (April 1980), 82–86.

Howe, Elizabeth, and Jerome Kaufman. "The Ethics of Contemporary American Planners." *Journal of the American Planning Association* 45 (July 1979), 243–255.

Inglehart, R. "Policy Problems of Advanced Industrial Society." *Comparative Policy Studies* 10 (October 1977), 291–472.

Kaikati, Jack G. "The Arab Boycott: Middle East Business Dilemma." *California Management Review* 20 (Spring 1978), 32–46.

Klosterman, Richard E. "Foundations of Normative Planning." *Journal of the American Institute of Planners* 44 (January 1978), 37–46.

Marcuse, Peter. "Professional Ethics and Beyond: Values in Planning." *Journal of the American Institute of Planners* 42 (July 1976), 264–274.

May, William F. "Between Ideology and Interdependence." *California Management Review* 19 (Summer 1977), 88–90.

Mitroff, Ian I., and Ralph H. Kilmann. "Teaching Managers to Do Policy Analysis: The Case of Corporate Bribery." *California Management Review* 20 (Fall 1977), 47–54.

Newgren, Kenneth, and Archie B. Carroll. "Integrating Social Treatment into the Strategic Planning Process to Achieve Corporate Social Involvement." *National AIDS Proceedings* (1976).

Nielsen, Richard P. "International Marketing of Public Policy: U.S. Penetration of the Canadian Television Program Market." *Columbia Journal of World Business* 11 (Spring 1976), 130–139.

Nielsen, Richard P. "Public Policy and Price Discrimination in Favor of Nonprofit and against Profit Seeking Organizations." *Academy of Management Review* 2 (April 1977), 316–319.

Olasky, Marvin. "Efficiency, Equity, and Equality of Result: What Should Business Be Doing?" *Columbia Journal of World Business* 13 (Winter 1978), 15–21.

Ostrow, Philip B. "A Planner's Burden: Social Responsibility Programs." *Managerial Planning* 25 (July–August 1976), 22–24+.

Parvin, Manoucher. "Technology, Environment, and Economic Policies." *American Economist* 20 (Fall 1976), 16–23.

Post, James E. "SMR Forum: The Corporation in the Public Policy Process—A View toward the 1980's." *Sloan Management Review* 21 (Fall 1979), 45–52.

Richardson, Elliot L. "Business Ready to Support Public Interest . . . Once It's Defined." *Commerce America* 1 (June 7, 1976), 6–8.

Rosenman, Linda S. "Unemployment of Women: A Social Policy Issue." *Social Work* 24 (January 1979), 20–25.

Rusk, Dean. "The Interdependence of All Peoples." *California Management Review* 19 (Summer 1977), 79–83.

Sawyer, George C. "Social Policy for Growth." *Managerial Planning* 25 (March–April 1977), 37–40.

Schelling, Thomas C. "Economic Reasoning and the Ethics of Policy." *The Public Interest* 63 (Spring 1981), 37–61.

Shetty, Y. K. "New Look at Corporate Goals." *California Management Review* 22 (Winter 1979), 71–79.

"Should Big Oil Companies Be Broken Up? 'Yes' by James Abourzek, 'No' by Dewey F. Bartlett." *American Legion Magazine* 100 (April 1976), 20–21.

Sims, Henry P., Jr., and W. Harvey Hegarty. "Policies, Objectives, and Ethical Behavior: An Experiment." *Academy of Management Proceedings, 37th Annual Meeting* 1977, 295–299.

Tipgos, Manuel A. "Integrating Social Goals into Corporate Strategic Planning." *Managerial Planning* 25 (March–April 1977), 26–30.

Weidenbaum, Murray L. "A Free Market Approach to Economic Policy." *Challenge* 21 (March–April 1978), 40–41.

Weidenbaum, Murray L. "Business Policy and the Public Welfare: The Excesses of Government Regulations." *Vital Speeches of the Day* 43 (March 1, 1977), 317–320.

Wriston, Walter B. "Let's Create Wealth, Not Allocate Shortages." *Challenge* 20 (September–October 1977), 44–47.

Corporate Law

Books

The Business Lawyer: Ethical Responsibilities of Corporate Lawyers. Chicago: American Bar Association, 1978.

Elzinga, Kenneth G., and William Breit. *The Antitrust Penalties: A Study in Law and Economics.* New Haven: Yale University Press, 1976.

Freedman, Monroe H. *Lawyer's Ethics in an Adversary System.* New York: Bobbs-Merrill, 1975.

Gorovittz, Samuel, and Bruce Miller. *Professional Responsibility in the Law: A Curriculum Report from the Institute on Law and Ethics.* College Park, Md.: Council for Philosophical Studies, 1977.

Hazard, Geoffrey C., Jr. *Ethics in the Practice of Law.* New Haven: Yale University Press, 1978.

Kaufman, Burton I. *The Oil Cartel Case: A Documentary Study of Antitrust Activity in the Cold War Era.* Westport, Conn.: Greenwood Press, 1978.

Kintner, Earl W. *A Primer on the Law of Deceptive Practices: A Guide for Business.* New York: Macmillan, 1978.

Nader, Ralph, and Mark Green. *Verdicts on Lawyers.* New York: T. Y. Crowell, 1977.

Stevenson, Russell B., Jr. *Corporations and Information: Secrecy, Access, and Disclosure.* Baltimore: John Hopkins, 1980.

Waldman, Don E. *Antitrust Action and Market Structure.* Lexington, Mass.: Lexington Books, 1978.

Articles

"ABA Statement for Policy Regarding Lawyer's Responses to Auditor's Request for Information: Second Report of the Committee on Audit Inquiry Responses regarding Initial Implementation." *Business Lawyer* 32 (November 1976), 177–186.

Aultman, Mark H. "Scrambling for a New Ethics Code: State High Courts Put on the Spot as Disciplinary Enforcers." *National Law Journal* 3AZ-NK-aa (November 10, 1980), 15.

Blair, Roger D., and David L. Kaserman. "Vertical Integration, Tying, and Antitrust Policy." *American Economic Review* 68 (June 1978), 397–402.

Carnahan, George R. "The Ethics Question, Legally Speaking." *Management World* (April 1976), 7–10.

"Challenge to Corporate Privacy." *Business Week* (October 9, 1978), 44–46.

Coffee, John C., Jr. "Beyond the Shut-Eyed Sentry: Toward a Theoretical View of Corporate Misconduct and an Effective Legal Response." *Virginia Law Review* 63 (November 1977), 1100–1278.

Cromartie, William A. "Civil and Criminal Sanctions Applicable to the Corporate Taxpayer, Its Officers, Directors, and Employees." *Taxes* 55 (December 1977), 786–793.

Dunfee, Thomas W. "Privity in Antitrust: Illinois Brick v. Illinois." *American Business Law Journal* 16 (Spring 1978), 107–117.

Ferrara, Ralph C., and Marc Steinberg. "The Role of Inside Counsel in the Corporate Accountability Process." *Corporation Law Review* 4 (Winter 1980), 3–22.

Ferren, John M. "The Corporate Lawyer's Obligation to the Public Interest." *Business Lawyer* 33 (March 1978), 1253–1289.

Fletcher, Stephen H. "The Role of the Corporate Legal Department." *Business Lawyer* 33 (March 1978), 1537–1541.

Forrow, Brian D. "Special Problems of Inside Counsel for Industrial Companies." *Business Lawyer* 33 (March 1978), 1453–1462.

Freedman, Monroe H. "Lying and the Lawyers' Code." *The Hastings Center Report* 10 (October 1980), 4.

Freund, P. A. "The Moral Education of a Lawyer." *Emory Law Journal* 26 (1977), 3–12.

Friedman, Stephen J. "Limitations on the Corporate Lawyer's and Law Firm's Freedom to Serve the Public Interest." *Business Lawyer* 33 (March 1978), 1475–1488.

Fuld, James J. "Lawyers' Standards and Responsibilities in Rendering Opinions." *Business Lawyer* 33 (March 1978), 1295–1319.

Goedeche, Walter R. "Corporations and the Philosophy of Law." *Journal of Value Inquiry* 10 (1976), 83–88.

Hazard, Geoffrey C., Jr. "An Historical Perspective on the Attorney-Client Privilege." *California Law Review* 66 (September 1978), 1061–1091.

Hershman, Mendes. "Special Problems of Inside Counsel for Financial Institutions." *Business Lawyer* 33 (March 1978), 1435–1451.

Hoffman, Junius. "On Learning of a Corporate Client's Crime or Fraud: The Lawyer's Dilemma." *Business Lawyer* 33 (March 1978), 1389–1431.

Honnold, John O., ed. "Unification of International Trade Law: UNCITRAL's First Decade." *American Journal of Comparative Law* 27 (Spring–Summer 1979), 201–563.

Inman, James E. "The Uniform State Antitrust Net: A Review and Commentary." *American Business Law Journal* 14 (Fall 1976), 171–193.

"Law to Be Strengthened on Conduct of Company Directors." *Accountancy* 89 (January 1978), 14–15.

Leete, Burt A. "An Analysis of the Standard for Determining the Requisite Economic Control Necessary for a Tying Contract to Amount to a Violation of the Sherman Act: The Lessons of Fortner I and II." *American Business Law Journal* 16 (Fall 1978), 189–202.

Leigh, Monroe. "The Challenge of Transnational Corporate 'Wrongdoing' to the Rule of Law." *Department of State Bulletin* 74 (May 24, 1976), 642–647.

Lieberman, Jethro K. "New Fire in the Drive to Reform Corporation Law." *Business Week* (November 21, 1977), 98–100.

Lilley, William, III, and James C. Miller III. "The New 'Social' Regulation." *Across the Board* 15 (January 1978), 32–39.

Lorne, Simon M. "The Corporate and Securities Adviser, the Public Interest, and Professional Ethics." *Michigan Law Review* 76 (January 1978), 423–496.

Luban, David. "Professional Ethics: A New Code for Lawyers?" *The Hastings Center Report* 10 (June 1980), 11–15.

McAdams, Tony, and Robert C. Miljus. "Growing Criminal Liability for Executives." *Harvard Business Review* 55 (March–April 1977), 36+.

McKinney, Luther C., and Donald A. Washburn. "Antitrust—A Route to Centralized Governmental Planning?" *American Journal of Agricultural Economics* 58 (December 1976), 861–866.

Marcus, Ruth. "Key Corporate Issue Tested: Attorney-Client Privilege." *National Law Journal* 2 (March 31, 1980), 3.

Marcus, Ruth. "SEC: Ethics Dilemma a Bar Issue: Should Lawyers Disclose Corporate Misbehavior? *National Law Journal* 2 (May 12, 1980), 3.

Miller, Arthur Selwyn, and Lewis D. Solomon. "Constitutional Chains for the Corporate Beast." *Business and Society Review* 27 (Fall 1978), 15–19.

Miller, Gale T. "Getting to the Bottom or Digging Your Own Grave: The Applicability of the Attorney-Client Privilege and Work-Product Doctrines to Internal Corporate Investigations." *Colorado Law* 9 (May 1980), 945–951.

Mundheim, Robert H. "Should Code of Professional Responsibility Forbid Lawyers to Serve on Boards of Corporations for Which They Act as Counsel." *Business Lawyer* 33 (March 1978), 1507–1518.

O'Donovan, Vincent. "Where Ignorance Is Bliss: Directors Need Not Be Wise." (Britain) *The Accountant* 176 (April 14, 1977), 419–421.

O'Leary, Howard E., Jr. "Criminal Antitrust and the Corporate Executive: The Man in the Middle." *American Bar Association Journal* 63 (October 1977), 1389–1392.

Parker, Russell C. "Antitrust Issues in the Food Industries." *American Journal of Agricultural Economics* 58 (December 1976), 854–860.

Perry, Martin K. "Vertical Integration: The Monopsony Case." *American Economic Review* 68 (September 1978), 561–570.

"A Practical Guide to the Conduct of Lawyer Directors." *International Business Law* 8 (June 1980), 182–184.

Reed, Jean D. "Corporate Self-Investigators under the Foreign Corrupt Practices Act." *University of Chicago Law Review* 47 (Summer 1980), 803–823.

"Rewriting the Rules Lawyers Should Live By." *Business Week* (February 18, 1980), 66–67.

Riger, Martin. "The Lawyer-Director—'A Vexing Problem.' " *Business Lawyer* 33 (July 1978), 2381–2388.

Ritholz, Jules. "Defenses of the Corporate Taxpayer Accused in Connection with Sensitive Foreign Payments." *Taxes* 55 (December 1977), 806–810.

Sethi, S. Prakash. "Liability without Fault? The Corporate Executive as an Unwitting Criminal." *Employee Relations Law Journal* 4 (Autumn 1978), 185–219.

Seymour, W. N. "New Look at Responsibilities of Corporate Counsel." *Business Lawyer* 31 (1976), 1271–1275.

Siegel, Alan. "To Lift the Curse of Legalese—Simplify, Simplify." *Across the Board* 14 (June 1977), 64–70.

Solomon, Stephen. "The Corporate Lawyer's Dilemma: He May Be Betraying His Client If He Blows the Whistle, but He May Be in Trouble with the Law If He Doesn't." *Fortune* 100 (November 5, 1979), 138–140.

Stephenson, Kay Eileen. "Conflicting Standards for Applying the Corporate Attorney–Client Privilege." *Vanderbilt Law Review* 33 (May 1980), 999–1015.

Tankersley, Michael W. "The Corporate Attorney-Client Privilege: Culpable Employees, Attorney Ethics, and the Joint Defense Doctrine." *Texas Law Review* 58 (April 1980), 809–843.

Van Dusen, Lewis H., Jr. "Ethics and Specialized Practice—An Overview of the Momentum for Re-Examination." *Business Lawyer* 33 (March 1978), 1565–1577.

"Which Client Secrets Must a Lawyer Reveal?" *Business Week* (August 15, 1977), 124+.

Wilcox, Thomas R. "Law and Ethics: The Banking Community." *Vital Speeches of the Day* 44 (February 15, 1978), 283–286.

Williams, Harold M. "Professionalism and the Corporate Bar." *Los Angeles Daily Journal* 93 (October 24, 1980), 5–22.

Williams, Harold M. "The Role of Inside Counsel in Corporate Accountability." *Los Angeles Daily Journal* 93 (March 7, 1980), 5–12.

Employee Relations and Personnel Management

Books

Arvey, Richard D. *Fairness in Selecting Employees*. Reading, Mass.: Addison-Wesley, 1979.

Berg, Ivar, Marcia Freedman, and Michael Freeman. *Managers and Work Reform: A Limited Engagement*. New York: Free Press, 1978.

Bernstein, Paul. *Workplace Democratization: Its Internal Dynamics*. Kent, Ohio: Comparative Administration Research Institute, College of Business Administration, Graduate School of Business Administration, Kent State University; distributed by Kent State University Press, 1976.

Boothe, Ben B. *To Be or Not to Be an S.O.B.* Fort Worth: Hulme, 1979.

Carvell, Fred J. *Human Relations in Business*. 3d ed. New York: Macmillan, 1980.

Carson, Charles R. *Managing Employee Honesty*. Los Angeles: Security World Publishing Co., 1977.

Conway, Mimi. *Rise Gonna Rise: A Portrait of Southern Textile Workers*. Garden City, N.Y.: Doubleday Co., 1979.

Desatuick, R. L., and M. L. Bennett. *Human Resource Management in the Multinational Company*. New York: Nichols Publishing, 1978.

Deutsch, Arnold R. *The Human Resources Revolution: Communicate or Litigate*. New York: McGraw-Hill, 1979.

Duckles, R. *Work, Workers, and Democratic Change*. Berkeley: The Wright Institute, 1976.

Dunlop, John T., and Walter Galinson, eds. *Labor in the Twentieth Century*. New York: Academic Press, 1978.

Elliott, Robert K., and John J. Willingham. *Management Fraud: Detection and Deterrence*. Princeton, N.J.: Petrocelli, 1980.

Foulkes, Fred K. *Personnel Policies in Large Nonunion Companies*. Englewood Cliffs, N.J.: Prentice-Hall, 1980.

Garson, G. David, ed. *Worker Self Management in Industry: The West European Experience*. New York: Praeger, 1977.

Gyllenhammer, Pehr G. *People at Work*. Reading, Mass.: Addison-Wesley Publishing Co., 1977.

Heisler, William J., and John W. Houck, eds. *A Matter of Dignity: Inquiries into The Humanization of Work*. Notre Dame, Ind.: University of Notre Dame Press, 1977.

Janger, Allen R. *The Personnel Function: Changing Objectives and Organizations.* New York: The Conference Board, 1977.

King, Charles D., and Mark van Devall. *Models of Industrial Democracy: Consultation, Codetermination, and Workers Management.* Hawthorne, N.Y.: Mouton, 1978.

Lieberstein, Stanley H. *Who Owns What Is in Your Head? Trade Secrets and the Mobile Employee.* New York: Hawthorn Books, 1979.

Maccoby, Michael. *The Gamesman.* New York: Simon and Schuster, 1977.

Machlowitz, Marilyn. *Workaholics: Living with Them, Working with Them.* New York: Addison-Wesley, 1980.

McLean, Alan A. *Work Stress.* New York: Addison-Wesley Publishing Co., 1979.

O'Toole, James. *Work, Learning, and the American Future.* San Francisco: Jossey-Bass, 1977.

Price, R. Masters. *Unions and Men.* New York: Cambridge University Press, 1980.

Schumacher, E. F. *Good Work.* New York: Harper and Row, 1979.

Stokes, Brian. *Worker Participation.* Washington, D.C.: Wordsworth Institute, 1978.

Walker, James W., and Harriet L. Lazer.*The End of Mandatory Retirement: Implications for Managers.* New York: John Wiley, 1978.

Watson, Tony J. *The Personnel Manager: A Study in the Sociology of Work and Employment.* Boston: Routledge and Kegan Paul, 1978.

Westin, Alan F., and Stephan Salisbury, eds. *Individual Rights in the Corporation: A Reader on Employee Rights.* New York: Pantheon Books, 1980.

Wolf, William B., ed. *Top Management of the Personnel Function: Current Issues and Practices.* Ithaca: New York School of Industrial Relations, 1980.

Zwerdling, Daniel. *Workplace Democracy.* New York: Harper and Row, 1980.

Articles

Aileen, O. "Wrongful Dismissal." *Personnel Management* 8 (January 1976), 40.

Allen, George R. "Liberty, Equality, and Anxiety at Worker-Run IGP." *Business and Society Review* 24 (Winter 1977–78), 43–46.

Baker, John C. "Are Corporate Executives Overpaid?" *Harvard Business Review* 55 (July–August 1977), 51–56.

Bateman, D. N. "Employees' Right to Know Issues and Corporations' Responsibility to Communicate." *Journal of Business Communication* 14, no. 2 (1977), 3–9.

Becker, Stephen P. "The Trainer's Changing Ethics." *Training* 13 (November 1976), 20.

Beer, Michael, and Robert A. Ruh. "Employee Growth through Performance Management." *Harvard Business Review* 54 (July–August 1976), 59–66.

Bellamy, G. Thomas, E. Francis Bertrand, and Robert H. Horner. "The Severely Retarded Employee: A New Face in the Labor Force." *Journal of Contemporary Business* 8, no. 4 (1979), 99–106.

Belt, John A., and Peter B. Holden. "Polygraph Use among Major U.S. Corporations." *Personnel Journal* 57 (February 1978), 80–86.

Benson, Miles. "Lying to Management: A Legitimate Solution?" *Computerworld* 12 (September 11, 1978), 30–31.

Boling, T. Edwin. "The Management Ethics 'Crisis': An Organizational Perspective." *Academy of Management Review* 3 (April 1978), 360–365.

Brewer, Richard. "Personnel's Role in Participation." *Personnel Management* 10 (September 1978), 27–29+.

Buchholz, Rogene A. "The Work Ethic Reconsidered." *Industrial and Labor Relations Review* (July 1978), 450–459.

Bulmer, Charles, and John L. Carmichael, Jr. "Labor and Employment Policy: An Overview of the Issues." *Policy Studies Journal* 6 (Winter 1977), 255–263.

Carter, Byrum. "Some Reflections on Merit." *Business Horizons* 21 (December 1978), 3–6.

Cascio, Wayne F. "Turnover, Biographical Data, and Fair Employment Practice." *Journal of Applied Psychology* 61 (October 1976), 576–580.

Chamot, Dennis. "Professional Employees Turn to Unions." *Harvard Business Review* 54 (May–June 1976), 119–127.

Cherrington, David J. "Teaching the Work Ethic at Work." *Personnel Administrator* 21 (October 1976), 24–28.

Clarkson, Kenneth W. "What Humphrey-Hawkins Asks, but Doesn't Answer." *Business and Society Review* 20 (Winter 1976–77), 68–71.

"Clearer Rules on Confidentiality." *Business Week* (June 11, 1979), 35+.

Clement, Ronald W., Patrick R. Pinto, and James W. Walker. "Unethical and Improper Behavior by Training and Development Professionals." *Training and Development Journal* 32 (December 1978), 10–12.

Davis, Louis E. "Enhancing the Quality of Working Life—Developments in the United States." *International Labour Review* 116 (July–August 1977), 53–65.

Delaney, William A. "When It Comes to Ethics Golden Rule Applies to DP'er Changing Jobs." *Computerworld* 11 (August 8, 1977), 15.

Donnelly, John F. "Participative Management at Work." *Harvard Business Review* 55 (January–February 1977), 117–127.

Erdlen, John D. "Ethics and the Employee Relations Function." *Personnel Administrator* 24 (January 1979), 41–43+.

Ewing, David W. "What Business Thinks about Employee Rights." *Harvard Business Review* 55 (September–October 1977), 81–94.

Filipowicz, Christine A. "The Troubled Employee: Whose Responsibility?" *Personnel Administrator* 24 (June 1979), 17–22+.

Finkelstein, James, and James T. Ziegenfuss, Jr. "Diagnosing Employees' Personal Problems." *Personnel Journal* 57 (November 1978), 633–636+.

Foster, Lawrence W., and Marilyn L. Liebrenz. "Corporate Moves—Who Pays the Psychic Costs?" *Personnel* 54 (November–December 1977), 67–75.

Friedman, Barry A. "Seniority Systems and the Law." *Personnel Journal* 55 (July 1976), 334–336.

Fuller, Stephen H., and Bertha Jonsson. "Corporate Approaches to the Quality of Work Life." *Personnel Journal* 59 (August 1980), 632–638.

Fulmer, William E. "When Employees Want to Oust Their Union." *Harvard Business Review* 56 (March–April 1978), 163–170.

Guest, Robert H. "Quality of Work Life: Prospects for the 80's." *Vital Speeches of the Day* 46 (March 1, 1980), 310–313.

Gyllenhammer, Pehr G. "How Volvo Adopts Work to People." *Harvard Business Review* 55 (July–August 1977), 102–113.

Haessel, Walter, and John Palmer. "Market Power and Employment Discrimination." *Journal of Human Resources* 13 (Fall 1978), 545–560.

Hair, Joseph F., Jr., Ronald F. Bush, and Paul Busch. "Employee Theft: Views from Two Sides." *Business Horizons* 19 (December 1976), 25–29.

Hall, Douglas T., and Samuel Rabinowitz. "Caught Up in Work." *Wharton Magazine* 2 (Fall 1977), 19–25.

Hastings, Robert E. "Examining Employee Evaluations." *Business Horizons* 19 (February 1976), 77–83.

Hayden, Trudy. "How Much Does the Boss Need to Know?" *Civil Liberties Review* 3 (August–September 1976), 23–32+.

Herzberg, Frederick I. "New Perspectives on the Will to Work." *Personnel Administrator* 24 (December 1979), 72–76.

Hines, John. "Overcoming the Obstacles to Disabled Employment." *Personnel Management* 11 (March 1979), 40–43.

Hirsch, R., and C. Berman. "When Your Best Friend Becomes Your Boss . . ." *Working Woman* 3 (August 1978), 32–35+.

Hoke, W. G. "Equity for Exempt Personnel." *Personnel Administrator* 21 (July 1976), 41–46.

Holley, William H., and Hubert S. Field. "Equal Employment Opportunity and Its Implications for Personnel Practices." *Labor Law Journal* 27 (May 1976), 278–286.

Jacobs, Robert B. "Employee Resistance to OSHA Standards: Toward a More Reasonable Approach." *Labor Law Journal* 30 (April 1979), 219–230.

Jungblut, M. "Technology and Unemployment." *Atlas* 25 (October 1978), 56.

Kaagen, Stephen S. "Terminating People from Key Positions." *Personnel Journal* 57 (February 1978), 96–98.

Kearney, William J. "Pay for Performance? Not Always." *MSU Business Topcis* 27 (Spring 1979), 5–16.

Kempe, Richard L. "Merit Promotion and Equal Employment Opportunity." *GAO Review* 12 (Winter 1977), 80–82.

Kepner, Les. "Arbitration and Ethics." *Real Estate Today* 11 (September 1978), 1+.

Kleinschrod, Walter A. "Mandatory Retirement: The New Law May Not Be As Bad As Some Now Fear." *Administrative Management* 38 (December 1977), 25.

Koehn, Hank E. "Trends to the Future: I'm Entitled." *Journal of Systems Management* 30 (March 1979), 40–41.

Kotter, John P. "Power, Dependence, and Effective Management." *Harvard Business Review* 55 (July–August 1977), 125–136.

Kramer, Otto P. "Reporting Employee Fraudulent Acts." *Journal of Systems Management* 29 (January 1978), 22–23.

Kuffel, Tom, Peter P. Schoderbek, and Donald L. Plambeck."The Role of Continuing Responsibilities: Some Empirical Results." *Public Personnel Management* 8 (January–February, 1979), 26–31.

Lawler, E. E., III. "Should the Quality of Work Life Be Legislated?" *Personnel Administrator* 21 (January 1976), 17–21.

Lecht, Leonard A. "Women at Work: The Numbers Improve, But the Problem Remains the Same." *Conference Board Record* 13 (September 1976), 16–21.

Levering, Robert. "Is Business Pro or Con Illegal Immigration?" *Business and Society Review* 24 (Winter 1977–78), 55–59.

Levinson, Harry. "The Abrasive Personality." *Harvard Business Review* 56 (May–June 1978), 86–94.

Levitan, Sar A., and Richard S. Belous. "Workers Should Be Counted as (a) Employed or (b) Forced into Idleness. Right? Wrong?" *Across the Board* 14 (December 1977), 23–28.

Lillard, Lee A. "Inequality: Earnings vs. Human Wealth." *American Economic Review* 67 (March 1977), 42–53.

Linowes, David F. "Is Business Giving Employees Privacy?" *Business and Society Review* 32 (Winter 1979–1980), 47–49.

McCarville, William J. "Wisdom in the Workplace: Career and the Chemical Industry." *Vital Speeches of the Day* 46 (December 15, 1979), 136–138.

McClelland, David C., and David H. Burnham. "Power Is the Great Motivator." *Harvard Business Review* 54 (March–April 1976), 100–110.

Maccoby, Michael. "The Corporate Climber Has to Find His Heart." *Fortune* 94 (December 1976), 98–101+.

McIsaac, George S. "What's Coming in Labor Relations." *Harvard Business Review* 55 (September–October 1977), 22–36+.

MacLeod, J. S. "Importance of Social Diversity." *Personnel Administrator* 21 (October 1976), 20–23.

Malone, Paul B., III. "Baring Your Managerial Soul (Philosophically Speaking)." *Supervisory Management* 25 (June 1980), 31–35.

Marks, Charles W. "Is Your Bias Showing?" *Personnel Journal* 56 (August 1977), 381.

Meyer, Herbert E. "Personnel Directors Are the New Corporate Heroes." *Fortune* 93 (February 1976), 84–88+.

Miller, D. B. "Privacy: A Key Issue between Employees and Managers." *University of Michigan Business Review* 28 (January 1976), 7–12.

Miller, Neil. "The Accountability Chart—A Tool for Team Building." *Personnel* 54 (November–December 1977), 51–56.

Moore, Philip R. "Equal Pay for Equal Work of Equal Value?" *Enterprise* 3 (August 1979), 13–14.

Norwood, J. M. "But I Can't Work on Saturdays." *Personnel Administrator* 25 (January 1980), 25–30.

"OSHA's New Medical Disclosure Standard: Fundamental Right or Threat to Privacy?" *Occupational Hazards* 42 (August 1980), 47–49.

Peck, Cornelius J. "Unjust Discharges from Employment: A Necessary Change in the Law." *Ohio State Law Journal* 40 (1979), 1–49.

Pinder, Craig C. "Concerning the Application of Human Motivation Theories in Organizational Settings." *Academy of Management Review* 2 (July 1977), 384–397.

Radest, Howard B. "Work and Work: Felix Adler." *Journal of Historical Philosophy* 16 (January 1978), 71–81.

Rains, Harry H. "Industrial Relations in the Public Sector." *Employee Relations Law Journal* 3 (Summer 1977), 139–144.

Rhine, Shirley H. "The Senior Worker—Employed and Unemployed." *Conference Board Record* 13 (May 1976), 5–14.

Rittenoure, R. Lynn. "Measuring Fair Employment Practices: The Search for a Figure of Merit." *American Journal of Economics and Sociology* 37 (April 1978), 113–128.

Rosow, Jerome M. "Changing Attitudes to Work and Life Styles." *Journal of Contemporary Business* 8, no. 4 (1979), 5–18.

Saint, Paul F. "The Ethics of Performance." *Managers Magazine* 55 (May 1980), 26–32.

Schein, Virginia E. "Individual Privacy and Personnel Psychology: The Need for a Broader Perspective." *Journal of Social Issues* 33 (Summer 1977), 154–168.

Schrader, Alec D., and H. G. Osburn. "Biodata Faking: Effects of Induced Subtlety and Position Specificity." *Personal Psychology* 30 (Autumn 1977), 395–404.

Schroeder, Leila Obier. "Invasion of Privacy Limitations on Employee Theft Control." *Louisiana Business Review* 40 (May 1976), 2–5.

Shaffer, David R., Pamela V. Mays, and Karen Etheridge. "Who Shall Be Hired: A Biasing Effect of the Buckley Amendment on Employment Practices." *Journal of Applied Psychology* 61 (October 1976), 571–575.

Shapiro, Irving S. "Quality: The Underlying Theme of America's Third Century." *Personnel Administrator* 21 (January 1976), 16.

Sonnenfeld, Jeffrey. "Dealing with the Aging Work Force." *Harvard Business Review* 56 (November–December 1978), 81–92.

Stanton, Roger R. "Professional Managers and Personal Liability." *Public Personnel Management* 7 (January–February 1978), 43–48.

Stevenson, Russell B., Jr. "How Much Privacy Does Business Need?" *Business and Society Review* 30 (Summer 1979), 45–48.

Stondemire, Robert H. "Grievances of Employees and Personnel Administration." *University of South Carolina Governmental Review* 18 (May 1976), 1–4.

Stuart-Kotze, Robin, and Graham Cole. "Defeating the Peter Principle." *Optimum* 9 (1978), 54–61.

Sullivan, Frank W. "Peer Review and Professional Ethics." *American Journal of Psychiatry* 134 (February 1977), 186–188.

Summers, Clyde W. "Individual Protection against Unfair Dismissal: Time for a Statute." *Virginia Law Review* 62 (April 1976), 481–532.

Suojanen, Waino W., and Donald R. Hudson. "Coping with Stress and Addictive Work Behavior." *Atlantic Economic Review* 27 (March–April 1977), 4–9.

Taddeo, Kenneth, and Gerald Lefebvre. "The New Work Ethic." *Labour Gazette* 77 (July 1977), 305–308.

Taylor, Alan. "Don't Risk Getting Sacked for Being Ethical." *Computerworld* 11 (September 12, 1977), 23–24.

Taylor, Alan. "Readers See Some Dangers in Headhunting." *Computerworld* 12 (April 24, 1978), 15.

Taylor, Ronald N., and Mark Thompson. "Work Value System of Young Workers." *Academy of Management Journal* 19 (December 1976), 522–536.

Thimm, Alfred L. "The False Promise of Employee Codetermination." *Business and Society Review* 32 (Winter 1979–1980), 36–41.

Tronsen, M. Anders. "Protecting Personnel Policy from Further Government Regulation." *Personnel Journal* 55 (August 1976), 400–401+.

Upton, Molly. " 'Who Owns a Program' Depends on Type of Software." *Computerworld* 11 (June 27, 1977), 5.

Walker, James W. "Human Resource Planning: Managerial Concerns and Practices." *Business Horizons* 19 (June 1976), 55–59.

Weaver, K. M., and R. I. Hartman. "When a Corporation Starts Talking." *Personnel Administrator* 21 (September 1976), 19–23.

Westcott, Robert F. "How to Fire an Executive." *Business Horizons* 19 (April 1976), 33–36.

Wiggins, Ronald L., and Richard D. Steade. "Job Satisfaction as a Social Concern." *Academy of Management Review* 1 (October 1976), 48–55.

"Winning and Holding Employee Loyalty." *Nation's Business* 65 (April 1977), 40–44.

Winstanley, N. B. "Legal and Ethical Issues in Performance Appraisals." *Harvard Business Review* 58 (November–December 1980), 186+.

Wolters, Roger S. "Moral Turpitude in the Industrial Environment: A Real Dilemma." *Labor Law Journal* 27 (April 1976), 245–254.

Youngdahl, James E. "Arbitration of Discrimination Grievances: A Novel Approach under One Collective Agreement." *Arbitration Journal* 31 (September 1976), 145–163.

Zakraishek, Edward A. "Ethical Considerations and the Supervisor." *Supervision* 40 (March 1978), 1–3.

Ziskind, David. "Affirmative Action v. Seniority-Retroactive Seniority: A Remedy for Hiring Discrimination." *Labor Law Journal* 27 (August 1976), 480–490.

Finance and Banking

Books

Adams, Silas W. *The Legalized Crime of Banking.* New York: Gordon Press, 1979.

Bank Business Ethics and Conflict of Interest. Park Ridge, Ill.: Bank Administration Institute, 1977.

Bauman, W. Scott. *Professional Standards in Investment Management.* Charlottesville: The Financial Analysts Research Foundation, University of Virginia, 1980.

Greenwald, Carol S. *Banks Are Dangerous to Your Wealth.* Englewood Cliffs, N.J.: Prentice-Hall, 1980.

Lechner, Alan. *Street Games: Inside Stories of the Wall Street Hustle.* New York: Harper and Row, 1980.

Myer, Martin. *Don't Bank on It.* Rockville Center, N.Y.: Farnsworth Publishing Co., 1979.

Articles

Adam, John, Jr. "The Power to Destroy." *United States Banker* 89 (November 1978), 159+.

Adams, E. "Have Banks Gone Too Far?" *Bankers Magazine* 159 (Autumn 1976), 84–88.

Albrecht, W. Steve, and Marshall B. Romney. "Deterring White-Collar Crime in Banks." *Bankers Magazine* 163 (November–December 1980), 60–64.

Alexander, Gordon J., and Rogene A. Buchholz. "Corporate Social Responsibility and Stock Market Performance." *Academy of Management Journal* 21 (September 1978), 479–486.

"Answering Questions about Codes of Ethics." *Banking* 70 (June 1978), 8–14.

Bancroft, Al. "Ethical Issues in Marketing Financial Services." *Managerial Finance*, no. 3 (1980), 257–270.

Baron, C. David, D. Gerald Searfoss, Douglas A. Johnson, and Charles H. Smith. "Corporate Irregularities: Banker's Expectations and the New Audit Standards." *Journal of Commercial Bank Lending* 59 (July 1977), 45–58.

Basi, Bart A. "The Responsibility of the Broker-Dealer to the Investing Public." *American Business Law Journal* 13 (Winter 1976), 371–384.

Berry, Leonard L. "Banking in the Age of the People." *Bankers Magazine* 159 (Winter 1976), 62–66.

Bleiberg, Robert M. "Shareholder Constituency? The Liabilities Probably Outweight the Assets." *Barron's* 57 (August 29, 1977), 7+.

Callan, Eugene J. "Who Is the Competition?" *Bankers Monthly* 93 (July 15, 1976), 22–24.

Cheng, Jeanette. "White Collar Crime: Common Schemes and How to Spot Them." *Credit and Financial Management* 81 (January 1979), 10+.

Cook, James A., Jr. "An Expanded Look at Codes of Ethics for Bank Officers." *Magazine of Bank Administration* 55 (January 1979), 22–25.

"Corporate Responsibility in the Financial Accounting and Disclosure Areas: Who Makes and Who Implements the Rules?" *Business Lawyer* 34 (July 1979), 1979–1981.

Demott, John. "Inside Information: The Equity Funding Aftermath." *The Institutional Investor* (March 1977), 196–197.

Eirinberg, Alan B. "Consumer Education Is In: Banks, Savings Institutions Start to Tell It Like It Is." *Advertising Age* 47 (September 13, 1976), 78+.

Fabian, Robert H. "The Preservation of Privacy in Banking." *Bankers Magazine* 159 (Summer 1976), 60–64.

Feldman, Sidney. "Accounting for Bank Annual Reports: Everyone from the SEC to Ralph Nader Wants Banks to Report More in Their Annual Reports. Are the Banks Moving in the Right Direction?" *Bankers Magazine* 161 (Autumn 1977), 37–41.

Ferrara, Ralph C. "Accountant-Banker Credibility: How to Restore a Public Image." *Journal of Commercial Bank Lending* 60 (July 1978), 13–27.

"Financial Marketers Adopt Voluntary Advertising Ethics Guidelines." *Marketing News* 10 (October 22, 1976), 1+.

"Financing Apartheid—Citibank in South Africa." *Interfaith Center on Corporate Responsibility* (May 1980), 3A–3B.

Green, Wayne E. "Breaking Faith? Takeover Fights Pose an Ethical Question for Banks and Brokers." *Wall Street Journal* (December 12, 1977), 1+.

Grossman, Steven, Thomas Oxner, and Richard Rivers. "Financial Disclosures for Diversified Companies." *Atlanta Economic Review* 28 (July–August 1978), 27–31.

Haas, Peter C., Jr. "Closing the Door on Internal Bank Fraud." *Personnel Administrator* 23 (November 1978), 45–48.

Hanenburg, Don. "Integrity Pays Dividends." *Credit and Financial Management* 79 (January 1977), 32–33.

Harris, Daniel L. "Responding to External Pressure on Redlining: A Case Study." *Issues in Bank Regulation* 2 (Summer 1978), 24–29.

Harrison, Michael A. "Reciprocity in International Banking." *Bankers Magazine* 160 (Winter 1977), 31–34.

"How SEC Plans to Boost Disclosure for Non-U.S. Securities." *Public Relations Journal* 35 (April 1979), 13–15.

Jarrett, Charles B., Jr. "Developing a Bank's Code of Ethics and Conflict of Interest Policy." *Magazine of Bank Administration* 53 (January 1978), 10–11+.

Johnson, Herbert E. "Corporate Responsibility: Words into Substance." *Magazine of Bank Administration* 53 (July 1977), 22–27.

Kane, Edward J. "Can FDIC Regulation Deliver Us from Self Dealing?" *Bankers Monthly* 159 (Autumn 1976), 13–15.

Kempin, Frederick G., Jr. "The Use and Misuse of Inside Information by Corporate Managers and Other Insiders." *American Business Law Journal* 14 (Fall 1976), 136–169.

Landau, Theodore K. "Don't Avoid Lending Responsibility." *Bankers Magazine* 159 (Summer 1976), 10–12.

Leff, Gary. "How Secret Should Bank Problem Lists Be?" *Bankers Magazine* 161 (September–October 1978), 37–40.

Leigh-Pemberton, Robin. "O.R. and the Changing Banking Scene." *Journal of the Operations Research Society* 30 (January 1979), 1–9.

"Limiting the Players in the Options Game." *Business Week* (March 5, 1979), 28.

Mandell, Lewis, and Harold Black. "Monitoring Discrimination in Lending." *Bankers Monthly* 160 (Winter 1977), 80–82.

"Marketers See Link in Industry Economic Social Challenges." *Savings Bank Journal* 59 (July 1978), 12–17.

Mitchell, Dan W. "Ethics in Loan Management." *Journal of Commercial Bank Lending* 62 (April 1980), 2–10.

Mobley, Louis R. "Should Finance Officers Be Concerned with Ethics?" *Governmental Finance* 6 (February 1977), 31–35.

Moskowitz, Milton R. "Bank of America's Rocky Road to Responsibility." *Business and Society Review* 22 (Summer 1977), 61–64.

Murray, Edwin A., Jr. "The Social Response Process in Commercial Banks: An Empirical Investigation." *Academy of Management Review* 1 (July 1976), 5–15.

"New Help in Writing a Code of Conduct for Your Bank." *Banking* 70 (October 1978), 128+.

Pace, Edmond E. "A Banker's Code of Conduct (A Training Feature)." *Journal of Commercial Bank Lending* 60 (November 1977), 8–12.

"Personal Loans and Bank Ethics." *Time* 110 (August 29, 1977), 49–50.

Prentice, P. I. "Urban Financing for Jobs, Profits, and Prosperity: Broader Policy Issues in Property Tax Reform." *American Journal of Economics and Sociology* 36 (January 1977), 65–78.

"Redlining and Urban Reinvestment." *Corporate Information Center Brief* (November 1977), 3A–3D.

"Regulators' Survey of Banking Practices Finds Abuses Are 'Not Widespread.' " *Banking* 70 (April 1978), 53–54.

"RMA Revises Code of Ethics for the Exchange of Credit Information." *Journal of Commercial Bank Lending* 59 (October 1976), 2–13.

Rose, Peter S. "Social Responsibility in Banking." *The Canadian Banker and ICB Review* 86 (April 1979), 62–67.

Rubin, Harvey W. "A Banker's Guide to Directors' and Officers' Liability." *Bankers Magazine* 161 (May–June 1978), 27–31.

Siegel, Joel, and Johnson Bank. "Should Companies Publish Financial Forecasts?" *Atlanta Economic Review* 26 (January–February 1976), 33–36.

"Simsa Faces Up to Ad Ethics Code." *Savings and Loan News* 98 (September 1977), 86–88.

Sjaastad, Larry A., and Daniel L. Wisecarver. "The Social Cost of Public Finance." *Journal of Political Economy* 85 (June 1977), 513–547.

Stalder, Henri. "Ethical and Material Values in Swiss Banking." *Canadian Banker and ICB Review* 85 (May–June 1978), 20–23.

Stein, Herbert. "Price-Fixing as Seen by a Price-Fixer." *Across the Board* 15 (December 1978), 32–43.

Thomas, Donald L. "The Banks and Redlining: Regulations, Responsibilities, and Reality." *Vital Speeches of the Day* 44 (April 15, 1978), 407+.

Thompson, Thomas. "Postscript to the Lance Affair: A Banker Code of Ethics." *United States Banker* 88 (November 21, 1977), 5–6+.

"U.S. Bank Loans to Chile." *Corporate Information Center Brief* (December 1978), 3A–3B.

Via, J. William. "Antitrust and the Rescue of Distressed Banks by Acquisition." *Banking Law Journal* 94 (June–July 1977), 508–524.

Weiss, Elliott J. "Disclosure and Corporate Accountability." *Business Lawyer* 34 (January 1979), 575–603.

Willacy, Aubrey B., and Hazel M. "Conglomerate Bank Mergers and Clayton 7 (Section 7 of the Clayton Act): Is Potential Competition the Answer?" *Banking Law Journal* 93 (February 1976), 148–195.

Wu, H. K. "Does Banking Need a Code of Ethics?" *Bankers Magazine* 160 (Summer 1977), 11–14.

Insurance

Books

Code of Professional Ethics of the American Institute for Property and Liability Underwriters. Malvern, Pa.: American Institute for Property and Liability Underwriters, 1979.

Grant, Roger H. *Insurance Reform: Consumer Action in the Progressive Era.* Iowa City: Iowa State University Press, 1979.

Hershey, Barry J. *Billion Dollar Bankruptcies: The Potential Crisis in the Insurance Industry.* Cambridge, Mass.: ABT Associates, 1980.

Horn, Ronald C. *On Professions, Professionals, and Professional Ethics.* Malvern, Pa.: American Institute for Property and Liability Underwriters, 1978.

Spielman, Peter, and Aaron Zelman. *The Life Insurance Conspiracy: Made Elementary by Holmes and Watson.* Hamden, Conn.: Fireside Press, 1979.

Zelezer, Viviara A. Rotman. *Morals and Markets: The Development of Life Insurance in the United States.* New York: Columbia University Press, 1979.

Articles

Brandon, L. G. "Value Orientations of Insurance Industry Chief Executives: A Study of the Identification and Role of Personal Values in Decision Making?" *CPCU Annuals* 29 (September 1976), 205–211.

Christensen, Burke A. "Is the Sale of Life Insurance a Profession?" *Trusts and Estates* 119 (September 1980), 72–73.

"Coping with Consumerism—Three Viewpoints." *National Underwriter* (Life edition) 80 (June 5, 1976), 15+.

"Equality Drive Threat to Risk System?" *National Underwriter* (Life edition) 80 (December 18, 1976), 2+.

Everett, Martin. "The Dark Side of Insurance Sales." *Sales and Marketing Management* 122 (February 5, 1979), 25–29.

"Insurance Redlining: Do We Need Insurance against Insurance Companies?" *Interfaith Center on Corporate Responsibility* (July 1979), 3A–3D.

Karson, Stanley G. "Insurance Industry and Social Responsibility: A Successful Effort." *Journal of Contemporary Business* 8, no. 1 (1979), 103–114.

Klimon, E. L. "Attempt to Define Dishonesty." *National Underwriter* (Property edition) 83 (May 25, 1979), 37–38.

O'Connell, Jeffrey. "Business and the Products Liability Crisis: Legal Aspects of No-Fault Insurance." *Vital Speeches of the Day* 43 (February 15, 1977), 278–280.

Young, James R. "Consumer Problems with Industrial Life Insurance." *Journal of Consumer Affairs* 10 (Winter 1976), 255–260.

Marketing

Books

Balderston, Frederick E., and James M. Carman, eds. *Regulation of Marketing and the Public Interest.* Elmsford, N.Y.: Pergamon Press, 1981.

Balderston, Frederick E., and Francesco M. Nicosia, eds. *Public Policy for Marketing.* Elmsford, N.Y.: Pergamon Press, 1980.

Bork, Robert H. *The Antitrust Paradox.* New York: Basic Books, 1978.

Dominquez, George S. *Marketing in a Regulated Environment* New York: John Wiley & Sons, 1978.

Henion, Karl E., II, and Thomas C. Kinnear, eds. *Ecological Marketing.* New York: American Marketing Association, 1976.

Reynolds, Fred D., and Hiram C. Burkesdale, eds. *Marketing and the Quality of Life.* Chicago: American Marketing Association, 1978.

Robertson, Andrew. *Strategic Marketing: A Business Response to Consumerism.* New York: Halstead Press, 1978.

Rosenberg, Larry J. *Marketing.* Englewood Cliffs, N.J.: Prentice-Hall, 1977.

Uhr, Ernest B., and Lance P. Jarvis, eds. *Social Responsibility in Marketing: A Selected and Annotated Bibliography.* Chicago: American Marketing Association, 1977.

Articles

Adler, Lee. "The Privacy Issue Arouses Concern about Ethics in Marketing Research." *Sales and Marketing Management* 125 (December 1980), 88–89.

"All Market Research Is Potential Evidence: Presnick." *Marketing News* 12 (May 18, 1979), 16+.

"Are We Doing the Wrong Things Right?" *Marketing and Media Decisions* 14 (May 1979), 64–67.

Bezilla, R., J. B. Haynes, and C. Elliott. "Ethics in Marketing Research." *Business Horizons* 19 (April 1976), 83–86.

Blair, Roger D., and Yoram C. Peles. "Private Brands and Antitrust Policy." *UCLA Law Review* 25 (October 1977), 46–69.

Blois, K. J. "Social Responsibility and the Industrial Marketer." *Management Decision* 18 (1980), 246–253.

Buchanan, James M. "Markets, States, and the Extent of Morals." *American Economic Review* 68 (May 1978), 364–368.

Bumpass, Donald. "The Social Costs of Monopoly: They May Be Greater Than We Thought." *Antitrust Law and Economics Review* 9, no. 2 (1977), 91–101.

Coney, K. A., and J. K. Murphy. "Attitudes of Marketers toward Ethical and Professional Marketing Research Practices." *Southern Marketing Association Proceedings of Conference* (October 1976), 172–174.

Crosier, Keith. "How Effective Is the Contribution of Market Research to Social Marketing?" *Journal of the Market Research Society* 21 (January 1979), 3–16.

Demonthoux, P. G. "Marketing and Corruption." *Management Decision* 15, no. 6 (1977), 494–503.

Denenberg, Herb. "Companies That Pretend They're Perfect Are Missing Out on Some Big Sales." *Sales and Marketing Management* 122 (March 1979), 82+.

Divita, Salvatore F. "Marketing Quality Control: An Alternative to Consumer Affairs." *California Management Review* 20 (Summer 1978), 74–78.

Dubinsky, Alan J., Eric N. Berkowitz, and William Rudelius. "Ethical Problems of Field Sales Personnel." *MSU Business Topics* 28 (Summer 1980), 11–16.

Dunn, Albert H. "Case of the Suspect Salesman." *Harvard Business Review* 57 (November–December 1979), 38–40+.

Erickson, W. Bruce. "Price Fixing Conspiracies: Their Long-Term Impact." *Journal of Industrial Economics* 24 (March 1976), 189–202.

Ewing, J. "Honesty, Salesmen, and College Students." *Sales and Marketing Management* 116 (May 10, 1976), 73–75.

Finney, F. Robert. "Reciprocity: Gone but Not Forgotten." *Journal of Marketing* 42 (January 1978), 54–59.

Frass, Arthur G., and Douglas F. Greer. "Market Structure and Price Collusion: An Empirical Analysis." *Journal of Industrial Economics* 26 (September 1977), 21–44.

Frey, Cynthia J., and Thomas C. Kinnear. "Legal Constraints and Marketing Research: Review and Call to Action." *Journal of Marketing Research* 16 (August 1979), 295–302.

Friedman, M. "Standards for Professional Conduct in Consumer Research: Can We Get There from Here?" *Advances in Consumer Research* 4 (1977), 254–255.

Friedman, M. "Establishing Standards for Professional Conduct in Consumer Research: A Suggested Role for the Association for Consumer Research." *Advances in Consumer Research* 4 (1977), 261.

Gibson, Frank F. "Location Restrictions—A Legitimate Limitation on Product Distribution?" *Bulletin of Business Research* 52 (June 1977), 1–3+.

Gilbert, Richard J., and Steven M. Goldman. "Potential Competition and the Monopoly Price of Our Exhaustible Resource." *Journal of Economic Theory* 17 (April 1978), 319–331.

Gravereau, Victor P., Leonard J. Konopa, and Jim L. Grimm. "Attitudes of Industrial Buyers toward Selected Social Issues." *Industrial Marketing Management* 7 (June 1978), 199–207.

Gray, Roger. "When Does Aggressive Trading Become Market Tampering?" *The Business Lawyer* 35 (March 1980), 745–750.

Gross, Charles W., and Harish L. Verma. "Marketing and Social Responsibility." *Business Horizons* 20 (October 1977), 75–82.

Hargraves, R. "Promotion of Prescription and Proprietary Drugs." *Journal of Drug Issues* 6, no. 1 (1976), 1–5.

Holzmann, Henry. "How to Avoid the Kick-Back Trap." *Agency Sales Magazine* 8 (March 1978), 14–15.

Jacoby, J. "History and Objectives Underlying the Formation of ACR's Professional Affairs Committee." *Advances in Consumer Research* 4 (1977), 256–257.

Keller, Edmund R. "The Trouble with Monopoly Is the Price." *Antitrust Law and Economics Review* 9, no. 2 (1977), 73–90.

Kushner, Joseph, and Isidore J. Masse. "Patents as a Basis for International Price Discrimination." *Antitrust Bulletin* 21 (Winter 1976), 639–656.

Laczniak, Gene R., and D. A. Michie. "Broadened Marketing and Social Disorder: A Reply." *Academy of Marketing Science Journal* 7 (Summer 1979), 239–242.

Laczniak, Gene R., and D. A. Michie. "Social Disorder of the Broadened Concept of Marketing." *Academy of Marketing Science Journal* 7 (Summer 1979), 214–232.

Laczniak, Gene R., Robert F. Lusch, and Patrick E. Murphy. "Social Marketing: Its Ethical Dimensions." *Journal of Marketing* 43 (Spring 1979), 29–36.

Levy, S. J., and P. Kotter. "Toward a Broader Concept of Marketing's Role in Social Order." *Academy of Marketing Science Journal* 7 (Summer 1979), 233–238.

Luchsinger, L. Louise, and Patrick M. Dunne. "Fair Trade Laws—How Fair?" *Journal of Marketing* 42 (January 1978), 50–53.

Lundstrom, William J. "The Marketing Concept: The Ultimate in Bait and Switch." *Marquette Business Review* 20 (Fall 1976), 124–130.

McLintock, C. C. "Issues in Establishing and Enforcing Professional Ethics and Standards." *Advances in Consumer Research* 4 (1977), 258–260.

Moyer, Mel S. "Marketing Policies and Public Values." *Business Quarterly* 43 (Winter 1978), 50–57.

Munson, J. Michael, and Shelby H. McIntyre. "Developing Practical Procedures for the Measurement of Personal Values in Cross-Cultural Marketing." *Journal of Marketing Research* 16 (February 1978), 48–52.

Murphy, Patrick E., Gene R. Laczniak, and Robert F. Lusch. "Ethical Guidelines for Business and Social Marketing." *Journal of the Academy of Marketing Science* 6 (Summer 1978), 195–205.

Nelson, Robert H. "The Economics of Honest Trade Practices." *Journal of Industrial Economics* 24 (June 1976), 281–293.

Olshavsky, Richard W. "Marketing's Cigarette Scar." *Business Horizons* 21 (June 1978), 46–51.

Pauly, Mark V. "The Ethics and Economics of Kickbacks and Fee Splitting." *Bell Journal of Economics* 10 (Spring 1979), 344–352.

Penn, Stanley. "Little Data Company Charges That IBM Spread False Rumors of Link with Mafia." *Wall Street Journal* (July 8, 1976), 32.

Roering, Kenneth J., Robert D. Schooler, and Fred W. Morgan. "An Evaluation of Marketing Practices: Businessmen, Housewives, and Students." *Journal of Business Research* 4 (May 1978), 131–144.

Roward, Roger. "Ex-Employee Reveals AMC Kickbacks." *Automotive News* (September 26, 1977), 1+.

Schneider, Kenneth C. "Subject and Respondent Abuse in Marketing Research." *MSU Business Topics* 25 (Spring 1977), 13–19.

Sharman, Howard. "Unethical Exports." *Marketing* (London) (October 1976), 12–15.

Shilony, Yural. "Mixed Pricing in Oligopoly." *Journal of Economic Theory* 14 (April 1977), 373–388.

Snyder, James D. "Bribery in Selling: The Scandal Comes Home." *Sales and Marketing Management* 116 (May 10, 1976), 35–38.

Snyder, James D. "It's Time to Repeal the Right to Do Wrong." *Sales and Marketing Management* 117 (October 11, 1976), 39–42.

Sonnenfeld, Jeffrey, and Paul R. Lawrence. "Why Do Companies Succumb to Price Fixing?" *Harvard Business Review* 56 (July–August 1978), 145–157.

"Special Section: Social Issues and Public Policy in Marketing." *Journal of Marketing Research* 15 (February 1978), 1–57.

Stampfl, Ronald W. "Structural Constraints, Consumerism, and the Marketing Concept." *MSU Business Topics* 26 (Spring 1978), 5–16.

Townsend, Robert M. "The Eventual Failure of Price Fixing Schemes." *Journal of Economic Theory* 14 (February 1977), 190–199.

Trawick, I. Fred, and William R. Darden. "Marketers' Perceptions of Ethical Standards in the Marketing Profession." *Review of Business and Economic Research* 16 (Fall 1980), 1–17.

Walsh, Mike W. "Praise for ABP's New Research Practice Standards." *Marketing and Media Decisions* 14 (August 1979), 92–94.

Wise, Gordon L., Myron K. Cox, and Charles Floto. "Sex and Race Discrimination in the New-Car Showroom: A Fact or Myth?" *Journal of Consumer Affairs* 11 (Winter 1977), 107–113.

Zinn, John. "Let the Buyer Still Beware!" *Business Quarterly* 42 (Summer 1977), 54–58.

Organizational Life, Values, and Management Behavior

Books

Balzer, Richard. *Clockwork: Life in and outside an American Factory.* Garden City, N.Y.: Doubleday, 1976.

Barach, Jeffrey A., ed. *The Individual, Business, and Society.* Englewood Cliffs, N.J.: Prentice-Hall, 1977.

Bowen, Peter. *Social Control in Industrial Organizations.* Boston: Routledge and Kegan, 1976.

Brown, Courtney C. *Putting the Corporate Board to Work.* New York: Macmillan Publishing Co., 1976.

Burns, James MacGregor. *Leadership.* New York: Harper and Row, 1978.

Caves, Richard E. *American Industry—Structure, Conduct, Performance.* 4th ed. Englewood Cliffs, N.J.: Prentice-Hall, 1977.

Cornuelle, Richard. *De-Managing America: The Final Revolution.* New York: Random House, 1976.

Cray, Ed. *Chrome Colossus: General Motors and Its Times.* New York: McGraw-Hill, 1980.

Dill, William R. *Running the American Corporation.* New York: The American Assembly, Columbia University, 1978.

Dubin, Robert, ed. *Handbook of Work, Organization, and Society.* Chicago: Rand, 1976.

Edwards, Richard C. *Contested Terrain: The Transformation of the Workplace in the 20th Century.* New York: Basic Books, 1979.

England, George W., et al. *Organizational Functioning in Cross-Cultural Perspective.* Kent, Ohio: Kent State University Press, 1978.

Ermann, M. David, and Richard J. Lundman, eds. *Corporate and Governmental Deviance: Problems of Organizational Behavior in Contemporary Society.* New York: Oxford University Press, 1978.

Ewing, David W. *Freedom inside the Organization: Bringing Civil Liberties to the Workplace.* New York: E. P. Dutton, 1977.

Form, William H. *Blue-Collar Stratification: Autoworkers in Four Countries.* Princeton, N.J.: Princeton University Press, 1976.

Furlong, James. *Labor in the Boardroom, the Peaceful Revolution.* Princeton, N.J.: Dow Jones, 1977.

Golemdiewski, Robert. *Man, Management, and Morality: Toward a New Organizational Ethic.* New York: Pantheon Books, 1976.

Green, Mark, and Robert Massie, Jr., eds. *The Big Business Reader–Essays on Corporate America.* Washington, D.C.: Big Business Day–Publications Dept., 1980.

Haas, Frederick, and Niel Humphrey. *Business Man.* Reston, Va.: Reston Publishing Co., 1976.

Hackman, J. Richard, and J. Lloyd Suttle, eds. *Improving Life at Work: Behavioral Science Approaches to Organizational Change.* Santa Monica, Calif.: Goodyear, 1977.

Hammer, W. Clay. *Organizational Shock.* New York: John Wiley and Sons, 1980.

Hyde, J. Edward. *The Phone Book: What the Telephone Company Would Rather You Not Know.* Chicago: Regnery, 1976.

Jackall, Robert. *Workers in a Labyrinth: Jobs and Survival in a Bank Bureaucracy.* New York: Universe Books, 1978.

Jacques, Elliott. *A General Theory of Bureaucracy.* New York: Halsted Press, 1976.

Kanter, Rosabeth Moss, and Barry A. Stein, eds. *Life in Organizations.* New York: Basic Books, 1979.

Kanter, Rosabeth Moss. *Men and Women of the Corporation.* New York: Basic Books, 1977.

Katzell, Raymond A. *Work in America Institute.* New York: New York University Press, 1977.

Kelley, Joe. *How Managers Manage.* Englewood Cliffs, N.J.: Prentice-Hall, 1980.

Kerr, C., and Jerome M. Rosow, eds. *Work in America: The Decade Ahead.* New York: Van Nostrand-Reinhold, 1979.

Killran, Roy A. *Human Resource Management: An ROI Approach.* New York: Amacon, 1976.

King, Burt, et al. *Managerial Control and Organizational Democracy.* New York: Halsted Press, 1978.

Kleinfeld, Sonny. *The Biggest Company on Earth: A Profile of AT&T.* New York: Holt, Rinehart, and Winston, 1981.

Kraus, William A. *Collaboration in Organizations: Alternatives to Hierarchy.* New York: Human Sciences Press, 1980.

Levinson, Harry. *Psychological Man.* Cambridge: The Levinson Institute, 1976.

McDonald, John. *The Game of Business.* Garden City, N.Y.: Doubleday, 1977.

Macey, Stuart A. *The Degeneration of the American Corporate Managerial System.* Albuquerque, N.M.: American Classical Collection Press, 1981.

McGrath, Phyllis S. *Corporate Directorship Practices: The Public Policy Committee.* New York: Conference Board, 1980.

McSweeney, Edward. *Managing the Managers.* New York: Harper and Row, 1978.

Margolis, Diana R. *The Managers: Corporate Life in America.* New York: W. Morrow and Co., 1979.

Mueller, Robert Kirk. *New Directions for Directors: Behind the By-Laws.* Lexington, Mass.: Lexington Books, 1978.

Mueller, Robert Kirk. *Board Compass: What It Means to Be a Director in a Changing World.* Lexington, Mass.: Lexington Books, 1979.

Mulder, Mark. *The Daily Power Game.* Boston: Martinus Nijhoff, 1977.

Ollins, Wally. *The Corporate Personality: An Inquiry into the Nature of Corporate Identity.* Clifton, N.J.: Mayflower Press, 1979.

Osherson, Samuel D. *Holding On or Letting Go.* New York: Free Press, 1980.

Pfeffer, Richard M. *Working for Capitalism.* New York: Columbia University Press, 1979.

Presthus, Robert. *The Organizational Society.* New York: St. Martin's Press, 1978.

Roy, Robert H. *The Cultures of Management.* Baltimore: Johns Hopkins University Press, 1977.

Sayles, Leonard R. *Managerial Behavior: Administration in Complex Organizations.* 2d ed. Huntington, N.Y.: Krieger, 1979.

Sayre, Kenneth, ed. *Values in the Electric Power Industry.* Notre Dame, Ind.: University of Notre Dame Press, 1977.

Schrank, Robert. *Ten Thousand Working Days.* Cambridge: MIT Press, 1978.

Scott, William G., and David K. Hart. *Organizational America.* Boston: Houghton Mifflin, 1979.

Shorris, Earl. *The Oppressed Middle: Politics of Middle Management.* Garden City, N.Y.: Anchor Press/Doubleday, 1981.

Stevens, Mark. *"Like No Other Store in the World": The Inside Story of Bloomingdales.* New York: Thomas Y. Crowell, 1979.

Stevenson, Russell B., Jr. *Corporations and Information: Secrecy, Access, and Disclosure.* Baltimore: Johns Hopkins University Press, 1980.

Strauss, George, and Leonard R. Sayles. *The Human Problems of Management.* 4th ed. Englewood Cliffs, N.J.: Prentice-Hall, 1980.

Tarrant, John J. *Drucker: The Man Who Invented Corporate Society.* Boston: Cahners, 1976.

The Touche Ross Survey on the Changing Nature of the Corporate Board. New York: Research and Forecasts, 1978.

Westin, Alan F., and Stephan Salisbury. *Individual Rights in the Corporation.* New York: Pantheon, 1980.

Williams, Harold M., and Irving S. Shapiro. *Power and Accountability: The Changing Role of the Corporate Board of Directors.* New York: Columbia University Press, 1979.

Williams, J. Clinton. *Human Behavior in Organizations.* Cincinnati: Southwestern Publishing Co., 1978.

Witte, John F. *Authority and Alienation in Work: Workers' Participation in an American Corporation.* Chicago: University of Chicago Press, 1980.

Woodman, John, et al. *The World of a Giant Corporation: A Report from the GE Project.* Seattle: North County Press, 1976.

Wright, Patrick. *On a Clear Day You Can See General Motors.* Chicago: J. Patrick Wright Enterprises, 1979.

Articles

Aburdene, Patricia. "Beyond Executive Stress: Board Responsibility for CEO Mental Health." *Directors and Boards* 2 (Summer 1977), 27–40.

Allen, Robert F. "The Ik in the Office." *Organizational Dynamics* 8 (Winter 1980), 26–41.

Arbose, Jules. "The Changing Life Values of Today's Executive." *International Management* 35 (July 1980), 12–15+.

Argenti, John. "And Now for the New Masters." *Accountancy* 88 (January 1977), 94+.

Bartol, Kathryn M. "The Sex Structuring of Organizations: A Search for Possible Causes." *Academy of Management Review* 3 (October 1978), 805–815.

Bartolome, Fernando, and Paul A. Lee Evans. "Professional Lives versus Private Lives—Shifting Problems of Managerial Commitment." *Organizational Dynamics* 7 (Spring 1979), 3–29.

Bartusis, Connie. "My Boss Asked Me to Lie." *McCall's* 56 (July 1979), 85+.

Berry, Thomas. "Planetary Management: Observations on the Managerial Ethos." *FCR Review* 1 (Spring 1980), 6–12.

Bettauer, Arthur. "Internal Controls: The Corporate Directors' Vital Role." *Price Waterhouse Review* 24 (1979), 3–4+.

Bliss, Perry, and Jim McCullough. "The Tyranny of Small Decisions, Temporal Conflict, and the Necessity of Politicization of the Market." *Business and Society* 19 (Winter 1980), 48–55.

Boling, T. Edwin. "The Management Ethics Crisis: An Organizational Perspective." *Academy of Management Review* 3 (April 1978), 360–365.

Bowen, Donald D. "Value Dilemmas in Organization Development." *Journal of Applied Behavioral Science* 13, no. 4 (1977), 543–556.

Bowman, Edward H. "Some Reflections on Corporate Strategy and Corporate Governance." *International Studies of Management and Organization* 9 (Winter 1979–80), 100–107.

Brown, Martha A. "Values—A Necessary but Neglected Ingredient of Motivation on the Job." *Academy of Management Review* 1 (October 1976), 15–23.

Buchholz, Rogene A. "The Belief Structure of Managers Relative to Work Concepts Measured by a Factor Analytic Model." *Personnel Psychology* 30 (Winter 1977), 567–587.

Bunke, Harvey C. "Heroes, Values, and the Organization." *Business Horizons* 19 (October 1976), 33–41.

Burton, Gene E., Dev S. Pathak, and David B. Burton. "Brainstorming—Turning on the Creative Flow: Beware of the Effects of Group Loyalty." *Management World* 6 (December 1977), 3–5.

Carroll, Archie B. "Linking Business Ethics to Behavior in Organizations." *SAM Advanced Management Journal* 43 (Summer 1978), 4–11.

Cho, Jae H. "Moral Implication of Acquisitive Instinct under the Separation of Ownership and Control." *Review of Social Economy* 35 (October 1977), 143–148.

Cleary, C. B. "Corporate Governance." *AACSB Bulletin, Proceedings, Annual Meeting 1979*, 67–73.

Cohen, Allan R., Herman Gadon, and George Miaoulis. "Decision Making in Firms: The Impact of Non-Economic Factors." *Journal of Economic Issues* 10 (June 1976), 242–258.

Conrad, Alfred F. "Reflections on Public Interest Directors." *Michigan Law Review* 75 (April–May 1977), 941–961.

Cooper, M. R., B. S. Morgan, P. M. Foley, and L. B. Kaplan. "Changing Employee Values: Deepening Discontent?" *Harvard Business Review* 57 (January–February 1979), 117–125.

Cooper, Terry L. "Ethics Values and Systems." *Journal of Systems Management* 30 (September 1979), 6–12.

"The Corporate Mindset: Nice People Can Turn into Robber Barons." *Human Behavior* 7 (December 1978), 50.

Davis, Keith, and Robert L. Blomstrom. "Adapting the Organization for Social Response." *Arizona Business* 22 (June–July 1975), 12–16.

Davis, Louis E. "Individuals and the Organization." *California Management Review* 22 (Spring 1980), 4–14.

Denhardt, R. B. "Individual Responsibility in an Age of Organization." *Midwest Review of Public Administration* 11 (December 1977), 259–269.

Donaldson, J. Waller. "Ethics and Organization." *Journal of Management Studies* 17 (February 1980), 34–55.

England, George W. "Managers and Their Value Systems: A Five-Country Comparative Study." *Columbia Journal of World Business* 13 (Summer 1978), 35–44.

Estes, Robert M. "The Case for Counsel to Outside Directors." *Harvard Business Review* 54 (July–August 1976), 125–132.

Fottler, M. D. "Employee Participation in Social Action Programs: An Exploratory Study." *Academy of Management Proceedings, 37th Annual Meeting 1977*, 271–275.

Goodman, Steven E. "Quality of Life: The Role of Business." *Business Horizons* 21 (June 1978), 36–37.

Green, Mark. "The Case for Corporate Democracy." *Regulation* 4 (May–June 1980), 20–25.

Greenough, William Croan. "Keeping Corporate Governance in the Private Sector." *Business Horizons* 23 (February 1980), 71–74.

Hamilton, Walter A. "Corporate Behavior—A Status Report." *Conference Board Record* 13 (August 1976), 6–8.

Hegarty, W. Harvey, and Henry P. Sims, Jr. "Organizational Philosophy, Policies, and Objectives Related to Unethical Decision Behavior: A Laboratory Experiment." *Journal of Applied Psychology* 64 (June 1979), 331–338.

Hegarty, W. Harvey, and Henry P. Sims, Jr. "Some Determinants of

Unethical Decision Behavior: An Experiment." *Journal of Applied Psychology* 63 (August 1978), 451–457.

Holmes, Sandra L. "Structural Responses of Large Corporations to a Social Responsibility Ethic." *Academy of Management Proceedings, 37th Annual Meeting 1977*, 281–284.

Holmes, Sandra L. "Executives Should Be Seen and Heard." *Business Horizons* 20 (April 1977), 5–8.

Jantsch, Eric. "Ethics, Morals, and Systems Management." *Futures* 10 (December 1978), 459–468.

Kanter, Allen. "The Case for the Outside Director in the Closely Held Company." *Business Horizons* 22 (December 1979), 39–42.

Katz, Jack. "Cover-up and Collective Integrity: On the Natural Antagonisms of Authority Internal and External to Organizations." *Social Problems* 25 (October 1977), 3–17.

Keim, Gerald D. "Managerial Behavior and the Social Responsibility Debate: Goals versus Constraints." *Academy of Management Journal* 21 (March 1978), 57–68.

Kidron, Aryeh. "Work Values and Organizational Commitment." *Academy of Management Journal* 21 (June 1978), 239–247.

Kiechel, Walter, III. "Crime at the Top in Fruehauf Corporation." *Fortune* 99 (January 29, 1979), 32–35.

Kottcamp, E. H., Jr., and Brian M. Rushton. "Improving the Corporate Environment." *Research Management* 22 (November 1979), 19–22.

Kotter, John P. "Managing External Dependence." *Academy of Management Review* 4 (January 1979), 87–92.

Laudicina, Eleanor. "Management Is Management Is Management Is . . . (or Is It?)" *Public Administration Review* 38 (March–April 1978), 193–196.

Lehr, Lewis W. "The Role of Top Management." *Research Management* 22 (November 1979), 23–25.

Lewis, Marshall C. "How Business Can Escape the Climate of Mistrust." *Business and Society Review* 16 (Winter 1975–76), 70–71.

London, Paul. "Notes on Corporate Culture." *Business and Society Review* 23 (Fall 1977), 4–12.

Lovdal, Michael L., Raymond A. Bauer, and Nancy H. Treverton. "Public Responsibility Committees of the Board." *Harvard Business Review* 55 (May–June 1977), 40+.

McGuire, Joseph W. "The New Egalitarianism and Managerial Practice." *California Management Review* 19 (Spring 1977), 21–29.

McSweeney, John P. "Rumors—Enemy of Company Morale and Community Relations." *Personnel Journal* 55 (September 1976), 435–436.

Mainelli, V. P. "Democracy in the Workplace." *America* 136 (January 15, 1977), 28–30.

Mann, Michael. "Rockwell's B-1 Promotion Blitz." *Business and Society Review* 19 (Fall 1976), 28–32.

Marsh, Harold, Jr. "Relations with Management and Individual Financial Interests." *Business Lawyer* 33 (March 1978), 1227–1237.

Menzies, Hugh D. "Union Carbide Raises Its Voice." *Fortune* 98 (September 25, 1978), 86–90.

Montagu, Ashley. "Brainwashing Is the Biggest Business of All." *Business and Society Review* 29 (Spring 1979), 4–7.

"The More Things Change: For Every Barbara Jordan Selected to a Corporate Board There Are Dozens of Good Ol' Boys." *Forbes* 123 (June 11, 1979), 110+.

Morrison, R. H. "Nothing Succeeds like an SOB." *Business and Society Review* 28 (Winter 1978–79), 69–70.

Moskal, Brian S. "Executive Life-Styles: Shifting Priorities." *Industry Week* 196 (February 6, 1978), 32–35+.

Newstrom, John W., and William A. Ruch. "Managerial Values Underlying Intraorganizational Ethics." *Atlanta Economic Review* 26 (May–June 1976), 12–15.

Nikiforov, B. "Crime at the Top." *Atlas* 25 (August 1978), 35–36.

Nord, Walter R. "Dreams of Humanization and the Realities of Power." *Academy of Management Review* 3 (July 1978), 674–679.

Pascarella, Perry. "Humanagement." *Industry Week* 204 (January 7, 1980), 84–85+.

Payne, Stephen L. "Organization Ethics and Antecedents to Social Control Processes." *Academy of Management Review* 5 (July 1980), 409–14.

Pfeffer, Jeffrey, Gerald R. Salaneik, and Huseyin Leblebici. "The Effect of Uncertainty on the Use of Social Influence in Organizational Decision Making." *Administrative Science Quarterly* 21 (June 1976), 227–245.

"A Plan for Top Officials: More Pay, Higher Ethics." _U.S. News and World Report_ 82 (January 17, 1977), 49–50.

Purcell, Theodore V. "Institutionalizing Ethics on Corporate Boards." _Review of Social Economy_ 36 (April 1978), 41–54.

Quinn, Robert E. "Coping with Cupid: The Formation, Impact, and Management of Romantic Relationships in Organizations." _Administrative Science Quarterly_ 22 (March 1977), 30–45.

Ramsey, V. Jean, and Bernard J. White. "Some Unintended Consequences of 'Top Down' Organization Development." _Human Resource Management_ 17 (Summer 1978), 7–14.

Rayburn, John Michael. "Changing Role of Boards of Directors." _Southwest Business and Economic Review_ 18 (August 1980), 23–33.

Reeser, Clayton. "Managerial Obsolescence—An Organizational Dilemma." _Personnel Journal_ 56 (January 1977), 27–31+.

Rimler, George Warren. "The Death of Management—A Search for Causes." _Academy of Management Review_ 1 (April 1976), 126–218.

Roberts, Markley. "The Interlock of Corporate Power." _American Federationist_ 85 (August 1978), 5–8.

Rowe, Kenneth, and John Schlacter. "Integrating Social Responsibility into the Corporate Structure." _Public Relations Quarterly_ 23 (Fall 1978), 7–12.

Schrager, Laura Shill, and James F. Short, Jr. "Toward a Sociology of Organizational Crime." _Social Problems_ 25 (April 1978), 407–419.

Sethi, S. Prakash, Bernard Cunningham, and Carl Swanson. "The Catch-22 in Reform Proposals for Restructuring Corporate Boards." _Management Review_ 68 (January 1979), 27–28+.

Solomon, Lewis D. "Restructuring the Corporate Board of Directors—Fond Hope—Faint Promise?" _Michigan Law Review_ 76 (March 1978), 581–610.

Stewart, Judith. "Understanding Women in Organizations: Toward a Reconstruction of Organizational Theory." _Administrative Science Quarterly_ 23 (June 1978), 336–350.

Stone, Christopher D. "Public Directors Merit a Try." _Harvard Business Review_ 54 (March–April 1976), 20–22+.

Stone, Eugene F. "The Moderating Effect of Work-Related Values on the Job Scope-Job Satisfaction Relationship." _Organizational Behavior and Human Performance_ 15, no. 2 (April 1976), 147–167.

Toren, Nina. "Bureaucracy and Professionalism: A Reconsideration of Weber's Thesis." *Academy of Management Review* 1 (July 1976), 36–46.

Touretzky, Simeon J. "Changing Attitudes: A Question of Loyalty." *Personnel Administrator* 24 (April 1979), 35–36.

Velasquez, Manuel. "Ethics and Organizational Politics." *New Catholic World* 223 (November–December 1980), 248+.

Vogel, David. "Why Businessmen Distrust Their State: The Political Consciousness of American Corporate Executives." *British Journal of Political Science* 8 (January 1978), 45–78.

Votaw, Dow. "The New Equality: Bureaucracy's Trojan Horse." *California Management Review* 20 (Summer 1978), 5–17.

Walters, Kenneth D. "Corporate Governance Reforms of the 1970's: United States–European Comparisons." *Journal of Contemporary Business* 8, no. 1 (1979), 19–31.

Waters, James A. "Catch 20.5: Corporate Morality as an Organizational Phenomenon." *Organizational Dynamics* 6 (Spring 1978), 3–19.

Williams, Harold M. "Corporate Accountability—One Year Later: The Responsibility of Directors." *Vital Speeches of the Day* 45 (April 1, 1979), 354–360.

Williams, Harold M. "The Role of the Director in Corporate Accountability: The Necessity of Outside Directors." *Vital Speeches of the Day* 44 (July 1, 1978), 558–563.

Zuchert, Eugene M., and Vigo A. Nielsen. "Corporate Board Reform." *Enterprise* 2 (October 1978), 19–21.

Zenisek, Thomas J. "Corporate Social Responsibility: A Conceptualization Based on Organizational Literature." *Academy of Management Review* 4 (July 1979), 359–368.

Production and Product Management

Books

Abernathy, William J. *The Productivity Dilemma: Roadblock to Innovation in the Automobile Industry.* Baltimore: Johns Hopkins University Press, 1978.

Cumming, Thomas G., and Edmond S. Molloy. *Improving Productivity and the Quality of Work.* New York: Praeger, 1977.

Environmental Resources Ltd. *Product Planning: The Relationship between Product Characteristics and Environmental Impact.* New York: State Mutual Book, 1978.

Epstein, Richard A. *Modern Products Liability Law.* Westport, Conn.: Quorum Books, 1980.

Gussow, John Dye. *The Feeding Web.* Palo Alto, Calif.: Bull Publishing Co., 1978.

Hemenway, David. *Industrywide Voluntary Product Standards.* Cambridge, Mass.: Ballinger, 1975.

Hinrichs, John R. *Practical Management for Productivity.* New York: Van Nostrand Reinhold/Work in America Institute Series, 1978.

Moski, Bruno A. *The Human Side of Production Management.* Atlanta: Perkins, 1978.

Nader, Ralph, et al. *The Lemon Book.* Ossining, N.Y.: Caroline House Publishing, 1980.

Weinstein, Alvin S., et al. *Products Liability and the Reasonably Safe Product: A Guide for Management, Design, and Marketing.* New York: Wiley, 1978.

Wolf, Sidney M., and Christopher M. Coley. *Pills That Don't Work.* Washington, D.C.: Health Research Group, 1980.

Articles

"Armageddon, Inc.: The Manufacturers of the U.S. Nuclear Arsenal." *Corporate Information Center Brief* (April 1978), 3A–3D.

Bleiberg, Robert M. "Pajama Game? The Ban on Tris Is Very Serious Business." *Barron's* 57 (June 6, 1977), 7.

Brehm, H. E. "Product Safety." *Restaurant Management* 21 (January 1978), 21–23.

Brown, Donald D., Jr. "Products Liability: The Genesis of 'Second Collision.' " *New York State Bar Journal* 51 (January 1979), 21–23+.

Byington, B. John. "Perspectives in Product Safety." *Professional Safety* (May 1977), 20.

Cavers, David F. "The Proper Law of Producer's Liability." *International and Comparative Law Quarterly* 26 (October 1977), 703–733.

Chandran, Rajan, Jeffrey Lowenhar, and John Stanton. "Product Safety: The Role of Advertising." *Journal of Advertising* 8 (Spring (1979), 36–41+.

Collier, Calvin J. "Product Quality Regulation by the Federal Trade Commission." *Journal of Products Liability* 2 (1978), 187–191.

Epple, Dennis, and Artur Raviv. "Product Safety: Liability Rules, Market Structure, and Imperfect Information." *American Economic Review* 68 (March 1978), 80–95.

Faber, Ronald, and Scott Ward. "Children's Understanding of Using Products Safely." *Journal of Marketing* 41 (October 1977), 39–46.

Feldman, Lawrence P. "The Consumer Product Safety Commission: Benefit or Boondoggle?" *Journal of Consumer Affairs* 11 (Winter 1977), 25–42.

Fox, Harold W. "Product Management for Safety's Sake." *Akron Business and Economic Review* 7 (Spring 1976), 32–37.

Frantz, Alfred. "The Product Liability Crisis." *Credit and Financial Management* 79 (October 1977), 10–11+.

Grabowski, Henry G., and John M. Vernon. "Consumer Product Safety Regulation." *American Economic Review* 68 (May 1978), 284–289.

Greenwood, Peter H., and Charles A. Ingene. "Uncertain Externalities, Liability Rules, and Resource Allocation." *American Economic Review* 68 (June 1978), 300–310.

Grundy, Richard D. "Consumer Product Safety." *Challenge* 19 (November–December 1976), 34–36.

Henderson, James A., Jr., Richard A. Elestein, Jerry J. Phillips, and Anita Johnson. "Symposium on Products Liability Law: The Need for Statutory Reform." *North Carolina Law Review* 56 (1978), 625–692.

Irving, Robert R. "The Awful Truth about Products Liability." *Iron Age* 218 (September 27, 1976), 39–42+.

Kaapcke, Bernard. "Special Report: Product Liability: A Crisis in the Making." *Journal of Insurance* 37 (May–June 1976), 13–20.

Kaikati, Jack G. "The Product Liability Crisis: Perspective and Proposals." *Journal of Small Business Management* 16 (October 1978), 46–55.

Kytle, Rayford P., Jr. "New Dimensions for Quality and Product Safety." *Atlanta Economic Review* 26 (May–June 1976), 24–27.

"Let the Manufacturer Beware." *The Economist* 262 (January 22, 1977), 73–74.

Levy, Michael E. "We Must Rid Ourselves of the Myth of the Free Lunch and Refuel Our Powerful Productive System or We May

Be Doomed to Uncontrollable Inflation." *Across the Board* 16 (May 1979), 29–33.

McGuire, E. Patrick. "What's Ahead in Product Safety?" *Conference Board Record* 13 (August 1976), 32–34.

McIntyre, Kathryn J. "Workers Study Law to Learn to Foresee Product Liability Risk." *Business Insurance* 13 (June 11, 1979), 56–57.

Miller, Henry G. "Products Liability and the Safer Society." *New York State Bar Journal* 50 (June 1978), 304–307+.

Moellenberndt, Richard A. "Product Warranty Policy." *Atlanta Economic Review* 27 (May–June 1977), 29–34.

"New Programs Extend Product Responsibility." *Chemical Week* 125 (July 4, 1979), 53.

O'Brian, B. F., and R. B. Baldwin. "Products Liability: The Engineer's Role, and the Small Manufacturer's Concern." *National Underwriter* (Property Ed.) 80 (October 15, 1976), 52+.

O'Connell, Jeffrey. "Products and Services: No Fault without Legislation." *American Bar Association Journal* 62 (March 1976), 343–346.

Owen, David G. "Punitive Damages in Product Liability Litigation." *Michigan Law Review* 74 (June 1976), 1258–1371.

Perham, John C. "The Dilemma in Product Liability." *Dun's Review* 109 (January 1977), 48–50+.

Permut, Steven E., and James A. Firestone. "Consumer Product Safety in the International Marketplace." *Columbia Journal of World Business* 12 (Winter 1977), 77–85.

Peterson, James M. "Some Product Liability Problems." *South Dakota Business Review* 36 (November 1977), 2–3+.

Polsky, Norman. "Product Liability—How Does It Affect You?" *Management World* 7 (March 1978), 1+.

"Product Liability: Excellence by Edict or Effort?" *Technology Review* 82 (October 1979), 77+.

"Product Liability Plan: After-the-Fact Remedy." *Purchasing* 85 (September 13, 1978), 33–35.

"Product Liability: The Small Manufacturer's Side." *National Underwriter* (Property Ed.) 80 (March 26, 1976), 1+.

"The Product Liability Trap." *Enterprise* 2 (April 1978), 10–12.

"Production Liability: Profile of Big Cases." *Journal of American Insurance* 52 (Fall 1976), 18–21.

Rotfeld, Herbert J., and Kim B. Rotzoll. "Advertising and Product Quality: Are Heavily Advertised Products Better?" *Journal of Consumer Affairs* 10 (Summer 1976), 22–47.

Schmitt, M. A., and William W. May. "Beyond Products Liability: The Legal, Social, and Ethical Problems Facing the Automobile Industry in Producing Safe Products." *University of Detroit Journal of Urban Law* 56 (Summer 1979), 1021–1050.

Schroth, Peter W. "Products Liability." *American Journal of Comparative Law* 26 (1978), 67–89.

Schweig, Barry B. "Product Liability Problem." *Annals of the American Academy* 443 (May 1979), 94–103.

Shapiro, Benson P. "Can Marketing and Manufacturing Coexist?" *Harvard Business Review* 55 (September–October 1977), 104–114.

Singer, James W. "Who Will Set the Standards for Groups That Set Industry Product Standards?" *National Journal* 12 (May 3, 1980), 721–725.

Stratton, Debra J. "The Slow Road to Product Liability Reform." *Association Management* 30 (January 1978), 30–36.

Student, Kurt R. "Cost vs. Human Values in Plant Location." *Business Horizons* 19 (April 1976), 5–14.

Tomasch, Mark R. "Make Production a Human Activity." *Automation* 23 (January 1976), 48–52.

Trombetta, William L. "Products Liability and the Uniform Commercial Code." *Atlanta Economic Review* 27 (May–June 1977), 22–28.

Vinson, William D., and Donald F. Heany. "Is Quality Out of Control?" *Harvard Business Review* 55 (November–December 1977), 114–122.

Wolfe, R. C. "Product Stewardship: A Program That Works." *Industry Research and Development* 21 (September 1979), 114–119.

Public Relations

Articles

Adams, Kenneth. "Why We Should Preach the Gospel of Industry." *Director* 28 (May 1976), 66–68.

Anderson, James W. "The Art of Reputation Management." *Public Relations Journal* 33 (January 1977), 26–27.

Banks, Louis. "Taking on the Hostile Media." *Harvard Business Review* 56 (March–April 1978), 123–130.

Bernays, Edward L. "Hucksterism vs. Public Relations." *Public Relations Quarterly* 21 (Fall 1976), 16.

Blake, David H., and Vita Toros. "The Global Image Makers." *Public Relations Journal* 32 (June 1976), 10–12.

Brown, David H. "Let's Practice What We Preach." *Public Relations Journal* 33 (October 1977), 13.

"Business Explaining Itself Is Theme of Ad Workshop." *Automotive News* (October 4, 1976), 17.

Caldwell, Gregor T. "The Public Affairs Function: Management Response: Public Affairs Departments Have a Responsibility to Identify Social Trends That Have a Bearing on Their Business." *Canadian Business Review* 3 (Winter 1976), 32–35.

Clutterbuck, David. "How Texaco Salvaged Its Image after a Disaster." *International Management* 33 (May 1978), 30–34.

"Coping with Today's Major Public Policy Issues." *Public Relations Journal* 34 (January 1978), 16–31.

"The Corporate Image: PR to the Rescue." *Business Week* (January 22, 1979), 47–50+.

Finlay, J. Richard. "Toward a Neoenterprise Spirit: The Tasks and Responsibilities of the Public Affairs Function." *Business Quarterly* (Summer 1978), 50–58.

Gildea, Robert L. "Doubting Thomas Our Patron Saint?" *Public Relations Quarterly* 22 (Spring 1977), 25–27.

Harvey, David. "How Business Can Polish Up Its Public Image." *The Director* 30 (April 1978), 55–56.

Henderson, Malcolm. "Public Relations—The Ultimate Con?" *Director* 28 (May 1976), 34.

"How TV Helps Corporate Giants Enhance Their Public Images." *Broadcasting* 89 (November 24, 1976), 39–41.

Kilpatrick, James J. "Selling the Profit System to the Young." *Nation's Business* 64 (April 1976), 9–10.

Letton, Harry P., Jr. "Ways to Tell the Business Story." *Nation's Business* 64 (January 1976), 68–70.

Montgomery, Jim. "The Image Makers: In Public Relations Ethical Conflicts Pose Continuing Problems." *Wall Street Journal* (August 1, 1978), 1+.

Northart, Leo. J. "Employee Rights: Corporate PR's Newest Hot Potato." *Public Relations Journal* 34 (June 1978), 5+.

"Projecting and Protecting a Corporate Image." *Aerosol Age* 21 (February 1976), 32–33.

Roper, Burns W. "Scale, Scarcity, and Skepticism." *Public Relations Journal* 32 (January 1976), 9+.

Sethi, S. Prakash. "Advocacy Advertising and the Multinational Corporation." *Columbia Journal of World Business* 12 (Fall 1977), 33–46.

Sethi, S. Prakash. "Advocacy Advertising—The American Experience." *California Management Review* 2 (Fall 1978), 55–68.

Sethi, S. Prakash. "Management Fiddles While Public Affairs Flops." *Business and Society Review* 18 (Summer 1976), 9–11.

Sethi, S. Prakash. "The Role of Advocacy Advertising in External Communications." *Journal of General Management* 4 (Spring 1979), 3–14.

Spain, Jayne Baker. "Communication in a Crisis." *Across the Board* 15 (June 1978), 82–88.

Sullivan, Frank C. "The Dimensions of Disbelief." *Public Relations Quarterly* 23 (Spring 1978), 25–27.

Weaver, Paul H. "Corporations Are Defending Themselves with the Wrong Weapons: Teaching Economics Isn't Going to Turn the Anti-Business Tide." *Fortune* 95 (June 1977), 186–190+.

Wilck, C. Thomas. "Toward a Definition of Public Relations." *Public Relations Journal* 33 (December 1977), 26–27.

Wilcox, Dennis L. "Controversy: Criticism, Evaluation, and Professionalism." *Public Relations Journal* 35 (November 1979), 56–57.

Winks, Donald. "Speaking Out—With a Forked Tongue." *Business Week* (July 2, 1979), 9.

Wolff, Catherine W. "Activist Public Relations: Integrity and Respect." *Public Relations Journal* 33 (December 1977), 19–22.

Ylvisaker, Paul N. "When Your Personal Values Are under Pressure." *Public Relations Journal* 32 (January 1976), 8–9+.

Purchasing

Articles

Borath, Robert M., and Paul S. Hogstad. "The Effects of Professionalism on Purchasing Managers." *Journal of Purchasing and Materials Management* 15 (Spring 1979), 25–32.

Buchholz, Rogene, and William Rudelius. "Purchasing Standards Revisited." *Journal of Purchasing and Materials Management* 14 (Fall 1978), 23–26.

"Buyers Grapple with Sticky Issue." *Purchasing* 86 (June 27, 1979), 42–43.

Cummings, Gary F. "Are Purchasing Ethics Being Put to the Test?" *Iron Age* 222 (September 24, 1979), 21–24.

Decker, Russell. "Purchasing Law: Can You Sue Vendors' Suppliers for Price-Fixing?" *Purchasing* 83 (November 8, 1977), 63–65.

Decker, Russell. "Purchasing Law: Supreme Court Puts Tie-In Sales to New Test." *Purchasing* 83 (November 22, 1977), 97–99.

Dempsey, William F., Anthony Bushman, and Richard E. Plank. "Personal Inducement of Industrial Buyers." *Industrial Marketing Management* 9 (October 1980), 281–289.

Douglas, Richard C. "A Toast to the Suppliers, but Should We Accept Their Gifts?" *Advertising Age* 49 (December 25, 1978), 19.

Dowst, S. "Overseas Codes Could Cure Double Standards." *Purchasing* 84 (May 10, 1978), 87+.

Farmer, D. H., and K. MacMillan. "Voluntary Collaboration vs. Disloyalty to Suppliers." *Purchasing and Materials Management* 12 (Winter 1976), 3–8.

Goulet, Dennis. "The Supplies and Purchasers of Technology: A Conflict of Interests." *International Development Review* 18, no. 3 (1976), 14–20.

Green, Herbert J. "The Future of the 'Professional Expediter.' " *Journal of Purchasing and Materials Management* 14 (Spring 1978), 30–32.

Levy, Robert. "The Big Rip-Off in Purchasing." *Dun's Review* 109 (March 1977), 76–77+.

Lutz, Lillian, and John T. Seibert. "Pro and Con on Vender Integrity." *Administrative Management* 38 (April 1977), 124.

McLachlan, D. L. "Monopoly and Collusion in Public Procurement: A Survey of Recent American Experience." *Antitrust Law and Economic Review* 8, no. 2 (1976), 69–90.

"Overseas Buying: American, UK Buyers Seek One Ethics Code." *Purchasing* 84 (June 7, 1978), 47.

"Purchasers Consider Ethics Code with Teeth." *Industry Week* 198 (July 24, 1978), 31–32.

"Reciprocity Violates Antitrust Laws." *Purchasing* 84 (June 28, 1978), 18+.

Rudelius, William, and Rogene A. Buchholz. "Ethical Problems of Purchasing Managers." *Harvard Business Review* 57 (March–April 1979), 8.

Rudelius, William, and Rogene A. Buchholz. "What Industrial Purchasers See as Key Ethical Dilemmas." *Journal of Purchasing and Materials Management* 15 (Winter 1979), 2–10.

Spratlen, Thaddeus H. "The Impact of Affirmative Action Purchasing." *Journal of Purchasing and Materials Management* 14 (Spring 1978), 6–8+.

Werner, Ray O. "Robinson-Patman: Purchasing's Responsibility Still Unclear." *Journal of Purchasing and Materials Management* 14 (Spring 1978), 12–15.

Wiesner, Donald A. "Purchasing Law: Fudging the Facts Can Be Fraud." *Purchasing* 89 (May 25, 1976), 61+.

Research and Development

Books

Baum, Robert J., ed. *Ethical Problems in Engineering.* Troy, N.Y.: The Center for the Study of the Human Dimensions of Science and Technology, vol. 22, 1980.

Articles

Atkinson, Richard. "Responsibility in Scientific Research." *Chemical and Engineering News* 56 (April 10, 1978), 5.

Blickwede, Donald J. "The Societal Responsibilities of Industrial Research." *Research Management* 19 (September 1976), 7–8.

Blickwede, Donald J. "Society's Changing Attitudes and R & D." *Research Management* 20 (September 1977), 14–15.

Butler, J. K. "Is It Ethical to Conduct Volunteer Studies within Pharmaceutical Industry?" *Lancet* 1 (1978), 816–818.

Cheston, Warren, and Patricia McFate. "Ethics and Laboratory Safety." *The Hastings Center Report* 10 (August 1980), 7–8.

Delapalme, B. "Responsibility of Industrial Research with Regard to Society." *R & D Management* 7 (1977), 112–118.

Finnegan, Marcus B. "R & D for Developing Countries: The Code of Conduct Issue." *Research Management* 22 (May 1979), 39–41.

"Growing Government Role in R & D Criticized." *Chemical and Engineering News* 54 (November 29, 1976), 22.

List, Peter. "Engineers' Responsibilities within the Institutions: Some Reminders." *Business and Professional Ethics* 2 (Fall 1978), 4–5.

Malone, Donald J. "Industrial Research and Development for Ecology and Conservation." *Management International Review* 18 (February 1978), 51–62.

Oliver, Bernard M. "Innovation and Creativity in a Moral Atmosphere." *Center Magazine* 13 (January 1980), 35+.

Randal, Judith. "The DNA Debate." *Progressive* 41 (May 1977), 11+.

"The Research Associate: Where Familiarity Breeds Respect." *Commerce America* 1 (August 16, 1976), 4–6.

Rifkin, Jeremy. "DNA: Have the Corporations Already Grabbed Control of New Life Forms?" *Mother Jones* 2 (February–March 1977), 23–26+.

"The Silent Crisis in R & D." *Business Week* (March 8, 1976), 90.

Standke, K. H. "Responsibility of Industrial Research towards Society under Global Aspects." *R & D Management* 7 (1977), 150–154.

Toren, Nina. "The New Code of Scientists." *IEEE Transactions on Engineering Management* VEM-27 (August 1980), 78–84.

"Where Private Industry Puts Its Research Money: Survey of Corporate Research and Development Spending." *Business Week* (June 28, 1976), 62–69+.

Business and Social Responsibility

Business and Social Responsibility

Books

Ackerman, Robert W., and Raymond A. Bauer. *Corporate Social Responsiveness: The Modern Dilemma.* Reston, Va.: Reston Publishing Co., 1976.

Anshen, Melvin. *Corporate Strategies for Social Performance.* New York: Macmillan, 1980.

Aronoff, Craig. *Business and the Media.* Santa Monica, Calif.: Goodyear, 1979.

Barach, Jeffrey A., ed. *The Individual, Business, and Society.* Englewood Cliffs, N.J.: Prentice-Hall, 1977.

Beesley, Michael, and Tom Evans. *Corporate Social Responsibility—A Reassessment.* Totowa, N.J.: Biblio Distribution Centre, 1978.

Blair, John M. *The Control of Oil.* New York: Random House, 1978.

Bradshaw, Thornton F., and David Vogel, eds. *Corporations and Their Critics: Issues and Answers on the Problem of Corporate Social Responsibility.* New York: McGraw-Hill, 1980.

Carroll, Archie B., ed. *Managing Corporate Social Responsibility.* Boston: Little, Brown, and Co., 1977.

Crew, David F. *Industry and Community.* New York: Columbia University Press, 1979.

Davis, Keith, and Robert L. Blomstrom. *Business and Society: Environment and Responsibility.* New York: McGraw-Hill, 1977.

Deutsch, Jan G. *Selling the People's Cadillac: The Edsel and Corporate Responsibility.* New Haven: Yale University Press, 1976.

Eells, Richard, ed. *International Business Philanthropy.* New York: Free Press, 1979.

Epstein, Edwin M., and Dow Votaw, eds. *Legitimacy, Responsibility, and Rationality.* Santa Monica, Calif.: Goodyear, 1978.

Epstein, Marc J., et al. *Corporate Social Performance: The Measurement of Product and Service Contribution.* New York: National Association of Accountants, 1977.

Ewen, Lynda Ann. *Corporate Power and Urban Crisis in Detroit.* Princeton, N.J.: Princeton University Press, 1978.

Garfinkel, Irwin, and Robert H. Haveman. *Earnings Capacity, Poverty, and Inequality.* New York: Academic Press, 1977.

Giunta, Joanne. *Introduction to Corporate Social Responsibility Management.* Philadelphia: Human Resources Network, 1976.

Glueck, William F. *Readings in Business Policy from Business Week.* New York: McGraw-Hill, 1978.

Greenwood, William T. *Issues in Business and Society.* 3d ed. Boston: Houghton-Mifflin, 1976.

Harper, John D. *A View of the Corporate Role in Society.* New York: Columbia University Press, 1977.

Hodgetts, Richard M. *The Business Enterprise: Social Challenge, Social Response.* New York: Holt, Rinehart, and Winston, 1977.

Idris-Soven, Ahmed, Elizabeth Idris-Soven, and Mary K. Vaughn, eds. *The World as a Company Town.* Hawthorne, N.Y.: Mounton Publishers, 1979.

Klein, Thomas A. *Social Costs and Benefits of Business.* Englewood Cliffs, N.J.: Prentice-Hall, 1977.

Koch, Frank. *The New Corporate Philanthropy: How Society and Business Can Profit.* New York: Plenum Press, 1979.

Leonard, H. Jeffrey, J. Clarence Davies III, and Gordon Binder. *Business and Environment: Toward Common Ground.* Washington, D.C.: Conservation Foundation, 1977.

Luthans, Fred, and Richard M. Hodgetts, eds. *Social Issues in Business.* New York: Macmillan Co., 1976.

Maxwell, S. R., and Alister K. Mason. *Social Responsibility and Canada's Largest Corporations.* Lancaster: University of Lancaster, 1976.

Melrose, Woodman, Elizabeth Jonquil, and I. Kverndal. *Towards Social Responsibility: Company Codes of Ethics and Practice.* London: British Institute of Management, 1976.

Musselman, Vernon. *Introduction to Modern Business: Issues and Environment.* 7th ed. Englewood Cliffs, N.J.: Prentice-Hall, 1977.

Nadel, Mark V. *Corporations and Political Accountability.* Lexington, Mass.: Heath, 1976.

Nicolin, Curt. *Private Industry in a Public World.* Reading, Mass.: Addison-Wesley Publishing Co., 1977.

Pfeffer, Jeffrey. *The External Control of Organizations: A Resource Dependence Perspective.* New York: Harper and Row, 1978.

Sawyer, George C. *Business and Society: Managing Corporate Social Impact.* Boston: Houghton-Mifflin Co., 1979.

Schultze, Charles L. *The Public Use of Private Interest.* Washington, D.C.: Brookings Institution, 1977.

Sethi, S. Prakash. *Up against the Corporate Wall: Modern Corporations and Social Issues of the Seventies.* 3d ed. Englewood Cliffs, N.J.: Prentice-Hall, 1977.

Steiner, George A., and John F. Steiner. *Issues in Business and Society.* New York: Random House, 1977.

Stone, Christopher D. *Where the Law Ends: The Social Control of Corporate Behavior.* New York: Harper and Row, 1975.

Sturdivant, Frederick D. *Business and Society: A Managerial Approach.* Homewood, Ill.: Richard D. Irwin, 1977.

Sturdivant, Frederick D., and Larry M. Robinson. *The Corporate Social Challenge: Cases and Commentaries.* Homewood, Ill.: Richard D. Irwin, 1977.

Williams, Harold M., and Irving S. Shapiro. *Power and Accountability.* New York: Columbia University Press, 1980.

Wolfson, Joseph. *The Social Studies Student Investigates Business in the American Economy.* New York: Rosen Press, 1976.

Articles

Abbott, Walter F., and R. Joseph Monsen. "On the Measurement of Corporate Social Responsibility: Self-Reported Disclosures as a Method of Measuring Corporate Social Involvement." *Academy of Management Journal* 22 (September 1979), 501–515.

Abouzeid, Kamal M., and Charles N. Weaver. "Social Responsibility in the Corporate Goal Hierarchy." *Business Horizons* 21 (June 1978), 29–35.

Almeder, Robert. "The Ethics of Profit: Reflections on Corporate Responsibility." *Business and Society* 19 (Winter 1980), 7–14.

Armstrong, Scott. "Social Irresponsibility in Management." *Journal of Business Research* 5 (September 1977), 185–213.

Arrow, Kenneth J. "The Limitations of the Profit Motive: In a Profit Economy, Every Economic Activity Is Dependent on the Profit Motive, Whether or Not That Activity Is Beneficial or Harmful to Society; This Calls into Question the Legitimacy of the System Itself." *Challenge* 22 (September–October 1979), 23–27. (Excerpted from the book, *New Challenges to the Role of Profit,* ed. Benjamin M. Friedman.)

Atkinson, Christine, and Adrian Atkinson. "Corporate Social Responsibility—A Philosophical Approach." *Journal of Enterprise Management* 2 (1980), 131–135.

Attwood, James A. "The ABC's of Responsibility." *Business and Society Review* 18 (Summer 1976), 75–76.

Barovick, Richard L. "More Responsibility." *Business and Society Review* 24 (Winter 1977–78), 78.

Batten, Hal J. "Management's Responsibility to Whom?" *SAM Advanced Management Journal* 41 (Spring 1976), 31–34.

Benjamin, James J., Keith G. Stanga, and Robert H. Strawser. "Disclosure of Information regarding Corporate Social Responsibility." *Managerial Planning* 27 (July/August 1978), 23–27.

Beresford, Dennis R., and Scott S. Cowen. "Surveying Social Responsibility: Disclosure in Annual Reports." *Business* 29 (March–April 1979), 15–20.

Bock, Robert H. "Modern Values and Corporate Social Responsibility." *MSU Business Topics* 28 (Spring 1980), 5–17.

Bradshaw, Thornton F. "One Corporation's View of Social Responsibility." *Journal of Contemporary Business* 7 (Winter 1978), 19–24.

Bruyn, Severyn T. "Corporate Charters in the Public Interest." *Social Policy* 7 (May 1976), 44–49.

Buchholz, Rogene A. "An Alternative to Social Responsibility: Public Policy Has Certain Practical Advantages When It Comes to Meeting the Needs of Society." *MSU Business Topics* 25 (Summer 1977), 12–16.

Buehler, Vernon M., and Y. K. Shetty. "Managerial Response to Social Responsibility Challenge." *Academy of Management Journal* 19 (March 1976), 66–78.

Burford, Victor L., and Allison Esposito. "Today's Executive: Private Steward and Public Servant (An Interview with Irving S. Shapiro)." *Harvard Business Review* 56 (March–April 1978), 94–101.

Burton, Eric James. "Statement of Social Responsiveness: A Proposal." *Government Accountants' Journal* 25 (Winter 1976), 12–19.

Calitri, Joseph C. "The Pursuit of Very Goodness: Corporate Social Responsibility." *Vital Speeches of the Day* 45 (June 15, 1979), 524–528.

"Capitalizing on Social Change." *Business Week* (October 29, 1979), 105–106.

Carlson, Theodore J. "A Social View of the Public Utility." *Public Utilities Fortnightly* 98 (November 18, 1976), 23–28.

Carroll, Archie B. "Setting Operational Goals for Corporate Social Responsibility." *Long Range Planning* 11 (April 1978), 35–38.

Caudill, H. M. "Appalachian Life and Corporate Responsibility." *National Forum* 58 (Summer 1978), 15–19.

Chaikin, S. C. "A Labor Leader's Views on Corporate Governance and Responsibility." *AACSB Bulletin, Proceedings, Annual Meeting 1979*, 61–66.

Cheatham, Walter M. "Beyond Philanthropy." *Public Relations Journal* 34 (June 1978), 12–15.

Churchill, Neil C., and Arthur B. Toan, Jr. "Reporting on Corporate Social Responsibility: A Progress Report." *Journal of Contemporary Business* 7 (Winter 1978), 5–17.

Cleary, Robert E. "The Professional as Public Servant: the Decision-Making Dilemma." *International Journal of Public Administration* 2 (1980), 151–160.

Clutterbuck, David. "Bonus Pay-Outs Linked to Social Responsibility." *International Management* 33 (August 1978), 49–53.

Clutterbuck, David. "Making Social Responsibility Pay." *International Management* 32 (July 1977), 18–21.

Cohen, Stanley E. "Social Responsibility Can Win Friends in Government and the Marketplace." *Advertising Age* 47 (May 31, 1976), 6.

Collingsworth, E. T. "Corporate Accountability Is Alive and Well." *Business and Society Review* 27 (Fall 1978), 65–67.

Collins, Sheila D. "Alice in Wonderland (at Riverside Church)." *Christianity and Crisis* 36 (March 15, 1976), 49–51.

"Community Relations Project That Rang the Bell." *Public Relations Journal* 32 (December 1976), 20–23.

Conard, A. F. "Meaning of Corporate Social-Responsibility Variations on a Theme of Epstein, Edwin M.—Response." *Hastings Law Journal* 30, no. 5 (1979), 1321–1326.

Conover, Hobart H. "Meeting the New Social Concerns." *Management World* 6 (May 7, 1977), 25–27.

Cook, Suzanne H., and Jack L. Mendleson. "Androgynous Management: Key to Social Responsibility?" *SAM Advanced Management Journal* 42 (Winter 1977), 25–35.

"Coping with the New Rules of Conduct." *Business Week* (October 10, 1977), 76–77.

Crawford, Ronald L., and Harold A. Gram. "Social Responsibility as Interrorganizational Transaction." *Academy of Management Review* 3 (October 1978), 880–888.

D'Amore, Louis J. "An Executive Guide to Social Impact Assessment." *Business Quarterly* 43 (Summer 1978), 35–44.

Davis, Keith. "Social Responsibility Is Inevitable." *California Management Review* 19 (Fall 1976), 14–20.

Dawson, Leslie M. "Marketing for Human Needs in a Humane Future." *Business Horizons* 23 (June 1980), 72–82.

Dennis, Lloyd B. "Corporate Giving Goals Must Be Redefined by New Choices." *Fund Raising Management* 9 (January/February 1979), 26–31.

Donnell, John D. "Sixteen Commandments for Corporate Directors." *Business Horizons* 19 (February 1976), 45–58.

Dowie, Mark. "The Corporate Crime of the Century." *Mother Jones* (November 1979), 22+.

Doyle, Mortimer B. "Things Happen for the Public Good When Business Exercises Its Leadership Responsibility." *Association Management* 29 (November 1977), 48–50.

Dykeman, Francis C. "The Public's Great Expectations: Can We Measure Up?" *Price Waterhouse Review* 21 (1976), 40–45.

Edmonds, Charles P. III, and John H. Hand. "What Are the Real Long-run Objectives of Business?" *Business Horizons* 19 (December 1976), 75–81.

Edmunds, Stahrl W. "Unifying Concepts in Social Responsibility." *Academy of Management Review* 2 (January 1977), 38–45.

Eklund, Coy G. "Corporate Social Responsibility." *Vital Speeches of the Day* 43 (January 1, 1977), 168–170.

Elkins, Arthur. "Toward a Positive Theory of Corporate Social Involvement." *Academy of Management Review* 2 (January 1977), 128–133.

"Employee Task Forces Create Social Policies." *Banking* 71 (November 1979), 37.

Engel, D. L. "Approach to Corporate Social Responsibility." *Stanford Law Review*, no. 1 (1979), 1–98.

"Enlightened Social Policy." *Commerce America* 1 (July 19, 1976), 4–6.

Epstein, Edwin M. "Societal, Managerial, and Legal Perspectives on

Corporate Social Responsibility—Product and Process." *Hastings Law Journal* 30, no. 5 (1979), 1287–1320.

Epstein, Edwin M. "The Social Role of Business Enterprise in Britain: An American Perspective: Part 1." *Journal of Management Studies* 13 (October 1976), 213–233.

Epstein, Edwin M. "The Social Role of Business Enterprise in Britain: An American Perspective: Part II." *Journal of Management Studies* 14 (October 1977), 281–316.

Evans, M. Stanton. "Corporate Responsibility." *National Review* 31 (June 22, 1979), 823+.

Ewing, David W., S. Prakash Sethi, Herbert Schmertz, David Finn, and Robert Lekachman. "Public vs. Big Business: Who's Got the Upper Hand?" (Symposium) *Saturday Review* 5 (January 21, 1978), 11–16+.

Ferguson, James L. "The Chief Executive's Responsibility for Corporate Public Service." *Sloan Management Review* 20 (Fall 1978), 75–78.

Fitch, H. Gordon "Achieving Corporate Social Responsibility." *Academy of Management Review* 1 (January 1976), 38–46.

Ford, Henry, II, Phillip J. Drothing, Juanita M. Kreps, et al. "Is Corporate Responsibility a Dead Issue?" *Business and Society Review* 25 (Spring 1978), 4–20.

French, James P. "What Does Business Owe Society?" *Canadian Business Magazine* 49 (February 1976), 19–20+.

Friedman, Milton. "The Friedman Credo." *Across the Board* 15 (May 1978), 82–87.

Fry, Fred L., and Robert J. Hock. "Who Claims Corporate Responsibility? The Biggest and the Worst." *Business and Society Review* 18 (Summer 1976), 62–65.

Galvan, Frank. "U.S. Profits, Mexican Labor—Is It Moral?" *National Catholic Reporter* 15 (December 15, 1978), 13.

Goldston, Eli. "The Businessman's Role in the Urban Crisis." Address to the graduation class of the Program for Management Development, Harvard Business School (May 16, 1980).

Goodman, Steven E. "Quality of Life: The Role of Business." *Business Horizons* 21 (June 1978), 36–37.

Griffin, Carleton H. "How to Define the Limits of Responsibility." *Touche Ross Tempo* 22 (1976), 3–5.

Grunig, James E. "A New Measure of Public Opinions on Corporate Social Responsibility." *Academy of Management Journal* 22 (December 1979), 738–64.

"Guidelines for Business When Societal Demands Conflict: Responding to the Mandate for Social Responsibility." *Proceedings of the Fourth Panel Discussion of the Council of Better Business Bureaus.* Washington, D.C.: Better Business Bureau, 1978.

Haney, Camille. "Public Rights and Corporate Social Responsibility: A Profitable Marriage." *Retail Control* 48 (March 1980), 16–27.

Hazen, T. L. "Corporate Chartering and Securities Markets—Shareholder Suffrage, Corporate Responsibility and Managerial Accountability." *Wisconsin Law Review*, no. 2 (1978), 391–439.

Holmes, Sandra L. "Adapting Corporate Structure for Social Responsiveness." *California Management Review* 21 (Fall 1978), 47–54.

Holmes, Sandra L. "Corporate Social Performance: Past and Present Areas of Commitment." *Academy of Management Journal* 20 (September 1977), 433–438.

Holmes, Sandra L. "Executive Perceptions of Corporate Social Responsibility." *Business Horizons* 19 (June 1976), 34–40.

Holmes, Sandra L. "Who Gets the Corporate Social Dollar?" *Business and Society Review* 17 (Spring 1976), 62–63.

Humble, John. "A Practical Approach to Social Responsibility." *Management Review* (May 1978), 18–22.

Ingram, Robert W., and Katherine Beal Frazier. "Environmental Performance and Corporate Disclosure." *Journal of Accounting Research* 18 (Autumn 1980), 614–622.

Iyer, V. R. K. "Corporate Responsibility and Social Justice." *ASCI Journal of Management* 9, no. 2 (1980), 107–119.

Johnson, Harold L. "Business, Accounting, Law, and Medicine." *California Management Review* 18 (Summer 1976), 79–88.

Jones, Keith M. "Chelsea, the Adult Soft Drink: A Case Study of Corporate Social Responsibility." *Journal of Contemporary Business* 7, no. 4 (1978), 69–76.

Jones, Peter T., and Edward Engberg. "Christopher Stone's Prescription for Corporate Reform: Two Views." *Business and Society Review* 16 (Winter 1975–76), 73–78.

Jones, Thomas M. "Corporate Social Responsibility Revisited, Redefined." *California Management Review* 22 (Spring 1980), 59–67.

Kahalas, Harvey, and Ernest B. Uhr. "Social Responsibility Goal Perception." *Omega—International Journal of Management Science* 6, no. 1 (1978), 53–58.

Karp, Robert E. "Corporate Social Responsibility." *Training and Development Journal* 30 (November 1976), 10–15.

Keim, Gerald D. "Corporate Social Responsibility: An Assessment of the Enlightened Self-Interest Model." *Academy of Management Review* 3 (January 1978), 32–39. (Also Academy of Management *Proceedings*, 37th Annual Meeting, 1977, 285–289.)

Keim, Gerald D., and Roger E. Meiners. "Corporate Social Responsibility: Private Means for Public Wants?" *Policy Review* 5 (Summer 1978), 79–95.

Kinsman, Francis. "A British Bank Lends Old Executives to Charity." *Business and Society Review* 19 (Fall 1976), 73–76.

Kreps, Juanita M. "Corporate Responsibility in a Changing World." *Commerce America* 2 (April 25, 1977), 4–6.

Kreps, Juanita M. "The Administration's Position." *Public Relations Journal* 34 (June 1978), 10–11.

Kuhn, James W. "To Whom and for What Are Business Managers Responsible?" *Columbia Journal of World Business* 13 (Winter 1978), 52–61.

Kuntz, Edwin C., Banwari L. Kedia, and Carlton J. Whitehead. "Variations in Corporate Social Performance." *California Management Review* 22 (Summer 1980), 30–36.

Lange, R. W. "The True Social Responsibility of Business." *Arkansas Business and Economic Review* 9 (Summer 1976), 25–26.

Leontiades, Milton. "Social Demands: Continuing Pinch Threatens Business." *Planning Review* 7 (July 1979), 25–31.

Levitt, Theodore. "Corporate Responsibility: Taking Care of Business." *American Spectator* 11 (November 1977), 21–25.

Lovdal, Michael L., Raymond A. Bauer, and Nancy H. Treverton. "Public Responsibility Committees of the Board." *Harvard Business Review* 55 (May–June 1977), 40–42+.

Lowes, B., and G. Luffman. "A View from the Engine Room: Junior Managers' Attitudes towards Corporate Social Responsibility." *Management Decision* 16, no. 2 (1978), 75–92.

Lundborg, Louis B. "Making Profits Is Not Enough: If Businessmen Keep Talking like Computer Printouts, Then No Wonder People Think They Have Computers for Hearts." *Across the Board* 14 (February 1977), 54–58.

McAfee, Jerry. "Responsibilities Shared by Corporations and Society." *Credit and Financial Management* 80 (May 1978), 28–31.

McKersie, Robert B. " 'Plant Closed—No Jobs.' " *Across the Board* 17 (November 1980), 12–16.

MacNaughton, Donald S. "Managing Social Responsiveness." *Business Horizons* 19 (December 1976), 19–24.

McNulty, Paul J. "The Public Side of Private Enterprise: A Historical Perspective on American Business and Government." *Columbia Journal of World Business* 13 (Winter 1978), 122–130.

Mahoney, David. "Corporate Responsibility, More than Writing Checks." *Fund Raising Management* 10 (March/April 1979), 23–24.

Marsten, T. L. "Cummins Engine: The Role of Corporate Responsibility." *Personnel Administrator* 21 (October 1976), 29–33.

Marusi, Augustine R. "Balancing Power through Public Accountability." *Public Relations Journal* 35 (May 1979), 24–26.

Morgan, Thomas D. "The Evolving Concept of Professional Responsibility." *Harvard Law Review* 90 (February 1977), 702–743.

Moss, John E. "The Crisis of Corporate Accountability: A Legislator's View." *Journal of Corporate Law* 3 (Winter 1978), 251–265.

Murphy, Patrick E. "An Evolution: Corporate Social Responsiveness." *University of Michigan Business Review* 30 (November 1978), 19–25.

Ostlund, Lyman E. "Are Middle Managers an Obstacle to Corporate Social Policy Implementation?" *Business and Society* 18 (Spring 1978), 5–200.

Ostlund, Lyman E. "Attitudes of Managers toward Corporate Social Responsibility." *California Management Review* 19 (Summer 1977), 35–49.

Ostlund, Lyman E. "Managerial Attitudes towards Corporate Responsibility." *Journal of General Management* 5 (Autumn 1979), 68–79.

Palmieri, V. H. "Corporate Responsibility and the Competent Board." *Harvard Business Review* 59 (May 1979), 46+.

"Participation II: A Social Responsibility Report." *Computers and People* 26 (November 1977), 16+.

Peach, L., and John Hargreaves. "Social Responsibility: The Investment That Pays Off." *Personnel Management* 8 (June 1976), 20–24.

Pennings, Johannes M. "Corporate Social Responsibility: A Must or a

Virtue?" *New Catholic World* 223 (November–December 1980), 260+.

Phillips, Kenneth F. "Social Impact Strategies." *California Management Review* 19 (Fall 1976), 91–95.

"Plant Closing Acts: Social Responsibility or Industrial Hostage." *New England Business* 1 (May 16, 1979), 38–40.

Pledger, Rosemary, and Richard E. Vaden. "Traditional American Ideals and Corporate Responsibility." *Marquette Business Review* 20 (Summer 1976), 69–73.

Post, James E., and Marilyn Mellis. "Corporate Responsiveness and Organizational Learning." *California Management Review* 20 (Spring 1978), 57–63.

Preston, Lee E. "Analyzing Corporate Social Performance: Methods and Results." *Journal of Contemporary Business* 7 (Winter 1978), 135–150.

Preston, Lee E., Francoise Rey, and Meinolf Dierkes. "Comparing Corporate Social Performance: Germany, France, Canada, and the United States." *California Management Review* 20 (Summer 1978), 40–49.

Prout, G. "Expecting Corporate Ethical Reform." *Public Relations Review* 4, no. 2 (1978), 13–21.

Purcell, Theodore V. "Electing an 'Angel's Advocate' to the Board." *Management Review* 65 (May 1976), 4–11.

Reba, Marilyn. "Call It Irresponsible, but Know What You Mean." *Business and Society Review* 18 (Summer 1976), 73–74.

"Research Firm Report Examines Socially Responsible Companies." *Pensions and Investments* 6 (December 18, 1978), 1+.

Rinke, Delores F. "The Social Conscience and the Profit Motive." *Industrial Management* 21 (September–October 1979), 6–7.

Rivchun, Silvia. "Associations in Society: Learning to be a Better Neighbor." *Association Management* 32 (May 1980), 40–45.

Roberts, Markley. "Corporate Responsibility—A Goal for the 1980's." *American Federationist* 86 (November 1979), 8–11.

Roth, G. H., and H. Fitz. "Corporate Social Responsibility— European Models." *Hastings Law Journal* 30, no. 5 (1979), 1433–1462.

Sawyer, George C. "Corporate Allegiances to the Local Society." *Columbia Journal of World Business* 13 (Winter 1978), 39–44.

Schlesinger, James R. "In the Sense of Common Purpose." *Encounter/Social Action* 5 (October 1977), 18–22.

Schochet, Gordon J. "Social Responsibility, Profits, and the Public Interest." *Society* 16 (March–April 1979), 20–26.

Selto, Frank H. "Some Comments on Accounting for Social Performance." *Journal of Contemporary Business* 7 (Winter 1978), 171–174.

Sethi, S. Prakash. "A Conceptual Framework for Environmental Analysis of Social Issues and Evaluation of Business Response Patterns." *Academy of Management Review* 4 (January 1979), 63–74.

Shaffer, Butler D. "The Social Responsibility of Business: A Dissent." *Business and Society* 17 (Spring 1977), 11–18.

Shaffer, Butler D. "The Social Responsibility of Business: A *Flawed* Dissent: Response." *Business and Society* 18 (Spring 1978), 41–42.

Shanklin, William L."Corporate Social Responsibility: Another View." *Journal of Business Research* 4 (February 1976), 75–84.

Shinn, Richard R. "Social Rebirth and Corporate Responsibility." *Adherent* 3 (December 1976), 38–43.

Siegel, Joel, and Martin Lehman. "Own Up to Social Responsibility." *Financial Executive* 44 (March 1976), 44.

Sieghart, Paul. "Defining Corporate Responsibility: Major Ingredients of an Evolving Ethic." *Atlas* 25 (April 1978), 44.

Smart, S. Bruce, Jr. "A New Role for American Business." *FCR Review* 1 (Spring 1980), 3–5.

"Social Responsibility Disclosure." *Public Relations Journal* 35 (April 1979), 35.

"Social Responsiveness vs. Profits for the Company." *Management Review* 66 (December 1977), 56.

"A Social Strategy Aimed at Profits." *Business Week* (June 25, 1979), 118–123.

Spicer, Barry H. "Accounting for Corporate Social Performance: Some Problems and Issues." *Journal of Contemporary Business* 7 (Winter 1978), 151–170.

Spitzer, E. "Does Business Need a Social Responsiveness Index?" *Public Relations Journal* 34 (June 1978), 8–11.

Steiner, George A. "Institutionalizing Corporate Social Decisions." *Business Horizons* 18 (December 1975), 12–18.

Stemper, William. "An Approach to Corporate Responsibility: A Retrospective on the Forum." *FCR Review* 1 (Spring 1980), 13–15.

Stone, Christopher D. "The Place of Enterprise Liability in the Control of Corporate Conduct." *Yale Law Journal* 90 (November 1980), 1–77.

Strier, Franklin. "The Business Manager's Dilemma I. Defining Social Responsibility." *Journal of Enterprise Management* 2 (1979), 5–10.

Strier, Franklin. "The Business Manager's Dilemma II. Arguments pro and con Social Responsibility." *Journal of Enterprise Management* 2 (1979), 11–26.

Strier, Franklin. "The Business Manager's Dilemma III. Identifying the Social Responsibilities of Business." *Journal of Enterprise Management* 2 (1980), 119–126.

Stuart, Robert. "The Social Responsibility of People in Business." *Nation's Business* 65 (April 1977), 47–48.

Swart, J. Carroll. "Profits versus Social Responsibility: A Critical Analysis of Corporate Objectives from the Perspective of Communication Theory." *Academy of Management, Proceedings of the 36th Annual Meeting*, August 11–14, 1976, 320–323.

Swearingen, John E. "Business Leadership in National Affairs." (Based on address.) *Business Horizons* 19 (October 1976), 5–11.

Troub, R. M. "Industrial Growth, Technological Innovation, and Social Responsibilities of Large Corporations—Some Systemic Considerations." *Social Science Journal* 14, no. 1 (1977), 95–109.

Van Suken, Philip M., and R. Duane Ireland. "The Ethics of Business Social Responsibility." *Baylor Business Studies* 9 (August/October 1978), 33–40.

Walinsky, L. J. "A Businessman's Primer on Inflation and Social Justice." *Business and Society Review* 13 (Spring 1975), 16–24.

Walter, Ingo. "Social Responsibility and the Future of Guidance without Rules" *Intereconomics* (May 1976), 141–145.

Walters, Kenneth D. "Corporate Social Responsibility and Political Ideology." *California Management Review* 19 (Spring 1977), 40–51.

White, Donald D., Jr. "Social Responsibility of Business: An Opposing View." *Arkansas Business and Economic Review* 9 (Fall 1976), 1–5.

Wiggins, Ronald L., and Richard D. Steade. "Job Satisfaction as a

Social Concern." *Academy of Management Review* 1 (October 1976), 48–55.

Williams, Charles W. "Whither Private Enterprise: What Is Happening to Our Quality of Life?" *Financial Executive* 44 (February 1976), 28–33.

Williams, Harold M. "Corporate Accountability: The Board of Directors." *Vital Speeches of the Day* 44 (May 15, 1978), 468–472.

Williams, Harold M. "Accountability and the Corporate Board." *Enterprise* 4 (July 1980), 6–9.

Williams, Harold M. "The Dynamics of Corporate Accountability." *Los Angeles Business and Economics* 5 (Fall 1980), 29–31.

Wilson, Erika. "Social Responsibility of Business: What Are the Small Business Perspectives?" *Journal of Small Business Management* 18 (July 1980), 17+.

Zoffer, H. J. "New Dimensions for the Bottom Line: The View of Corporate Social Responsibility from the Contemporary Bridge." *Journal of General Management* 3 (Winter 1975–76), 22–34.

Business and Society: Particular Issues

Business and Society: Particular Issues

Bribery and Unusual Foreign Payments

Books

Adams, Gordon, et al. *The Invisible Hand: Questionable Corporate Payments Overseas.* New York: Council on Economics Priorities, 1976.

Basche, James R. *Unusual Foreign Payments: A Survey of the Policies and Practices of U.S. Companies.* New York: The Conference Board, 1976.

Boulton, David. *The Grease Machine.* New York: Harper and Row, 1979.

Jacoby, Neil H., Peter Nehemkis, and Richard Eells. *Bribery and Extortion in World Business.* New York: Macmillan, 1977.

Kennedy, Tom, and Charles E. Simon. *An Examination of Questionable Payments and Practices.* New York: Praeger, 1978.

Kugel, Yerachmiel, and Neal P. Cohen. *Government Regulation of Business Ethics: International Payoffs.* Dobbs Ferry, N.Y.: Oceana, 1977.

Kugel, Yerachmiel, and Gladys W. Gruenberg. *International Payoffs: Dilemma for Business.* Lexington, Mass.: Lexington Books, 1977.

Kugel, Yerachmiel, and Gladys W. Gruenberg, eds. *Selected Readings on International Payoffs.* Lexington, Mass.: Lexington Books, 1977.

Sampson, Anthony. *The Arms Bazaar: The Companies, The Dealers, The Bribes, from Vickers to Lockheed.* New York: Viking, 1977.

Securities and Exchange Commission. *Report on Questionable and Illegal Corporate Payments and Practices.* Washington, D.C.: May 12, 1976.

Articles

Ace, Goodman. "Here Comes the Bribes." *Saturday Review* 3 (May 1, 1976), 57.

Adelberg, Arthur H., and Sidney Feld. "Illegal Payments: Who's to Tell? When Clients Stray Should Auditors Pay?" *C.A. Magazine* 110 (April 1977), 31–33.

"All in the Normal Course of Selling Aeroplanes." *The Economist* 258 (January 24, 1976), 87–88.

"The Antibribery Bill Backfires." *Business Week* (April 17, 1978), 143.

" 'Anti-bribery' Law Overview." *Journal of Accountancy* 145 (June 1978), 84+.

"Are Congressmen for Sale to Business?" *Business and Society Review* 34 (Summer 1980), 10–14.

Balde, D. A., and W. E. Howard. "When Illegal Payments, Kickbacks, and Bribes Reduce Income." *Taxes* 57 (January 1979), 60–65.

Ballinger, Edward P., and Jesse Dillard. "The Foreign Corrupt Practices Act." *CPA Journal* 50 (February 1980), 37–46.

Banaszewski, J. "Mullane Calls Incentive a Bribe to Salesmen." *Automotive News* (January 17, 1977), 2+.

Barone, Sam, and Suk H. Him. "International Payoffs: Profits and Morality." *International Journal of Comparative and Applied Criminal Justice* 4 (Spring 1980), 57–62.

Barovick, Richard L. "The SEC Unleashes a Foreign Payoffs Storm." *Business and Society* Review 19 (Fall 1976), 48–53.

Baruch, Hurd. "The Foreign Corrupt Practices Act." *Harvard Business Review* 57 (January-February 1979), 32–34+.

Basche, James R. "Questionable Payments and the Regulation of Multinational Corporations." *Journal of Contemporary Business* 6 (Autumn 1977), 165–177.

Basche, James R. "Those 'Questionable Payments': A Code Would Be Questionable, Too." *Across the Board* 14 (July 1977), 23–26.

"The Basics of Bribery." *Wall Street Journal* (February 27, 1976), 8.

Bates, Homer L., and Philip M. J. Reckers. "Complying with the Foreign Corrupt Practices Act." *Business* 27 (July-August 1979), 35–38.

Beresford, Dennis R., and Ray J. Groves. "SEC Reports to Congress on Questionable Corporate Payments." *Financial Executive* 44 (July 1976), 8.

Beresford, Dennis R., and James D. Bond. "The Foreign Corrupt Practices Act—Its Implication to Financial Management." *Financial Executive* 46 (August 1978), 26–32.

Blumenthal, W. Michael. "Top Management's Role in Preventing Illegal Payments." *Conference Board Record* 13 (August 1976), 14–16.

Blumenthal, W. Michael. (Treasury Secretary Blumenthal testifies on legislation concerning illicit payments abroad.) *Department of State Bulletin* 76 (April 11, 1977).

Borgida, Chester J. "SEC and the 'Questionable Payments' Controversy." *Public Relations Journal* 33 (April 1977), 10–11+.

"Bribery: A Shocker in U.S., but a Tradition Overseas." *U.S. News and World Report* 80 (April 12, 1976), 33–34.

"Bribery and Brokerage: An Analysis of Bribery in Domestic and Foreign Commerce under Section 2(c) of the Robinson-Patman Act." *Michigan Law Review* 76 (August 1978), 1343–1370.

"The Bribery Epidemic." *Atlas* 23 (May 1976), 29–37.

"Bribery: Hard Soap for Foreigners." *The Economist* 260 (September 11, 1976), 85–86.

"Bribery: Not All Publicity Is Good Publicity." *The Economist* 265 (December 3, 1977), 105–106.

"Bribery: Pure but Not Too Pure." *The Economist* 259 (May 22, 1976), 105–106.

Buckley, William F., Jr. "Bribery International." *National Review* 28 (January 23, 1976), 52.

"Business against Bribery." *The Economist* 265 (November 26, 1977), 86.

"CPI Firms Tackle Payments Problem." *Chemical Week* 118 (May 19, 1976), 20–21.

Calame, Byron E. "After the Fall: At Gulf Oil Nowadays, a 'Questionable' Deal Is One to Be Shunned." *Wall Street Journal* (January 25, 1977), 1+.

"Canada's Flexible Bribery Standards." *Business Week* (June 13, 1977), 35.

Chazin M. "Bribery and Kickbacks Are Commonplace and Expensive." *Inland Printer/American Lithographer* 180 (February 1978), 40–43.

Chu, Morgan, and Daniel Magraw. "The Deductibility of Questionable Foreign Payments." *Yale Law Journal* 87 (May 1978), 1091–1124.

Cohen, Richard E. "Corporate Bribery—Something's Wrong, but What Can Be Done about It?" *National Journal* 8 (May 15, 1976), 658–668.

Coshnear, Theodore A. "The Lockheed Scandal and the U.S. Congress—The Evils and Virtues of the Foreign Corrupt Practices Act of 1977." *Italian American Business* 29 (October 1978), 32–34+.

Council on Economic Priorities. "Corporate Payoffs: The Tally So Far." *Business and Society Review* 19 (Fall 1976), 54–57.

Cousins, Norman. "Bribery and Human Rights." *Saturday Review* 4 (May 2, 1977), 4.

Cushman, Robert. "The Norton Company Faces the Payoff Problem." *Harvard Business Review* 54 (September–October 1976), 6–7.

Cutler, Lloyd N. "The Sunlight Cure for Briber's Disease." *Business and Society Review* 21 (Spring 1977), 32–35.

"Disclosure Seen Curb to Foreign Payoffs." *Commerce America* 1 (August 16, 1976), 16.

Dolanski, Anthony P. "Improper Payments." *World* 10 (Winter 1976), 2–5.

Duncan, Sue. "Corporate Payoffs Abroad: Issues and Answers." *Directors and Boards* 1 (Fall 1976), 12–35.

"Elliot Richardson on Bribery." *New Republic* 175 (July 24, 1976), 3–4.

Esty, John S., and David W. Marston. "Pitfalls (and Loopholes) in the Foreign Bribery Law." *Fortune* 98 (October 9, 1978), 182–183.

"The Ethics of Bribery." *Nation* 224 (March 5, 1977), 260.

Feldman, Mark B. "U.S. Proposes System of Disclosure in Treaty on Illicit Payments." *Department of State Bulletin* 75 (December 6, 1976), 696–699.

Ferrera, Gerald R. "Corporate Board Responsibility under the Foreign Corrupt Practices Act of 1977." *American Business Law Journal* 18 (Summer 1980), 259–267.

Fitzgerald, Richard D. "Combating Extortion and Bribery in Business Transactions." *Price Waterhouse Review* 23, no. 4 (1978), 40–45.

Ford, Gerald R. "Task Force on Questionable Corporate Payments Abroad Established." *Department of State Bulletin* 74 (May 3, 1976), 583–584.

"Foreign Bribes and the Securities Acts' Disclosure Requirements." *Michigan Law Review* 74 (May 1976), 1222–1242.

"Foreign Corrupt Practices Act Called Vague." *National Underwriter* 83 (June 1, 1979), 59–60.

Gillespie, G. Robert. "Questionable Payments." *Internal Auditor* 36 (October 1979), 61–65.

"The Global Costs of Bribery." *Business Week* (March 15, 1976), 22–24.

"Governments Asked to Take All Measures to Halt Bribery by Transnationals." *UN Chronicle* 13 (January 1976), 50–51.

Granroge, John T. "Multinational Corporations and the Ethics of Questionable Payments." *Business and Professional Ethics* 2 (Spring/Summer 1979), 5–6.

"Group on Practices of Transnationals Reaches Agreement on Major Issues." *UN Chronicle* 14 (March 1977), 31.

Guillet de Monthoux, Pierre. "Marketing and Corruption." *Management Decision* 15 (1977), 531–541.

Gustman, David C. "The Foreign Corrupt Practices Act of 1977: A Transactional Analysis." *Journal of International Law and Economics* 13 (1979), 367–401.

Guzzardi, Walter, Jr. "An Unscandalized View of Those 'Bribes' Abroad." *Fortune* 94 (July 1976), 118–121+.

Halbrooks, John R. "Business Bribery—How Big Is It?" *Purchasing* 81 (August 17, 1976), 22–37.

Hancock, William A. "New 'Bribery' Statute: Your Accounting Standards May Not Pass the Test." *Journal of Applied Management* 43 (May–June 1979), 12–19.

Hanson, Simon G. "Questionable Payments? Notes on Business Practices in Latin America." *Inter-American Economic Affairs* 31 (Autumn 1977), 25–40.

Heindel, Richard H. "American Business Bribery Shakes the World—Can Americans Remake It?" *Intellect* 105 (April 1977), 312+.

Heine, Andrew N. "Curbs on Overseas Bribes Are Hurting U.S. Business." *Dun's Review* 114 (September 1979), 123–124+.

Heller, Robert. "Review of Bribery and Extortion." *Harvard Business Review* 56 (July–August 1978), 68–69+.

Herlihy, Edward D., and Theodore A. Levine. "Corporate Crisis: The Overseas Payment Problem." *Law and Policy in International Business* 8 (1976), 547–629.

Hershey, Robert D., Jr. "Payoffs: Are They Stopped or Just Better Hidden?" *New York Times* (January 9, 1977), 23.

Hibey, Richard A. "New Rules for an Old Game." *Perspective* 4 (Spring–Summer 1978), 2–6.

Hollier, Derek. "Bribery: One in Five Top Men Are Bribes Targets." *Business Administration* (April 1976), 16–19.

Horn, Stephen A. "How to Cope with the Corrupt Practices Act." *Tax Executive* 31 (January 1979), 154–163.

"Hot on the Scent of Payoffs at Home." *Business Week* (March 8, 1976), 29–30.

"How Boeing Passed $52 Million under the Table." *Business and Society Review* (Winter 1978–79), 36–40.

Ingersoll, Robert S. "Department Proposes Two New Actions to Deal with International Problem of Bribery." *Department of State Bulletin* 74 (March 29, 1976), 412–415.

"International Chamber of Commerce: Commission on Ethical Practices Recommendations to Combat Extortion and Bribery in Business Transactions." *International Legal Materials* 17 (March 1978), 417–421.

"International Corporations: Foreign Payola Policy?" *Senior Scholastic* 108 (May 4, 1976), 16–19.

Jacoby, Neil H. "Naiveté: Foreign Payoffs Law." *California Management Review* 22 (Fall 1979), 84–87.

Jensen, Michael C. "Many U.S. Executives Reported in Favor of Overseas Bribes." *New York Times* (February 13, 1976), 45+.

John, Douglas A., and Kurt Pany. "Arizona Firms and the Foreign Corrupt Practices Act." *Arizona Business* 26 (February 1979), 10–14.

Kaikati, Jack G. "The Phenomenon of International Bribery." *Business Horizons* 20 (February 1977), 25–37.

Kaikati, Jack G., and Wayne A. Label. "American Bribery Legislation: An Obstacle to International Marketing." *Journal of Marketing* 44 (Fall 1980), 38–43.

Kaikati, Jack G., and Wayne A. Label. "Foreign Antibribery Law: Friend or Foe?" *Columbia Journal of World Business* 15 (Spring 1980), 46–51.

Kaplan, Philip T. "The Foreign Corrupt Practices Act." *Journal of Corporate Taxation* 5 (Autumn 1978), 287–290.

"A Kingdom for a Bribe?" *The Economist* 260 (August 21, 1976), 12.

Kneedler, Robert L., and Grant W. Newton. "The Foreign Corrupt Practices Act: Coping with Internal Accounting Control Provisions." *Los Angeles Business and Economics* 5 (Winter 1980), 22–27.

Korbin, Stephen J. "Morality, Political Power and Illegal Payments by Multinational Corporations." *Columbia Journal of World Business* 11 (Winter 1976), 105–110.

Kotchian, A. Carl. "The Payoff: Lockheed's 70-Day Mission to Tokyo." *Saturday Review* 4 (July 9, 1977), 1+.

Kraut, Richard S. "No Sermon on the Mount but Recent Developments Involving Questionable Payments." *Management Review* 67 (April 1978), 29–31.

Kroll, Jules B., and Sanford E. Beck. "White Collar Crime: Security's Role in Combatting Commercial Bribery." *Security Management* 22 (July 1978), 6–8.

Kugel, Yerachmiel, and Gladys W. Gruenberg. "Criteria and Guidelines for Decision Making: The Special Case of International Payoffs." *Columbia Journal of World Business* 12 (Fall 1977), 113–123.

Kugel, Yerachmiel, and Gladys Gruenberg. "International Payoffs: Where We Are and How We Got There." *Challenge* 19 (September–October 1976), 13–20.

Lang, John S. "Drive to Curb Kickbacks and Bribes by Business." *U.S. News and World Report* 85 (September 4, 1978), 41–44.

Lapham, Edward. "Chrysler, Ford Admit Illegal Foreign Payouts." *Automotive News* (June 20, 1977), 2.

Lashbrooke, E. C., Jr. "The Foreign Corrupt Practices Act of 1977: A Unilateral Solution to an International Problem." *Cornell International Law Journal* 12 (Summer 1979), 227–243.

Lernoux, Penny. "Bribes by Big Business in Latin Countries." *National Catholic Reporter* 15 (March 16, 1979), 4.

Lowenfels, Lewis D. "Questionable Corporate Payments and the Federal Securities Laws." *New York University Law Review* 51 (April 1976), 1–33.

McClenahen, John S. "Clearer Bribe Rules May Be Even Worse." *Industry Week* 199 (December 11, 1978), 19–23.

McCloy, John J. "Improper Payments and the Responsibility of the Board of Directors." *Conference Board Record* 13 (August 1976), 9–13.

McCloy, John J., Nathan W. Pearson, and Beverley Matthews. "The Boy Scouts at Gulf Oil." *Business and Society Review* 19 (Fall 1976), 58–60.

Mace, Myles L., ed. "John J. McCloy on Corporate Payoffs." *Harvard Business Review* 54 (July–August 1976), 14–16+.

McGehee, Fielding M., III. "Bribery for 'National Security.'" *Progressive* 42 (March 1978), 7–8.

McKee, Thomas E. "Auditing under the Foreign Corrupt Practices Act." *CPA Journal* 49 (August 1979), 31–35.

McManus, Charles R. "Questionable Corporate Payoffs Abroad: An Antitrust Approach." *Yale Law Journal* 86 (December 1976), 215–257.

Marchione, Anthony R. "Illegal Payments—Unnecessary Cost for Free Enterprise." *Michigan Business Review* 29 (July 1977), 22–26.

Mark, B.S. "Commercial Bribes: Are They Deductible?" *Taxes* 58 (August 1980), 593–597.

Mette, William R., Jr., and Charles A. Werner. "Stopping Illegal Corporate Payments." *Business Week* (July 26, 1976), 19.

Middleton, Thomas H. "Baksheesh, Cumshaw, and All That Grease." *Saturday Review* 4 (July 9, 1976), 20–21.

Miller, Jennifer L. "Accounting for Corporate Misconduct Abroad: The Foreign Corrupt Practices Act of 1977." *Cornell International Law Journal* 12 (Summer 1979), 293–307.

"Misinterpreting the Antibribery Law." *Business Week* (September 3, 1979), 150–151.

Morgenthaler, E., and Byron E. Calame. "Do's and Don't's: More Concerns Issue Guidelines on Ethics in Payoffs Aftermath." *Wall Street Journal* (March 16, 1976), 1+.

Murphy, Michael E. "Payoffs to Foreign Officials: Time for More National Responsibility." *American Bar Association Journal* 62 (April 1976), 480–482.

Nelson, David K. "Bribes, Kickbacks, and Political Contributions in Foreign Countries." *Wisconsin Law Review* (1977), 1231–1268.

Neumann, Frederick L. "Corporate Audit Committees and the Foreign Corrupt Practices Act." *Business Horizons* 23 (June 1980), 62–71.

Noonan, John T., Jr. "Bribes and the Boycott: The Responsibilities of American Lawyers." *American Bar Association Journal* 62 (December 1976), 1607–1609.

North, James. "The Economics of Extortion." *Washington Monthly* 10 (November 1978), 29–30+.

Parker, C. Wolcott, II. "Bribery in Foreign Lands." *Vital Speeches of the Day* 42 (February 15, 1976), 281–284.

Pastin, Mark, and Michael Hooker. "Ethics and the Foreign Corrupt Practices Act." *Business Horizons* 23 (December 1980), 43–47.

Phillips, Susan Daunhauer. "The Federal Bribery Statute: An Argument for Cautious Revision." *Kentucky Law Journal* 68 (1979–80), 1026–1053.

Phillips, William J. "Deductibility of Overseas Commercial Bribes." *Columbia Journal of Law and Social Problems* 13 (1977), 235–255.

Pomeranz, Felix. "A Corporate Response to the Foreign Corrupt Practices Act." *Journal of Accounting, Auditing, and Finance* 2 (Fall 1978), 70–75.

Proxmire, William, Emmett R. Tyrrell, Jr., et al. "American Grease and Foreign Palms—A Roundup." *Business and Society Review* 21 (Spring 1977), 23–31.

"Questionable or Illegal Corporate Payments and Practice." *CPA Journal* 47 (June 1977), 50–52.

"Questionable Payments: 1—Setting Policies to Eliminate Them." *Business International* (January 28, 1977), 27+.

"Reduction in Earnings and Profits Resulting from Illegal Payment." *CPA Journal* 48 (July 1978), 42.

Ricchiute, David N. "Foreign Corrupt Practices: A New Responsibility for Internal Auditors." *Internal Auditor* 35 (December 1978), 58–64.

Ricchiute, David N. "Illegal Payments, Deception of Auditors, and Reports on Internal Control." *MSU Business Topics* 28 (Spring 1980), 57–63.

Richman, Barry. "Can We Prevent Questionable Foreign Payments?" *Business Horizons* 22 (June 1979), 14–19.

Richman, Barry. "Stopping Payments under the Table: Doing Business Overseas Should Not Mean Forgetting about Ethical Standards." *Business Week* (May 22, 1978), 18.

Robinson, Herbert, and J. Karl Fishbach. "Commercial Bribery—The Corporation as Victim." *Financial Executive* 47 (April 1979), 16–19+.

Rodgers, William. "The Bribe Came COD: Corruption in the Computer Industry." *Computer Decisions* 8 (September 1976), 66+.

Ross, Irwin. "Bribery Is Bad Business." *Reader's Digest* 109 (September 1976), 123–126.

Roth, Allan. "The Foreign Corrupt Practices Act of 1977: Background and Summary." *Corporation Law Review* 1 (Fall 1978), 347–356.

Ryans, John K., Jr., and Henry W. Woudenberg, Jr. "The MNC Bribery Question." *Atlanta Economic Review* 28 (November–December 1978), 28–33.

Scheibla, Shirley Hobbs. "Accountable for What? Executives Push Changes in Foreign Corrupt Practices Act." *Barron's* 60 (December 29, 1980), 9–10+.

Singer, James W. "The Crackdown on Improper Corporate Payments Made Abroad." *National Journal* 10 (June 3, 1978), 880–883.

" 'Slush Money': Beyond the Fringe Benefit." *Banker* 127 (June 1977), 29–30.

Solomon, Kenneth I., and Hyman Muller. "Illegal Payments: Where the Auditor Stands." *Journal of Accountancy* 143 (January 1977), 51–57.

Solomon, Lewis D., and Leslie G. Linville. "Transnational Conduct of American Multinational Corporations: Questionable Payments Abroad." *Boston College Industrial and Commercial Law Review* 17 (March 1976), 303–345.

Sommer, A. A. "Parting Look at Foreign Payments." *Arthur Andersen Chronicle* 36 (April 1976), 13–25.

Sorensen, Theodore C. "Improper Payments Abroad: Perspectives and Proposals." *Foreign Affairs* 54 (July 1976), 719–733.

Sprow, Howard T., and James N. Benedict. "The Foreign Corrupt Practices Act of 1977: Some Practical Problems and Suggested Procedures." *Corporation Law Review* 1 (Fall 1978), 357–363.

Stentzel, James. "Fallout of Bribery: Lockheed Aids Japan's Militarists." *Nation* 222 (March 6, 1976), 262–264.

Stevenson, Russell B., Jr. "The SEC and Foreign Bribery." *Business Lawyer* 32 (November 1976), 53–73.

Sumutka, Alan R. "Questionable Payments and Practices: Why? How? Detection? Prevention?" *Journal of Accountancy* 149 (March 1980), 50–52+.

Taylor, John C., III. "Preventing Improper Payments through Internal Controls." *Conference Board Record* 13 (August 1976), 17–19.

"They Paid and Paid." *Chemical Week* 119 (July 21, 1976), 17.

"Two Viewpoints: Are Payoffs Abroad Ever Justified? Sometimes—When the 'National Interest' Is at Stake." *U.S. News and World Report* 80 (April 12, 1976), 35–36.

"U.S. Moves to Ban Overseas Payments." *Aviation Week and Space Technology* 106 (June 6, 1977), 197–199.

Walker, Michael A. "The Foreign Corrupt Practices Act of 1977: An Auditor's Perspective." *CPA Journal* 48 (May 1978), 71–75.

Wambold, Judson J. "Prohibiting Foreign Bribes: Criminal Sanctions for Corporate Payments Abroad." *Cornell International Law Journal* 10 (May 1977), 231–254.

Wolfson, Nicholas. "The Foreign Corrupt Practices Act." *Corporation Law Review* 1 (Summer 1978), 258–261.

Changing Business and Society

Books

Backman, Jules. *Business Problems of the Eighties.* Indianapolis: Bobbs, 1980.

Blair, Roger D., and Robert F. Lanzillotti, eds. *The Conglomerate Corporation: A Public Policy Problem?* Cambridge, Mass.: Oelgeschlager, Gunn & Hain, 1980.

Blumberg, Phillip I. *The Megacorporation in American Society.* Englewood Cliffs., N.J.: Prentice-Hall, 1976.

Brown, Courtney C. *Toward the Next Corporation.* New York: Macmillan, 1979.

Brown, Courtney C., et al. *The Future of Business: Global Issues in the Eighties and Nineties.* Elmsford, N.Y.: Pergamon Press, 1979.

Brown, James K. *This Business of Issues: Coping with the Company's Environments.* New York: The Board, 1979.

Cavanaugh, Gerald F. *American Business Values in Transition.* Englewood Cliffs, N.J.: Prentice-Hall, 1976.

Chamberlain, Neil W. *Remaking American Values: Challenge to a Business Society.* New York: Basic Books, 1977.

Chandler, Alfred D., Jr. *The Visible Hand: The Managerial Revolution in American Business.* Cambridge, Mass.: Harvard University Press, 1977.

Chandler, Alfred D., Jr., and Daems Herman, eds. *Managerial Hierarchies: Comparative Perspectives on the Rise of Modern Industrial Enterprise.* Cambridge, Mass.: Harvard University Press, 1980.

Curtiss, Ellen T., and Philip A. Unterfee. *Corporate Responsibilities and Opportunities to 1990.* Lexington, Mass.: Lexington Books, 1979.

DeMott, Deborah A., ed. *Corporations at the Crossroads.* New York: McGraw-Hill, 1980.

Drucker, Peter F. *Managing in Turbulent Times.* New York: Harper and Row, 1980.

Drucker, Peter F. *The Unseen Revolution.* New York: Harper and Row, 1976.

Easley, Eddie, et al. *Contemporary Business: Challenges and Opportunities.* St. Paul: West Publishing Co., 1978.

Greenfield, Sidney M., et al., eds. *Entrepreneurs in Cultural Context.* Albuquerque: University of New Mexico Press, 1979.

Guinther, John. *Moralists and Managers: Public Interest Movements in America.* Garden City, N.Y.: Doubleday and Co., 1976.

Haas, John J. *Corporate Social Responsibility in a Changing Society.* New York: Vantage, 1976.

Hargreaves, John, and Jan Dauman. *Business Survival and Social Change: A Practical Guide to Responsibility and Partnership.* New York: Halstead Press, 1975.

Hay, Robert D., Edmund R. Gray, and James E. Gates, eds. *Business and Society.* Cincinnati: Southwestern Publishing Co., 1976.

Heilbroner, Robert L. *Beyond Boom and Crash.* New York: W. W. Norton, 1978.

Ivancevich, John M., et al. *Business in a Dynamic Environment.* St. Paul: West Publishing Co., 1979.

Jacoby, Neil H. *Corporate Power and Social Responsibility: A Blueprint for the Future.* New York: Free Press, 1977.

Kay, Lillian. *The Future Role of Business in Society.* New York: Conference Board, 1977.

Madden, Carl H. *Clash of Culture: Management in an Age of Changing Values.* Washington, D.C.: National Planning Association, 1976.

O'Toole, James. *Energy and Social Change.* Cambridge, Mass.: MIT Press, 1976.

Paluszek, John L. *Will the Corporation Survive?* Englewood Cliffs, N.J.: Prentice-Hall Publications, 1977.

Post, James E. *Corporate Behavior and Social Change.* Englewood Cliffs, N.J.: Prentice-Hall, 1978.

Reid, Samuel Richardson. *The New Industrial Order.* New York: McGraw-Hill, 1976.

Report of the Task Force on Corporate Social Performance. *Business and Society: Strategies for the 1980's.* Washington, D.C.: Department of Commerce, 1980.

Rubin, Bernard. *Big Business and the Mass Media.* Lexington, Mass.: D.C. Heath and Co., 1977.

Shephard, Wilham G., ed. *Public Policies toward Business: Reading and Cases.* Homewood, Ill.: Richard D. Irwin, 1979.

Sheppard, C. Stewart, ed. *Working in the Twenty-first Century.* New York: Wiley–Interscience, 1980.

Starling, Grover. *The Changing Environment of Business.* Belmont, Calif.: Doxbury Press, 1980.

Tavel, Charles. *The Third Industrial Age: Strategy for Business Survival.* Elmsford, N.Y.: Pergamon Press, 1980.

Warner, Rawleigh, Jr., and Leonard Silk. *Ideals in Collision: The Relationship between Business and the News Media.* New York: Columbia University Press, 1979.

Ways, Max, ed. *The Future of Business: Global Issues in the 80's and 90's.* Elmsford, N.Y.: Pergamon Press, 1979.

Articles

Ablon, Ralph. "Financing of the Corporate Structure for the 1980's: The Social Responsibility of the Businessman." *Vital Speeches of the Day* 43 (April 15, 1977), 398–401.

Bell, Daniel. "Communications Technology—For Better or for Worse." *Harvard Business Review* 57 (May–June 1979), 20–42.

Berry, Leonard L. "Corporate Leadership in the Age of the People." *Atlanta Economic Review* 26 (May–June 1976), 4–7.

Blumenthal, W. Michael. "Business Morality Has Not Deteriorated— Society Has Changed." *New York Times* (January 9, 1977), 9.

Boe, Archie R. "Fitting the Corporation to the Future." *Public Relations Quarterly* 24 (Winter 1979), 4–5.

Boris, Elizabeth Trocolli. "Private Enterprise and Public Values." *Society* 16 (March–April 1979), 18–19.

Bowman, James S. "Ethics in the Federal Service—A Post-Watergate View." *Midwest Review of Public Administration* 11 (March 1977), 3–20.

Brown, Marilyn V. "Corporate Reporting in a Changing Environment." *Public Relations Journal* 32 (April 1976), 14–15.

Burgen, Carl. "How Companies React to the Ethics Crisis." *Business Week* (February 9, 1979), 78–79.

Canham, E. D. "Management and Social Values." *Advanced Management Journal* (October 1976), 12–17.

"Capitalizing on Social Change." *Business Week* (October 29, 1979), 105–106.

Cardinal, Robert J., and Ronald J. Sanderson, et al. "The Changing

Private Market System." *Journal of Advertising* 6 (Summer 1977), 34–40.

Chamberlain, Neil W. "Managerial Response to Social Change in Western Europe." *Columbia Journal of World Business* 13 (Winter 1978), 31–38.

Chase, W. Howard. "Adjusting to a Different Business/Social Climate." *Administrative Management* 40 (January 1979), 29–30+.

Cherrington, David J. "The Values of Younger Workers." *Business Horizons* 20 (December 1977), 18–30.

Dam, Andre van. "Management in the 1980's: An Awakening of Social Consciousness." *Association Management* 30 (August 1978), 47–50.

Druck, Kalman B. "Dealing with Exploding Social and Political Forces: A Whole New Ball Game for Public Relations and Top Management." *Vital Speeches of the Day* 45 (December 1, 1978), 110–114.

Edmonds, Charles P., III, and John H. Hand. "What Are the Real Long-Run Objectives of Business?" *Business Horizons* 19 (December 1976), 75–81.

Englebert, Renny. "The CA's Role in a Changing Society." *The Accountant* 175 (September 30, 1976), 378–380.

Finlay, J. Richard. "Rethinking the Corporate-Social Predicament: An Agenda for Mutual Survival." *Business Quarterly* 42 (Summer 1977), 59–69.

Gillies, Jim "Managing in Times of Rapid Social Change." *Business Quarterly* 41 (Winter 1976), 59–64.

Greenberg, Stanley B. "Business Enterprise in a Racial Order." *Politics and Society Review* 6, no. 2 (1976), 213–240.

Henderson, Hazel. "The Changing Corporate-Social Contract in the 1980's: Creative Opportunities for Consumer Affairs Professionals." *Human Resource Management* 17 (Winter 1978), 15–22.

Henderson, Hazel. "A Farewell to the Corporate State." *Business and Society Review* 17 (Spring 1976), 49–56.

Hessen, Robert. "Creatures of the State? The Case against Federal Chartering of Corporations." (Editorial.) *Barron's* 56 (May 24, 1976), 7.

"Industry's Challenge, Society's Demands." *National Underwriter* (Property Ed.) 83 (June 8, 1979), 55–56.

Jacoby, Neil H. "Six Big Challenges Business Will Face in the Next Decade." *Nation's Business* 64 (August 1976), 36–38+.

Kumar, Krishan. "Industrialism and Post-Industrialism: Reflections on a Putative Transition." *Sociological Review* 24 (August 1976), 439–478.

Lahiff, James M., and John D. Hatfield. "The Winds of Change and Managerial Communication Practices." *Journal of Business Communication* 15 (Summer 1978), 19–28.

Levitt, Theodore. "Legitimacy of Business." *Management* 24 (June 1977), 94–99.

Lodge, George Cabot. "Ethics and the New Ideology: Can Business Adjust?" *Management Review* 66 (July 1977), 10–19.

London, Paul. "Business in the Modern World." *Current* 201 (March 1978), 30–38.

Lurie, William L. "How Justice Loads the Scales against Big Corporations." *Fortune* 102 (December 29, 1980), 86+.

McCarthy, Charles. "Legitimacy, Individualism, and Motivation." *Management* 24 (June 1977), 100–102.

McNulty, Paul J. "The Public Side of Private Enterprise: A Historical Perspective on American Business and Government." *Columbia Journal of World Business* 13 (Winter 1978), 122–130.

McQuaid, Kim. "Young, Swope, and General Electric's 'New Capitalism': A Study in Corporate Liberalism, 1920–1933." *American Journal of Economics and Sociology* 36 (July 1977), 323–334.

Meechan, Charles J. "The Problem of a Changing Business Environment." *Research Management* 22 (November 1979), 35–38.

Nader, Ralph, and Mark Green. "Is Bigness Bad for Business?" *Business and Society Review* 30 (Summer 1979), 20–24.

Nader, Ralph, Mark Green, and Joel Seligman. "Who Rules the Giant Corporation?" *Business and Society Review* 18 (Summer 1976), 40–48.

Newgren, Kenneth E., and Archie B. Carroll. "Social Forecasting in U.S. Corporations—A Survey." *Long Range Planning* 12 (August 1979), 59–64.

Orr, David. "New Responsibilities for Management." *Management Today* (January 1979), 90+.

Peterson, Wallace C., et al. "How Big Should Big Business Be?" *Business and Society Review* 31 (Winter 1979–80), 4–27.

Post, James E. "The Challenge of Managing under Social Uncertainty." *Business Horizons* 20 (August 1977), 51–60.

Robinson, Charles W. "U.S. Business and Government in a World of Change." *Department of State Bulletin* 75 (October 11, 1976), 441–446.

Schwartz, R. L. "Changing Values, Entrepreneurs, and the Corporation." *Research Management* 21 (March 1978), 7–11.

Sethi, S. Prakash. "Grassroots Lobbying and the Corporation." *Business and Society* 29 (Spring 1979), 8–14.

Shapiro, Irving S. "The Future Role of Business in Society." *Vital Speeches of the Day* 43 (October 15, 1976), 16–19.

Silk, Leonard. "Business in the Public Forum." *Challenge* 19 (November–December 1976), 54–55.

Silk, Leonard, and David Vogel. "A Question of Legitimacy." *Across the Board* 13 (October 1976), 4–14.

Steiner, John F., and Stahrl W. Edmunds. "Ascientific Beliefs about Large Organizations and Adaptation to Change." *Academy of Management Review* 4 (January 1979), 107–112.

Stone, Christopher D. "Law and the Culture of the Corporation." *Business and Society Review* 15 (Fall 1975), 5–17.

Sturdivant, Frederick O. "Executives and Activists: Test of Shareholder Management." *California Management Review* 22 (Fall 1979), 53–59.

Thackray, John. "America's Changing Boardroom." *Management Today* (May 1978), 58–61.

Udell, Jon G., Gene R. Laczniak, and Robert F. Lusch. "The Business Environment of 1985." *Business Horizons* 19 (June 1976), 45–54.

Van Dam, Andre. "The Business Environment in the 1980's." *Long Range Planning* 10 (August 1977), 8–12.

Van Dam, Andre. "The Future of Management: A Growing Social Consciousness Will Spur a New Business Ideology." *Management World* 7 (January 1978), 3–6.

Verity, C. William, Jr. "Multiplication by Division—An Organic View of the Changing Role of the Board Chairman in Corporate Governance." *Michigan Business Review* 31 (January 1979), 9–12.

Vogel, David. "Ralph Naders All over the Place: Citizens vs. the Corporations." *Across the Board* 16 (April 1979), 26–31.

Wilson, Ian H. "Business Management and the Winds of Change." *Journal of Contemporary Business* 7 (Winter 1978), 45–54.

Winthrop, Henry. "Some Instabilities and Moral Deficiencies of the Post-Industrial Society." *American Journal of Economics and Sociology* 35 (October 1976), 373–390.

Consumerism

Books

Aaker, David A., and George S. Day, eds. *Consumerism: Search for the Consumer Interest.* 2d ed. New York: Free Press, 1978.

Cartwright, Joe, and Jerry Patterson. *Been Taken Lately? The Comprehensive Consumer Fraud Digest.* New York: Grove, 1977.

Graedon, Joe. *The People's Pharmacy.* New York: St. Martin's Press, 1976.

Jones, Mary Gardiner, and David M. Gardner. *Consumerism: A New Force in Society.* Lexington, Mass.: Lexington Books, 1976.

Katz, Robert N., ed. *Protecting the Consumer Interest.* Cambridge, Mass.: Ballinger Publishing Co., 1976.

Kastrup, E. K., ed. *Facts and Comparison.* St. Louis: Facts and Comparisons, 1980.

Long, J. W. *The Essential Guide to Prescription Drugs.* New York: Harper and Row, 1977.

Maney, Ardith. *Representing the Consumer Interest: Mayors, Political Parties, and Interest Groups in Bureaucratic Politics.* Washington, D.C.: University Press of America, 1978.

Moffitt, Donald, ed. *Swindled!* Princeton, N.J.: Dow Jones Books, 1976.

Penna, R. P. ed. *Handbook of Nonprescription Drugs.* 6th ed. Washington, D.C.: American Pharmaceutical Association, 1979.

Robertson, Andrew. *Strategic Marketing: A Business Response to Consumerism.* New York: John Wiley and Sons, 1978.

Silverman, Milton M. *The Drugging of the Americas.* Berkeley: University of California, 1976.

Steele, Eric H. *Dispute the Consumer: Responding to Consumer Complaints.* Chicago: American Bar Foundation, 1975.

Woodside, Arch G., et al. *Foundations of Consumer and Industrial Buying Behavior.* New York: American Elsevier, 1977.

Articles

Andreasen, Alan R., and Arthur Best. "Consumers Complain—Does Business Respond?" *Harvard Business Review* 55 (July–August 1977), 93–101.

Ankvisiti, Sak, and John J. Shaw. "American and Foreign Consumer Concerns toward American Business." *Journal of Business* 17 (December 1978), 27–36.

Barksdale, Hiram C., William R. Darden, and William D. Perreault, Jr. "Changes in Consumer Attitudes toward Marketing, Consumerism, and Government Regulation: 1971–1975." *Journal of Consumer Affairs* 10 (Winter 1976), 117–139.

Best, Arthur, and Alan R. Andreasen. "Consumer Response to Unsatisfactory Purchases: A Survey of Perceiving Defects, Voicing Complaints, and Obtaining Redress." *Law and Society Review* 11 (Spring 1977), 701–742.

Bickerstaffe, George. "A New Direction for Consumerism." *International Mangement* 35 (October 1980), 35–36+.

Bloom, Paul N., and Mark J. Silver. "Consumer Education: Marketers Take Heed." *Harvard Business Review* 54 (January–February 1976), 32–42+.

"The Consumer Confronts the Businessman." *Across the Board* 14 (November 1977), 79–84.

Cox, Steven M., and Robert J. Zimmer. "Corporate Responsiveness to Consumer Requests for Substantiation of Advertised Claims." *Akron Business and Economic Review* 9 (Winter 1979), 33–36.

Damon, Mary. "The Case for Being the Customer's Advocate." *Public Relations Journal* 34 (February 1978), 30.

Engledow, Jack L. "Was Consumer Satisfaction a Pig in a Poke?" *Business Horizons* 20 (April 1977), 87–94.

Fraser, Edie. "Consumer Fraud Act." *Public Relations Journal* 33 (February 1977), 31.

Gelb, Betsy D., Gabriel M. Gelb, and Ricky W. Griffin. "Managing with the Consumer's Help." *Business Horizons* 19 (April 1976), 69–74.

George, William W. "Manufacturing to Meet Consumer Needs." *Industrial Management* 19 (January–February 1977), 16–20.

Gustafson, Alberta W. "Consumerism and the Free Enterprise System: An Overview of Recent Trends." *Alabama Business* 46 (August 1976), 2–4+.

Haney, Camille. "Business and Consumerism: Emerging Patterns of Partnership." *Columbia Journal of World Business* 13 (Winter 1978), 81–88.

Hinds, James Andrew, Jr. "To Right Mass Wrongs: A Federal Consumer Class Action Act." *Harvard Journal of Legislation* 13 (June 1976), 776–844.

Hise, Richard T., Peter L. Gillett, and Kelly J. Patrick. "The Corporate Consumer Affairs Effort." *MSU Business Topics* 26 (Summer 1977), 17–26.

Hoffman, Matthew E. "The Consumer Product Safety Commission: In Search of a Regulatory Pattern." *Columbia Journal of Law and Social Problems* 12 (1976), 393–450.

Johansson, J. K. "The Theory and Practice of Swedish Consumer Policy." *Journal of Consumer Affairs* 10 (Summer 1976), 19–32.

Jones, Mary Gardiner. "The Consumer Affairs Office: Essential Element in Corporate Policy and Planning." *California Management Review* 20 (Summer 1978), 63–73.

Keiser, Stephen K., and James R. Krum. "Consumer Perceptions of Retail Advertising with Overstated Price Savings." *Journal of Retailing* 52 (Fall 1976), 27–36.

Krattenmaker, Thomas G. "The Federal Trade Commission and Consumer Protection." *California Management Review* 18 (Summer 1976), 89–104.

McNeal, James U. "Consumer Education as a Competitive Strategy." *Business Horizons* 21 (February 1978), 50–56.

Margolius, Sidney. "The Consumer's New Concerns." *American Federationist* 85 (September 1978), 1–5.

Mayo, Robert P. "The Business Environment: Consumer Opinion vs. the Consumer Advocate." *Vital Speeches of the Day* 42 (May 7, 1976), 434–436.

Miller, Kenneth E., and Frederick D. Sturdivant. "Consumer Responses to Socially Questionable Corporate Behavior: An Empirical Test." *Journal of Consumer Research* 4 (June 1977), 1–7.

Moyer, Mel S. "Consumerism in the Future: Complex Questions and Collaborative Answers." *Business Quarterly* 41 (Winter 1976), 28–33.

Mueller, Willard F. "Social Costs of Market Power: Consumer Overcharges and Unemployment." *Antitrust Law and Economics Review* 9, no. 4 (1977), 31–39.

Munkirs, John R., Michael Ayers, and Al Grandys. "Rape of the Rate Payer: Monopoly Overcharges in the 'Regulated' Electric-Utility Industry." *Antitrust Law and Economics Review* 8, no. 2 (1976), 57–68.

Myerson, Bess. "Who Speaks for the Consumer?" *Redbook* 146 (January 1976), 29+.

Nader, Ralph. "Consumerism and Legal Services: The Merging of Movements." *Law and Society Review* 91 (December 1977), 402–426.

Nagdeman, Julian J. "Out with Gobbledygook: Simple Legal Language Is an Ideal Whose Time Has Come." *Barron's* 57 (July 25, 1977), 3.

O'Grady, M. James. "Protecting Consumers around the World." *Canadian Business Review* 5 (Spring 1978), 16–19.

Olley, Robert E. "The Canadian Consumer Movement: Basis and Objectives." *Canadian Business Review* 4 (Autumn 1977), 26–29.

Pertschuk, Michael. "Consumer Priorities, Macroconcentration, and the Scope of the FTC's Deconcentration Authority." *Antitrust Law and Economics Review* 9 (November 2, 1977), 31–42.

Pittle, R. David. "The Consumer Product Safety Commission." *California Management Review* 18 (Summer 1976), 105–109.

Reich, Robert B. "Business Can Profit from Consumer Protection." *Business and Society Review* 35 (Fall 1980), 60–63.

Rosenberg, Larry J., John A. Czepiel, and Lewis C. Cohen. "Consumer Affairs Audits: Evaluation and Analysis." *California Management Review* 19 (Spring 1977), 12–20.

Trahey, Jane. "Can We Have Detente between Advertisers and Consumerists?" *Advertising Age* 47 (August 9, 1976), 34.

Tsaklanganos, A. "The Evolution of Consumerism." *Arkansas Business and Economic Review* 9 (Spring 1976), 9–13.

Vogel, David, and Mark V. Nadel. "Who Is a Consumer? An Analysis of the Politics of Consumer Conflict." *American Politics Quarterly* 5 (January 1977), 27–56.

Voorhis, Jerry. "The Consumer Movement and the Hope of Human Survival." *The Journal of Consumer Affairs* 11 (Summer 1977), 1–16.

Wilkinson, J. B., and J. Barry Mason. "Unavailability and Mispricing of Advertised Specials: The Food Shopper's Knowledge, Experience, and Response." *Journal of Consumer Affairs* 12 (Winter 1978), 355–363.

Yanowich, Murray. "Protecting the Consumer." *Challenge* 20 (September–October 1977), 24–28.

Credibility Crisis and the Fallen Image of Business

Books

Bradshaw, Thornton F., and David Vogel. *Corporations and Their Critics.* New York: McGraw-Hill, 1981.

D'Aprix, Roger M. *The Believable Corporation.* New York: American Management Association, 1977.

Diamond, Sigmund. *The Reputation of the American Businessman.* Magnolia, Mass.: Peter Smith, 1980.

Hulteng, John. *The Messenger's Motives: Ethical Problems of the News Media.* Englewood Cliffs, N.J.: Prentice-Hall, 1976.

Johnson, M. Bruce, ed. *The Attack on Corporate America: The Corporate Issues Sourcebook.* New York: McGraw-Hill Book Co., 1978.

McGrath, Phyllis S., ed. *Business Credibility: The Critical Factors.* New York: Conference Board, 1976.

Silk, Leonard, and David Vogel. *Ethics and Profits: The Crisis of Confidence in American Business.* New York: Simon and Schuster, 1976.

Articles

Askin, Steve. "Corporate Executives Open Fire on Critics." *National Catholic Reporter* 16 (July 18, 1980), 3+.

Belliveau, Nancy. "Credibility: How Does a Company Get It? How Does a Company Lose It?" *The Institutional Investor* 11 (March 1977), 194–195.

Biegler, John C. "Rebuilding Public Trust in Business." *Financial Executive* 45 (June 1977), 28–31.

Biegler, John C. "Toward Closing the Corporate Credibility Gap." *Finance* 96 (May 1978), 3–5.

Bloom, Paul N., and Louis W. Stern. "Emergence of Anti-Industrialism." *Business Horizons* 19 (October 1976), 87–93.

Blumberg, Phillip I. "Corporate Morality and the Crisis of Confidence in American Business." *St. Louis: Beta Gamma Sigma* (January 1977).

Bork, Robert H. "Assault on the Corporation." *Across the Board* 15 (February 1978), 50–54.

Brown, Paul I. "Business vs. the Public: Why Protest Doesn't Work." *Management Review* 65 (March 1976), 4–10.

Coulson, Ron. "Corporate Credibility: What It's All About." *Business Quarterly* 45 (Spring 1980), 71–73.

"Credibility Issue Seen Crucial to U.S. Firms." *Commerce America* 1 (July 5, 1976), 11–12.

Edwards, J. O. "The Need for Business to Go Public." *Financial Executive* 44 (May 1976), 30–35.

Finlay, J. Richard. "Decoding the Corporate Credibility Dilemma." *Business Quarterly* 44 (Summer 1979), 43–55.

Gallagher, John P. "Marketers, as Communicators, Can Raise Public Esteem for Business." *Marketing News* 11 (April 7, 1978), 9.

Graham, Katherine. "If 'Business Credibility' Means Anything." *Conference Board Record* 13 (March 1976), 28–30.

Holton, Richard H. "Business in a Fishbowl." *Business and Society Review* 20 (Winter 1976–77), 74–75.

Jewkes, John. "Big Business as the Whipping Boy." *Challenge* 21 (July–August 1978), 52–53.

Jones, Reginald H. "The Legitimacy of the Business Corporation." *Business Horizons* 20 (August 1977), 5–9.

Krikorian, Robert V. "The Bridge to Public Trust." *Review of Business* (Summer 1980), 1–3.

Louviere, Vernon. "Clearing Up Muddy Thinking about Business." *Nation's Business* 64 (May 1976), 35.

Mikalachki, Alexander, and Dorothy Mikalachki. "Is Business a Four-Letter Word: Youth's Attitudes towards Business." *Business Quarterly* 43 (Summer 1978), 71–74.

Miller, Arjay. "The Improving Corporate Image." *Business and Society Review* 20 (Winter 1976–77), 75.

Miller, J. Irwin. "Blame Not the Socialistic College Professor." *Forbes* 120 (August 1, 1977), 48.

Mulcahy, John. "Credibility of Business." *Management* 24 (June 1977), 104–106.

Murphy, Thomas A. "The Corporation and Public Opinion." *Management Review* 66 (February 1977), 49–51.

"Public Trust in Business: It's Increasing, but—." *U.S. News and World Report, Special Report* 82 (June 27, 1977), 26–28.

Reilly, Ann M. "Assault on Corporate America." *Dun's Review* 115 (April 1980), 104–106+.

"Reputation and Ethics: Some Reflections from a Country Practitioner." *The Accountant* 179 (July 6, 1978), 13–14.

Roper, Burns W. "The Tarnished Image of Business: Some Thoughts for Improving It." *Public Relations Quarterly* (Summer 1977), 11–14.

Ruby, Michael et al. "Embattled Business." *Newsweek* 87 (February 16, 1976), 56–60.

Sethi, S. Prakash. "Alternative Viewpoints: Should Business Aid the Opposition?" *Public Relations Journal* 34 (November 1978), 18–20.

Sethi, S. Prakash, and Herbert Schmertz. "Industry Fights Back: The Debate over Advocacy Advertising." *Saturday Review* 5 (January 21, 1978), 20–22+.

Silk, Leonard, and David Vogel. "A Question of Legitimacy." *Conference Board Record* 13 (October 1976), 4–14.

Silk, Leonard, and David Vogel. "Rx for a Tarnished Image." *Saturday Review* 3 (July 10, 1976), 8–12.

Smith, Lee. "Business and the Media." *Dun's Review* 107 (March 1976), 31–34.

Steiner, John F. "The Business Response to Public Distrust." *Business Horizons* 20 (April 1977), 74–81.

Steiner, John F. "Cynicism toward Business." *Michigan Business Review* 30 (September 1978), 27–32.

Steiner, Robert L. "The Prejudice against Marketing." *Journal of Marketing* 40 (July 1976), 2–9.

Thackray, John, and Cary Reich. "The Credibility Crisis at Morgan Stanley." *The Institutional Investor* 13 (February 1979), 30–34+.

Tisch, Preston Robert. "The Credibility Crisis." *Best's Review* (Life/Health Insurance Ed.) 76 (January 1976), 14+.

Tisch, Preston Robert. "Businessmen and the Credibility Crisis." *National Underwriter* (Life ed.) 80 (January 24, 1976), 13–14+.

Trytten, J. M. "It's Unbelievable How Far a Little Credibility Will Take You." *Sales and Marketing Management* 117 (September 13, 1976), 104+.

"U.S. News Study: Americans Respect, Don't Trust Business." *Advertising Age* 47 (October 25, 1976), 100.

Vogel, David. "Ralph Naders All over the Place: Citizens vs. the Corporations." *Across the Board* 16 (April 1979), 26–31.

Ways, Max. "Myth of the 'Oppressive Corporation.'" *Fortune* 96 (October 1977), 149+.

"What Business Leaders Are Doing to Polish a Tarnished Image." *U.S. News and World Report* 81 (September 13, 1976), 42–44.

White, Arthur H. "Public Anti-Business Attitudes: What You Should Do about Them." *Advertising Age* 47 (May 10, 1976), 61–62+.

"Why Business Got a Bad Name." *Business and Society Review* 19 (Fall 1976), 10–27.

Zoffer, H. J. "Restoring Institutional Credibility." *MSU Business Topics* 25 (Autumn 1977), 5–10.

Ecology: Physical Environment and Energy

Books

Adamson, Wendy W. *Who Owns a River? A Study of Environmental Action.* Minneapolis: Dillon, 1977.

Baumol, William J., and Wallace E. Oates. *Economics, Environmental Policy, and the Quality of Life.* Englewood Cliffs, N.J.: Prentice-Hall, 1979.

Boyle, Robert H. *Malignant Neglect.* New York: Knopf, 1980.

Brown, Lester R. *The Twenty-Ninth Day: Accommodating Human Needs and Numbers to the Earth's Resources.* New York: W. W. Norton, 1978.

Brown, Michael. *Laying Waste.* New York: Pantheon, 1980.

Cahn, Robert. *Footprints on the Planet: A Search for an Environmental Ethic.* New York: Universe Books, 1978.

Chen, Edwin. *PBB: An American Tragedy.* Englewood Cliffs, N.J.: Prentice-Hall, 1979.

Costello, John, and Terry Hughes. *The Concorde Conspiracy.* New York: Scribners, 1976.

Coyne, John R., Jr., and Patricia S. Coyne. *The Big Breakup: Energy in Crisis.* Mission, Kans.: Sheed, 1977.

Davidson, D. J. *The Environmental Factor: An Approach for Managers.* New York: Halstead Press, 1978.

Doniger, David D. *The Law and Policy of Toxic Substances Control: A Case Study of Vinyl Chloride.* Baltimore: Johns Hopkins University Press for Resources for the Future, 1978.

Dusik, Dennis. *Electricity Planning and the Environment: Toward A New Role for Government in the Decision Process.* Cambridge, Mass.: Ballinger, 1980.

Fritsch, Albert J. *Environmental Ethics—Choices for Concerned Citizens.* Garden City, N.Y.: Doubleday, 1980.

Gladwin, Thomas N. *Environment, Planning, and the Multinational Corporation.* Greenwich, Conn.: JAI Press, 1977.

Leonard, H. Jeffrey, et al., eds. *Business and Environment: Toward Common Ground.* Washington, D.C.: Conservation Foundation, 1977.

Mikdashi, Zuhayr. *The International Politics of Natural Resources.* Ithaca, N.Y.: Cornell University Press, 1976.

Monttbrail, Thierry de. *Energy: The Countdown.* New York: Pergamon, 1979.

Nikolai, Loren A., et al. *The Measurement of Corporate Environmental Activity.* New York: National Association of Accountants, 1976.

Parsons, Howard L., ed. *Marx and Engels on Ecology.* Westport, Conn.: Greenwood, 1977.

Singh, Narindar. *Economics and the Crisis of Ecology.* London: Oxford University Press, 1979.

Sobel, Lester A., ed. *Jobs, Money, and Pollution.* New York: Facts on File, 1977.

Stretton, Hugh. *Capitalism, Socialism, and the Environment.* New York: Cambridge University Press, 1976.

Stobaugh, Robert, and Daniel Yergin. *Energy Future: The Report of the Harvard Business School Energy Project.* New York: Random House, 1979.

Tribe, Laurence H. *When Values Conflict: Essays on Environmental Analysis, Discourse, and Decision.* Cambridge, Mass.: Ballinger, 1976.

Whiteside, Thomas. *The Pendulum and the Toxic Cloud.* New Haven: Yale University Press, 1979.

Articles

Alexander, Tom. "It's Time for New Approaches to Pollution Control." *Fortune* 94 (November 1976), 128–131+.

Allan, John D. "Social Responsibility of Business As It Relates to Pollution." *Cost and Management* (Canada) 50 (September–October 1976), 17–20.

Anderson, Robert C. "Public Policies toward the Use of Scrap Materials." *American Economic Review* 67 (February 1977), 355–358.

Austin, Richard Cartwright. "Three Axioms for Lands Use." *Christian Century* 99 (October 12, 1977), 910–911+.

Bardach, Eugene, and Lucian Pugliaresi. "The Environmental-Impact Statement vs. Real World." *Public Interest* 49 (Fall 1977), 22–38.

Bowman, James S. "Business and the Environment: Corporate Attitudes, Actions in Energy-Rich States." *MSU Business Topics* 25 (Winter 1977), 37–49.

Brumm, Harold J., Jr., and Daniel T. Dick. "Federal Environmental Policy and R&D on Water Pollution Abatement." *American Economic Review* 66 (May 1976), 448–453.

Cahn, Robert. "A Place for Environment in the Corporate Structure." *Management Review* 68 (April 1979), 15–20.

Carey, Phillip. "Crisis in the Environment: A Sociological Perspective." *American Journal of Economics and Sociology* 36 (July 1977), 263–273.

"Case for an Environmental Ethic: A Discussion with Robert Cahn." *Center Magazine* 13 (March 1980), 5–13.

Chamousis, Nicholas. "The National Environmental Policy Act of 1969: What 'Alternatives' Must an Agency Discuss?" *Columbia Journal of Law and Social Problems* 12 (Winter 1976), 221–252.

Drengson, Alan R. "The Relevance of the Humanities to Environmental Studies." *Journal of Thought* 13 (July 1978), 196–204.

Dunphy, J. H., and A. Hall. "Waste Disposal: It's a Dirty Business." *Chemical Week* 122 (March 1, 1978), 25+.

Edmunds, Stahrl W. "Environmental Cost Trade-offs." *Pittsburgh Business Review* 45 (Summer 1976), 8–10.

Edmunds, Stahrl W. "Environmental Impacts: Conflicts and Trade-offs." *California Management Review* 19 (Spring 1977), 5–11.

Faramelli, Norman. "Reflections on Ethics and Energy." *Corporate Information Center Brief* (March 1979), 3A–3D.

Feiveson, Harold A., et al. "The Plutonium Economy: Why We Should and Why We Can Wait." *Bulletin of the Atomic Scientists* 32 (December 1976), 10–14.

French, Guy P. "Is the Conserver Society at Odds with the Real Environment?" *Business Quarterly* 44 (Summer 1979), 35–38.

Gladstone, Ken. "Hooker Chemical's Nightmarish Pollution Record." *Business and Society Review* 30 (Summer 1979), 25–28.

Gladwin, Thomas N. "Environmental Policy Trends Facing Multinationals." *California Management Review* 20 (Winter 1977), 81–93.

Goldfarb, William. "The Hazards of Our Hazardous Waste Policy." *Natural Resources Journal* 19 (April 1979), 249–260.

Harnik, Peter. "The Junking of an Anti-Litter Lobby." *Business and Society Review* 21 (Spring 1976), 46–51.

Harris, Robert H., et al. "An Epidemic of Environmental Cancer." *Business and Society Review* 21 (Spring 1977), 56–59.

"Has Environmental Regulation Gone Too Far? A Debate on the Costs versus the Benefits." *Chemical and Engineering News* 57 (April 23, 1979), 24–53.

Herman, Stewart W. "Solar Energy and Social Values: Why Industry Drags Its Heels." *Christianity and Crisis* 38 (June 12, 1978), 142–146.

"How Business Treats Its Environment." *Business and Society Review* 33 (Spring 1980), 56–65.

"How the Kepone Case Threatens the Cities." *Business Week* (May 24, 1976), 38–39.

Kahalas, Harvey, and David L. Groves. "Ecology, Pollution, and Business: A Proposed Planning Solution." *Long Range Planning* 11 (December 1978), 62–66.

Kirschten, Dick. "Should Environmental Impact Statements Have an Impact Abroad?" *National Journal* 10 (September 16, 1978), 1471–1474.

Kneese, Allen V., and William D. Schulze. "Environmental Problems: Environment, Health, and Economics—The Case of Cancer." *American Economic Review* 67 (February 1977), 326–332.

Kreps, Juanita M. "Energy: Keeping Our Priorities Straight." *Commerce America* 2 (July 4, 1977), 8–9.

Kury, Channing. "Prolegomena to Conservation: A Fisheye Review." *Natural Resources Journal* 17 (July 1977), 493–509.

Lambert, Douglas M., and James R. Stock. "The Corporate Energy Policy: A Management Planning Perspective." *Long Range Planning* 12 (April 1979), 45–51.

Libbey, Mary Beth. "Conservation and the Corporation." *Across the Board* 15 (April 1978), 4+.

Lund, Leonard. "Industrial Pollution Control Costs." *Conference Board Record* 13 (April 1976), 58–60.

Mason, Edward S. "Natural Resources and Environmental Restrictions to Growth." *Challenge* 20 (January–February 1981), 14–20.

Maxey, Margaret N. "The Trouble with the Extreme Environmentalists." *Across the Board* 14 (December 1977), 43–47+.

Mercuro, Nicholas, Lewis Zerby, Baldwin Ranson, and Lawrence W. Libbey. "When Values Conflict: Essays on Environmental Analysis, Discourses, and Decision." *Journal of Economic Issues* 12 (March 1978), 187–199.

Mighdoll, M. J., and Peter D. Weisse. "We Need a National Materials Policy." *Harvard Business Review* 54 (September–October 1976), 143–151.

Moskow, Michael H. "Environmental Regulation and Public Values." *Conference Board Record* 13 (April 1976), 47–50.

Navin, Thomas. "Arizona Smelters and Air Pollution." *Arizona Review* 25 (January 1976), 1–6.

Nelkin, Dorothy. "Ecologists and the Public Interest." *Hastings Center Report* 6 (February 1976), 38–44.

"Oil and Beyond: The Ownership of America's Energy." *Corporate Information Center Brief* (January 1978), 3A–3D.

Orloff, Neil. "Payoff for Business Initiative on the Environment." *Harvard Business Review* 55 (November–December 1977), 8–12.

Owensby, Walter L., ed. "Economic Justice within Environmental Limits: The Need for a New Economic Ethic." *Christian Society* 67 (September–October 1976), 5–78.

Quarles, John R., Jr. "Pollution Control—Not By Law Alone." *Conference Board Record* 13 (April 1976), 51–53.

Reese, Alexander. "Does Industry Really Want to Conserve Energy?" *Business and Society Review* 25 (Spring 1978), 62–66.

Rienow, R. "Business Corporations and Environmental Protection." *National Forum* 58 (Summer 1978), 20–22.

Russell, James, and Warren J. Samuels. "Corporate and Public Responsibility in Environmental Policy: A Case Study." *MSU Business Topics* 27 (Autumn 1979), 23–32.

Santmire, H. Paul. "Ecology and Ethical Ecumenics." *Anglican Theological Review* 59 (January 1977), 98–102.

"Slow Steps to an Energy Policy." *Business Week* (January 12, 1976), 23–24.

Speth, G. "Polluters versus Protectors—the Continuing Regulatory Conflict." *Center Magazine* 11 (May 1978), 66–69.

Spiegelman, Arthur. "Environmental Hazards: The Perils of Progress." *Journal of Insurance* 40 (May–June 1979), 9–12.

"The States Get Super-Tough: EPA Standards Look Better to Industry as Many States Crack Down Harder." *Business Week* (March 8, 1976), 74–75.

Strong, D. H., and E. S. Rosenfield. "Ethics or Expediency: An Environmental Question." *Environmental Affairs* 5 (1976), 255–270.

Train, Russell E. "Environment, Energy, Economic Equity: Can the World Balance These Vital Elements?" *Environmental Affairs* 6 (1977), 1–10.

Underwood, Richard C. "Ancient River Is Saved." *Christian Century* 93 (November 10, 1976), 973–974.

Wallace, Myles. "Energy Policy, the Price System, and the Future of the Energy Economy: A Comment." *Nebraska Journal of Economics and Business* 17 (Spring 1978), 67–68.

Wearly, William L. "Environmental Overkill?" *Akron Business and Economic Review* 10 (Summer 1979), 7–12.

Weaver, Paul H. "Noise Regulation Strikes a Sour Note." *Fortune* 93 (March 1976), 158–162+.

White, Ron P. "The Anatomy of a Nonmarket Failure: An Examination of Environmental Policies." *American Economic Review* 66 (May 1976), 454–458.

Wiedenbaum, Murray, et al. "Has Environmentalism Been Worth It?" *Business and Society Review* 24 (Winter 1977–78), 13–27.

Wood, Norman J. "Environmental Law and Occupational Health." *Labor Law Journal* 27 (March 1976), 152–162.

Government, Regulations, and Business Relations

Books

Bacon, Lawrence S. *Bargaining for Job Safety and Health.* Cambridge, Mass.: MIT Press, 1980.

Blair, Roger D., and Stephen Rubin. *Regulating the Professions.* Lexington, Mass.: Lexington Books, 1980.

DeMott, Deborah A., ed. *Corporations at the Crossroads: Government and Reform.* New York: McGraw-Hill, 1980.

Fedor, Kenneth, and John T. Dunlop, eds. *The Lessons of Wage and Price Controls—The Food Sector.* Boston: Division of Research, Harvard Business School (distributed by Harvard University Press, Cambridge, Mass.), 1977.

Holtz, Herman. *Government Contracts: Proposalmanship and Winning Strategies.* New York: Plenum, 1980.

Hughes, Jonathan R. T. *The Governmental Habit: Economic Controls from Colonial Times to the Present.* New York: Basic Books, 1977.

Katzmann, Robert A. *Regulatory Bureaucracy: The Federal Trade Commission and Antitrust Policy.* Cambridge, Mass.: MIT Press, 1979.

McCloy, John J., Nathan W. Pearson, and Beverly Matthews. *The Great Oil Spill: The Inside Report, Gulf Oil's Bribery and Political Chicanery.* New York: Chelsea House Publishers, 1976.

McGrath, Phyllis S. *Redefining Corporate-Federal Relations.* New York: Conference Board, 1979.

Marcus, Alfred A. *Promise and Performance: Choosing and Implementing an Environmental Policy.* Westport, Conn.: Greenwood Press, 1980.

Mazzolini, R. *Government Controlled Enterprises: International Strategic and Policy Decisions.* New York: Wiley, 1979.

Mendeloff, John. *Regulating Safety: A Political and Economic Analysis of the Federal Occupational Safety and Health Program.* Cambridge, Mass.: MIT Press, 1979.

Nader, Ralph. *Government Regulation: What Kind of Reform?* Washington, D.C.: American Enterprise, 1976.

Nader, Ralph, Mark Green, and Joel Seligman. *Taming the Giant Corporation.* New York: W. W. Norton and Co., Inc., 1976.

Reekie, W. Duncan, and Michael H. Weber. *Profits, Politics, and Drugs.* New York: Holmes and Meier, 1979.

Stone, Alan. *Economic Regulation and the Public Interest: The Federal Trade*

Commission in Theory and Practice. Ithaca, N.Y.: Cornell University Press, 1977.

Szenberg, Michael, et al. *Welfare Effects of Trade Restrictions: A Case Study of the U.S. Footwear Industry.* New York: Academic Press, 1977.

Walsh, Annmarie Hauck. *The Public's Business: The Politics and Practices of Government Corporations.* Cambridge, Mass.: MIT Press, 1978.

Weidenbaum, Murray L. *Business, Government, and the Press.* Englewood Cliffs, N.J.: Prentice-Hall, 1977.

Weidenbaum, Murray L. *The Future of Business Regulation.* New York: AMACOM, 1979.

Wilson, James Q., ed. *The Politics of Regulation.* New York: Basic Books, 1980.

Articles

Allen, Fred T. "Corporations, Ethics, and Regulation." *Public Utilities Fortnightly* 99 (January 6, 1977), 40–41.

Barber, Bernard. "Regulation and the Professions." *The Hastings Center Report* 10 (February 1980), 34–36.

Bell, Daniel. "Too Late Reacting, and Too Much Regulation." *Business and Society Review* 18 (Summer 1976), 4–8.

Biegler, John C. "It's Not Too Late to De-Regulate!" *Price Waterhouse Review* 21, no. 3 (1976), 4–9.

Bleiberg, Robert M. "Out of Thin Air: Regulators Seek to Fashion Novel Anti-Trust Doctrine." *Barron's* 56 (August 9, 1976), 7.

Braughcum, Alan. "Price Fixing and Economics in State Damage Cases." *Antitrust Law and Economics Review* 9, no. 4 (1977), 55–59.

Brooks, John. "The Businessmen and the Government: Corruption Yesterday and Today." *American Heritage* 28 (June 1977), 66–73.

Burt, Robert A. "Limits of Law in Regulating Health Care Decisions." *Hastings Center Report* 7 (December 1977), 29–32.

Callen, Earl. "A Freedom of Information Act Fable: What's in a Name File?" *Civil Liberties Review* 2 (June–July 1976), 58–66.

Callen, Jeffrey, G. Frank Matthewson, and Herbert Mohring. "The Benefits and Costs of Rate of Return Regulation." *American Economic Review* 66 (June 1976), 290–297.

Cohen, Rebecca A. "The FTC Assault on the Cost of Dying." *Business and Society Review* 27 (Fall 1978), 48–53.

DeButts, John D. "Regulation and Enterprise." *University of Michigan Business Review* 29 (July 1977), 1–5.

DeButts, John D. "Top Management's Public Role Defined." *Tax Executive* 30 (January 1981), 97–106.

DeMuth, Christopher C. "Defending Consumers against Regulation." *American Spectator* 11 (January 1978), 24–26.

Dismukes, Key. "Recombinant DNA: A Proposal for Regulation." *Hastings Center Report* 7 (April 1977), 25–30.

Dolan, Ronald J. "How an Association Is Investigated and What Is the Government Looking For—A Federal Trade Commission Perspective." *The Antitrust Bulletin* 22 (Summer 1977), 273–286.

Doron, Gideon. "Administrative Regulation of an Industry: The Cigarette Case." *Public Administration Review* 39 (March–April 1979), 163–170.

Dougherty, Alfred F., Jr. "Elimination of the 'Conduct' Requirement in Government Monopolization Cases: A Proposed Revision of the Sherman Act." *Antitrust Law and Economics Review* 10, no. 3 (1978), 37–62.

Fedders, John M., and Lauryn H. Guttenplan. "Document Retention and Destruction: Practical, Legal, and Ethical Considerations." *Notre Dame Lawyer* 56 (October 1980), 5–64.

Ferguson, John R. "The Case for Antitrust Suits against Selected Oligopoly Industries (II)." *Antitrust Law and Economics Review* 8, no. 1 (1976), 35–46.

Flamm, Alec. "The Impact of Regulation on Business Development: The Heyday of U.S Technology Is Past." *Vital Speeches of the Day* 44 (April 15, 1978), 386–389.

Guerrieri, Ursula A. "Economic Issues Raised by the Federal Corporate Chartering Proposal." *Business Economics* 13 (May 1978), 68–76.

Henteleff, Thomas O. "Individual Rights versus Pro Bono Publico (For the Public Good)." *Business Lawyer* 33 (July 1978), 2255–2261.

Herold, Arthur L. "The Cost-Benefit Approach: Tempering Government Regulation with Economic Realism." *Association Management* 31 (June 1979), 85–86.

Hewitt, Charles M. "The Collision between Professional Ethics and Antitrust." *Business Horizons* 22 (February 1979), 73–74.

Jaeniche, Douglas Walter. "Herbert Croly, Progressive Ideology, and the FTC Act." *Political Science Quarterly* 93 (Fall 1978), 471–493.

Kasper, Daniel M. "Competition and Regulation: Public Policy Considerations for Controlling Corporations." *Academy of Management, Proceedings of the 36th Annual Meeting* (August 11–14, 1976), 291–295.

Kelman, Steven. "Regulation for a Decent Society." *American Federationist* 86 (February 1979), 4–8.

Kendall, Donald M. "How to Halt Excessive Government Regulation." *Nation's Business* 64 (March 1976), 20–24.

Kleinschrod, Walter A. "Another Thing Government Might Try Is Zero-Base Regulation." *Administrative Management* 37 (December 1976), 19.

Kreps, Juanita M. "Thoughts about Government and Business: Changing Public Habits and Attitudes." *Vital Speeches of the Day* 43 (August 1, 1977), 610–612.

Kuhlman, John M. "Price Fixing, Nonprice Competition, and Focal Point Pricing: A Rose by Any Other Name?" *Antitrust Law and Economics Review* 10, no. 1 (1978), 75–86.

"Legal Affairs: Sticking Uncle Same for On-the-Job Injuries." *Business Week* (November 6, 1978), 182.

Leone, Robert A. "The Real Costs of Regulation." *Harvard Business Review* 55 (November–December 1977), 57–66.

Liebmann, George W. "The Proposed Federal Criminal Code: What Does It Mean for Business?" *Corporation Law Review* 2 (Winter 1979), 3–42.

Lilley, William, III, and James C. Miller III. "The New 'Social Regulation.' " *Public Interest* 47 (Spring 1977), 49–61.

Luthans, Fred, and Richard Hodgetts. "Government and Business: Partners in Social Action." *Labor Law Journal* 30 (December 1979), 763–770.

MacIntyre, Alasdair. "Regulation: A Substitute for Morality." *The Hastings Center Report* 10 (February 1980), 31–33.

McLaren, Richard, and Bruce Welling. "What Should Happen to Business Information Filed with Government?" *Business Quarterly* 43 (Spring 1978), 11+.

" 'Market Forces Are Best Path to Regulatory Reform': Kreps." *Commerce America* 2 (October 24, 1977), 9–16.

Martha, John P., and Sam M. Gibbons. "Should the United States Curb Imports? Opposing Views on a Question of Increasing Importance." *American Legion Magazine* 105 (July 1978), 26–27.

Melvin, Donald J. "The Commercial Banking Environment: The 1960's through the 1980's." *Journal of Commercial Bank Lending* 61 (June 1979), 46–69.

Morgan, Lee L. "Opportunities for Mutual Action: Government and Business Leaders in 1977." *California Management Review* 19 (Summer 1977), 91–93.

Moskow, Michael H. "Regulating Industry May Be Good, but It Isn't Free." *Commercial and Financial Chronicle* 22 (January 5, 1976), 16+.

Mueller, Charles E. "Trustbusting, Inflation, and the 'Ugly Face of Power': The Bottom Line." *Antitrust and Economics Review* 10, no. 3 (1978), 63–70+.

O'Toole, James. "What's Ahead for the Business-Government Relationship." *Harvard Business Review* 57 (March–April 1979), 94–105.

Peles, Yoram C., and Jerome L. Stein. "The Effect of Rate of Return Regulation Is Highly Sensitive to the Nature of the Uncertainty." *American Economic Review* 66 (June 1976), 278–289.

Peltzman, Sam. "Toward a More General Theory of Regulation." *Journal of Law and Economics* 19 (August 1976), 211–240.

Pertschuk, Michael. "An Inflation Paradox: Business Regulation of Business." *Antitrust Law and Economics Review* 10, no. 2 (1976), 53–59.

Pertschuk, Michael. "Needs and Licenses." *Regulation* 3 (March/April 1979), 14–16.

Pertschuk, Michael. "Regulatory Reform through the Looking Glass." *American Bar Association Journal* 65 (April 1979), 557–560.

Portis, Bernard, and Michael R. Pearce. "Managers Gravely Concerned over Increasing Government Regulation of Business." *Business Quarterly* 42 (Autumn 1977), 9–14.

Pustay, Michael W. "The Social Costs of Monopoly and Regulation: An Empirical Evaluation." *Southern Economics Journal* 45 (October 1978), 583–591.

Reagan, Ronald. "Get Government Out of Business." *Management World* 6 (October 1977), 1+.

Robie, Edward A. "Can Collaboration Outperform Litigation?" *Conference Board Record* 13 (September 1976), 22–24.

Robinson, Glen O. "The Federal Communications Commission: An Essay on Regulatory Watchdogs?" *Virginia Law Review* 64 (March 1978), 169–262.

Rose, Sanford. "Bank Regulation: The Reforms We Really Need." *Fortune* 96 (December 1977), 122–124.

Roth, Allan. "The Foreign Corrupt Practices Act of 1977: Background and Summary." *Corporation Law Review* 1 (Fall 1978), 347–356.

"Senators Carry Ten Foot Poles on Rewrite of FCC Legislation." *Broadcasting* 91 (November 29, 1976), 26.

Sierck, Alexander W., and Keith S. Watson. "Post-Watergate Business Conduct: What Role for the SEC?" *Business Lawyer* 31 (January 1976), 721–726.

Stratton, Debra J. "The FTC: Calling the Shots on Industry and the Professions: The ABC's of the Federal Trade Commission." *Association Management* 31 (January 1979), 28–33.

Trombetta, William L. "Patterns for Antitrust Confrontation?" *Atlanta Economic Review* 28 (November–December 1978), 12–18.

Van Dam, Andre. "The Challenge of Business/Government Cooperation." *Administrative Management* 38 (August 1977), 41–42+.

Weaver, Paul H. "Regulation, Social Policy, and Class Conflict." *Public Interest* (Winter 1978), 45–63.

Weidenbaum, Murray L. "A Way to Regulate the Regulatory Binge." *Business and Society Review* 20 (Winter 1976–77), 4–5.

Weimer, George A., and Ira G. Black. "Life in the Regulatory Jungle and How It Is Strangling Business." *Iron Age* 220 (November 21, 1977), 93–94+.

"Why an Ethics Law Makes the SEC Fidgety." *Business Week* (January 8, 1979), 17–18.

Williams, Roger M., Robert Crandall, et al. "Overregulation? Industry's Struggle with Government." *Saturday Review* 6 (January 20, 1979), 24+.

Wilson, Robert A. "Barriers to Trustbusting: 'Efficiency' Myths and Timid Trustbusters." *Antitrust Law and Economics Review* 9, no. 3 (1977), 19–39.

Wilson, Robert A. "The Verdict on Antitrust: Hiding the Corporate Rip-off from the Nice Folks Back in Peoria." *Antitrust Law and Economics Review* 8, no. 1 (1976), 11–28.

Ylvisaker, William T. "Regulation and the Public Interest: The Need to Act." *Vital Speeches of the Day* 44 (July 15, 1978), 604–607.

Investment Policy and Shareholder Responsibility

Books

Council on Economic Priorities. *Pension Funds and Ethical Investment: A Study of Investment Practices and Opportunities, State of California Retirement Systems.* New York: Council on Economic Priorities, 1980.

Haendel, Dan. *Foreign Investment: The Management of Political Risk.* Boulder, Colo.: Westview, 1978.

Kobrin, Stephen J. *Foreign Direct Investment, Industrialization, and Social Change.* Greenwich, Conn.: JAI Press, 1977.

Rogers, Barbara. *White Wealth and Black Poverty: American Investments in Southern Africa.* Westport, Conn.: Greenwood Press, 1976.

Schmidt, Elizabeth. *Decoding Corporate Camouflage: U.S. Business Support for Apartheid.* Washington, D.C.: Institute for Policy Studies, 1980.

Sloan, Michael P. *Investment Codes of Conduct: A Compendium.* New York: Carnegie Center for Transnational Studies, 1978.

Vogel, David. *Lobbying the Corporation: Citizen Challenges to Business Authority.* New York: Basic Books, 1978.

Webb, Lee, and William Schweke. *Public Employee Pension Funds: New Strategies for Investment.* Washington, D.C.: Conference Publications, 1979.

Articles

Baker, James C., and John K. Ryans, Jr. "Multinational Corporation Investment in Less Developed Countries: Reducing Risk." *Nebraska Journal of Economics and Business* 18 (Winter 1979), 61–69.

Buzby, Stephen L., and Haim Falk. "Demand for Social Responsibility Information by University Investors." *Accounting Review* 54 (January 1979), 23–37.

Chong, Leighton. "The Soft Energy Path: Opportunities for Ethical Investors." *Interfaith Center on Corporate Responsibility* (September 1980), 3A–3D.

Curzan, Myron P., and Mark L. Pelesh. "Revitalizing Corporate Democracy: Control of Investment Managers' Voting on Social Responsibility Proxy Issues." *Harvard Law Review* 93 (February 1980), 670–700.

Foster, Geoffrey. "The South African Connection." *Management Today* (April 1978), 86–88+.

Goldin, Harrison J. "Ethics and the Prudent Investor." *FCR Review* 1 (Spring 1980), 16–17.

Gustavsen, B. "Social Context of Investment Decisions." *Acta Sociologica* 19 (1976), 273–284.

Heard, Jamie. "Investor Responsibility: An Idea Whose Time Has Come?" *Journal of Portfolio Management* 4 (Spring 1978), 12–14.

Houser, George. "U.S. Policy in Southern Africa: Preaching Freedom, Investing in Oppression." *Christianity in Crisis* 37 (September 19, 1977), 197–201.

"How Pension Officers View Social Responsibility." *Institutional Investor* 13 (April 1979), 85–89.

Landau, Peter. "Do Institutional Investors Have a Social Responsibility?" *The Institutional Investor* 11 (March 1977), 124–126+.

Lange, Harry M. "Foreign Investments in Southern Africa: The Beginning of a Dialogue." *Economic Report* 29 (October 1977), 383–393.

Munsch, Virginia. "South African Equities Protested." *Pensions and Investments* 6 (August 28, 1978), 14+.

"Pension Fund Investments: Untapped Potential for Corporate Responsibility and Economic Development." *Interfaith Center on Corporate Responsibility* (June 1979), 3A–3D.

"Proxy Survey Reveals Corporate Activism." *Pensions and Investments* 7 (September 11, 1979), 31.

Purcell, Theordore V. "Management and the 'Ethical Investors.'" *Harvard Business Review* 57 (September–October 1979), 24–26+.

Roberts, Keith. "The Seven Veils of Ethical Investing." *Business and Society Review* 19 (Fall 1976), 70–72.

Roberts, Keith. "Shareholder Votes—Has Business Won Harvard's Heart?" *Business and Society Review* 20 (Winter 1976–77), 65–67.

Seligman, Daniel. "A Moral Victory for Yale." *Fortune* 99 (June 4, 1979), 66.

Sheinkman, Jacob. "The Union Role in the Boardroom." *Employee Relations Law Journal* 5 (Summer 1979), 14–20.

Smith, Timothy, and Valerie Heinonen. "The Church as Investor—A Voice in the Marketplace." *New Catholic World* 223 (November–December 1980), 267+.

Soderquist, L. D. "Reconciling Shareholders' Rights and Corporate Responsibility—Close and Small Public Corporations." *Vanderbilt Law Review* 33, no. 6 (1980), 1387–1420.

Stern, Les. "Social Investing: A Volatile Issue Surfaces." *Pensions and Investments* 6 (October 23, 1978), 1+.

Wallace, Anise. "In Whose Best Interest?" *Pensions and Investments* 6 (June 19, 1978), 27–28.

Weiss, Elliott J. "How to Make 'Ethical' Investments." *New York Times* (Sunday, July 30, 1978), 14.

Minorities and Justice

Books

Blackstone, William T., and Robert D. Heslep, eds. *Social Justice and Preferential Treatment: Women and Racial Minorities in Education and Business.* Athens: University of Georgia Press, 1977.

Cohen, Marshall, Thomas Nagel, and Thomas Scanlon, eds. *Equality and Preferential Treatment.* Princeton, N.J.: Princeton University Press, 1977.

Council on Economic Priorities, and Tina L. Simcich. *Women and Minorities in Banking: Shortchanged.* New York: Praeger, 1977.

Glazer, Nathan. *Affirmative Discrimination: Ethnic Inequality and Public Policy.* New York: Basic Books, 1976.

Glover, Robert W. *Minority Enterprise in Construction.* New York: Praeger Publishers, 1977.

Goldman, Alan H. *Justice and Reverse Discrimination.* Princeton, N.J.: Princeton University Press, 1979.

Gould, William B. *Black Workers in White Unions: Job Discrimination in the United States.* Ithaca, N.Y.: Cornell University Press, 1977.

Gross, B. R., ed. *Reverse Discrimination.* Buffalo, N.Y.: Prometheus Books, 1977.

Hayes, Harold P. *Realism in E.E.O.* New York: John Wiley and Sons, 1980.

Hill, Herbert. *Black Labor and the American Legal System: Race, Work, and the Law.* vol. 1. Washington, D.C.: Bureau of National Affairs, 1977.

Hoffman, Joan. *Racial Discrimination and Economic Development.* Lexington, Mass.: Lexington Books, 1975.

McNamara, Donna. *Preparing for Affirmative Action: A Manual for Practical Training.* Garrett Park, Md.: Garrett Park Press, 1978.

Marshall, Ray, et al. *Employment Discrimination: The Impact of Legal and Administrative Remedies.* New York: Praeger, 1978.

Northrup, Herbert R., and John A. Larson. *Impact of the AT&T-EEO Consent Decree.* Philadelphia: The Industrial Research Unit, the Wharton School, 1979.

Palley, Marian Lief, and Michael B. Preston, ed. *Race, Sex, and Policy Problems.* Lexington, Mass.: Lexington Books, 1979.

Peres, Richard. *Dealing with Employment Discrimination.* New York: McGraw-Hill, 1977.

Schlei, Barbara L., and Paul Grossman. *Employment Discrimination Law.* Washington, D.C.: Bureau of National Affairs, 1976.

Sherman, Herbert L., et al. *Discrimination in Employment Labor Relations and Social Problems.* Unit III. Washington, D.C.: Bureau of National Affairs, 1979.

Squires, Gregory D., ed. *Inequality and Public Policy: Ethics of Affirmative Action.* East Lansing: Michigan State University, Institute for Community Development and Services, 1977.

Sobel, Lester A., ed. *Quotas and Affirmative Action.* New York: Facts on File, 1979.

Articles

Anthony, William P., and Marshall Bowen. "Affirmative Action: Problems and Promises." *Personnel Journal* 56 (December 1977), 616–621.

Baron, A. S., and E. T. Reeves. "How Effective Has Affirmative Action Legislation Been?" *Personnel Administrator* 22 (January 1977), 47–49.

Becnel, Barbara. "Profiling the Black Worker, 1976." *American Federationist* 83 (July 1976), 11–17.

Bernard, Keith E. "The Business Cycle and the Occupational Distribution of Black Workers." *Growth and Change: A Journal of Regional Development* 7 (April 1976), 14–18.

Bleiberg, Robert M. "The Public Be Damned? Rights of Minority Shareholders Can't Be Ignored?" *Barron's* 56 (January 5, 1976), 7.

Bonepath, Ellen. "Black Businessmen and Community Responsibility." *Phylon* 37 (March 1976), 26–43.

Brereton, Thomas F. "The Problems of Race and Sex in Public Agency Staffs." *Public Administration Review* 37 (September/October 1977), 604–607.

Browne, Robert S. "Color the Board White, Then Add a Little Black." *Business and Society Review* 23 (Fall 1977), 22–24.

Browning, Edgar K. "Inequality, Income, and Opportunity: How Much More Equality Can We Afford?" *Public Interest* 43 (Spring 1976), 90–110.

"Business, Too, Tests Reverse Discrimination." *Business Week* (November 14, 1977), 40.

Capon, Noel. "Discrimination in Screening Credit Applicants." *Harvard Business Review* 56 (May–June 1978), 8–12+.

Chiplin, Brian. "Nonconvexity of Indifference Surfaces in the Case of Labor Market Discrimination: Note." *American Economic Review* 66 (December 1976), 921–924.

Churchill, Neil C., and John K. Shank. "Affirmative Action and Guilt-Edged Goals." *Harvard Business Review* 54 (March–April 1976), 111–116.

Conrad, T. R. "Debate about Quota Systems: An Analysis." *American Journal of Political Science* 20 (February 1976), 135–149.

Countryman, V. "Private Discrimination." *Center Magazine* 12 (July 19, 1979), 50–62.

Cruz, Nestor. " 'Realpolitik' and Affirmative Action." *Public Personnel Management* 9 (1980), 192–195.

D'Aprix, Roger M. "Blacks, Women, and the Conscience of a Company Man." *Business and Society Review* 18 (Summer 1976), 55–57.

Dipboye, Robert L., Richard D. Arvey, and David E. Terpstra. "Equal Employment and the Interview." *Personnel Journal* 55 (October 1976), 520–522+.

"Discrimination Cases Still on the Rise." *Banking* 68 (September 1976), 14.

"Do's and Don'ts of Equal Employment Legislation." *Commerce America* 1 (February 16, 1976), 7–9.

Dozier, Richard K. "Architects: Blacks Moving Ahead in a Profession Struggling Out of Three-Year Slump." *Black Enterprise* 7 (September 1976), 16–22+.

Dyer, Frederick C., and Chris W. Ford. "Training the Handicapped: Now It's Their Turn for Affirmative Action." *Personnel Journal* 55 (April 1976), 181–183.

"EEO Seminar: Update on Racism and Sexism." *Interfaith Center on Corporate Responsibility Brief* (December 1979), 3A–3D.

Etzioni, Amitai. "Making Up for Past Injustices: How Bakke Could Backfire." *Psychology Today* 11 (August 1977), 18.

Flores, Albert W., "Reverse Discrimination: Towards a Just Society." *Business and Professional Ethics* 1 (January 1978), 4.

Fulmer, William E. "Supervisory Selection: The Acid Test of Affirmative Action." *Personnel* 53 (November–December 1976), 40–46.

Gatewood, Robert D., and Lyle F. Schoenfeldt. "Content Validity and EEOC: A Useful Alternative for Selection." *Personnel Journal* 56 (October 1977), 520–522+.

Geary, Anne J. "Equal Credit Opportunity–An Analysis of Regulation B." *Business Lawyer* 31 (April 1976), 1641–1658.

Gery, Gloria J. "Equal Opportunity—Planning and Managing the Process of Change." *Personnel Journal* 56 (April 1977), 184–191+.

Goodman, Carl F. "Equal Employment Opportunity: Preferential Quotas and Unrepresented Third Parties." *Public Personnel Management* 6 (November–December 1977), 371–397.

Gregory, Karl D. "Some Alternatives for Reducing the Black-White Unemployment Rate Differential." *American Economic Review* 66 (May 1976), 324–327.

Hall, Francine S., and Douglas T. Hall. "Effects of Job Incumbents' Race and Sex on Evaluations of Managerial Performance." *Academy of Management Journal* 19 (September 1976), 476–481.

Halperin, Daniel. "Should Pension Benefits Depend upon the Sex of the Recipient?" *AAUP Bulletin* 62 (Spring 1976), 43–48.

Hewlett, Sylvia Ann. "Inflation and Inequality." *Challenge* 20 (July–August 1977), 50–51.

Higgins, James M. "Manager's Guide to the Equal Employment Opportunity Laws." *Personnel Journal* 55 (August 1976), 406–411+.

Holsendolph, E. "Blacks Can't Bank on Conventional Loans." *Black Enterprise* 9 (January 1979), 19+.

Husak, Douglas N., "Bakke and Compensatory Justice." *Business and Professional Ethics.* 1 (January 1978), 3.

Irons, Edward D. "Black Entrepreneurship: Its Rationale, Its Problems, Its Prospects." *Phylon* 37 (March 1976), 12–25.

Jacobs, Bruce A. "Homosexuals in Management." *Industry Week* 202–203 (July 23, 1979), 52–59.

Jain, Harish C., and Barrie O. Pettman. "The American Anti-Discrimination Legislation and Its Impact on the Utilization of

Blacks and Women." *International Journal of Social Economics* 3 (1976), 109–134.

Johnson, Deborah G., "Discrimination and Preferential Treatment." *Business and Professional Ethics* 1 (January 1978), 1–2.

Jones, H. "Fairness, Meritocracy, and Reverse Discrimination." *Social Theory and Practice* 4 (Spring 1977), 211–226.

Kelly, Richard S., and Mary M. Thorkelson. "Equal Employment Opportunity: Affirmative Action Programs for Federal Government Contractors." *Business Lawyer* 31 (April 1976), 1509–1515.

Lazer, Robert I. "The 'Discrimination' Danger in Performance Appraisal." *Conference Board Record* 13 (March 1976), 60–64.

Lim, Kim. "Asian American Employment: From Outright Exclusion to Modern Discrimination." *Civil Rights Digest* 9 (Fall 1976), 12–21.

Lodge, George Cabot. "Equality of *Result*, Not Equality of Opportunity." *Across the Board* 15 (March 1978), 56–58.

Loeb, M. "New Bridges between Blacks and Business." *Time* 113 (January 22, 1979), 62.

London, Paul. "How Equal Can We Be? An Interview with Irving Kristol." *Business and Society Review* 22 (Summer 1977), 12–19.

Lukaczer, Moses. "Assessing Progress: Employment among Americans of Spanish Origin." *Civil Rights Digest* 8 (Summer 1976), 30–37.

McAlmon, A. A. "Critical Look at Affirmative Action." *Center Magazine* 11 (March 1978), 43–55.

Moore, Joy, and Frank Laverty. "Affirmative Action: A Sadly Passive Event." (Canada) *Business Quarterly* 41 (Autumn 1976), 22–26.

Norton, Eleanor H. "Comment on the Bakke Decision." *Personnel Administrator* 23 (August 1978), 26–28.

Novick, M. R., and D. D. Ellis, Jr. "Equal Opportunity in Educational and Employment Selection." *American Psychologist* 32 (May 1977), 306–320.

Ogden, Warren C., Jr. "Justice and the Problem of the Volitional Victim." *Labor Law Journal* 28 (July 1977), 417–420.

Okun, Arthur M. "Equal Rights but Unequal Incomes." *New York Times Magazine* (July 4, 1978), 101–103+.

Pati, Gopal C., and Charles W. Reilly. "Reversing Discrimination: A

Perspective." *Labor Law Journal* 29 (January 1978), 9–25. *Human Resource Management* 16 (Winter 1977), 25–35.

Pati, Gopal C. "Reverse Discrimination: What Can Managers Do?" *Personnel Journal* 56 (July 1977), 334–338+.

Patterson, Pat. "Black Unemployment: It's Even Worse Than the Official Statistics Let On." *Black Enterprise* 7 (November 1976), 53+.

Richbell, S. "De Facto Discrimination and How to Kick the Habit. *Personnel Management* 8 (November 1976), 30–33.

Robertson, David E. "Update on Testing and Equal Opportunity." *Personnel Journal* 56 (March 1977), 144–147.

Saatkamp, Herman J., Jr. "Equal Employment Opportunity: Individual and Collective Merit." *Business and Professional Ethics* 1 (January 1978), 5.

Sargent, Alice G. "Affirmative Action: Total Systems Change." *Michigan Business Review* 30 (September 1978), 18–25.

Schiller, Bradley R. "Equality, Opportunity, and the 'Good Job.'" *Public Interest* 43 (Spring 1976), 111–120.

Sherman, Mitchell. "Equal Employment Opportunity: Legal Issues and Societal Consequences." *Public Personnel Management* 7 (March–April 1978), 127–134.

Sibal, Abner. "The EEOC's Dilemma." *Business and Society Review* 20 (Winter 1976–77), 76.

"Smart Firms Find Solution to Lackluster Workforce: America's Handicapped Adults." *Commerce America* 1 (September 27, 1976), 15.

Sowell, Thomas. "'Affirmative Action' Reconsidered." *Public Interest* 42 (Winter 1976), 47–65.

Stencel, Sandra. "Reverse Discrimination." *Editorial Research Reports* (August 6, 1976), 561–580.

Surett, Corey. "Fair Labor Standards, Age Discrimination, and Equal Pay." *Compensation Review* 9 (Fourth Quarter 1977), 55–61.

Swanson, Stephen C. "Quotas for Equal Opportunity in Employment." *Personnel Administrator* 23 (April 1978), 51–54.

Swinton, David H. "A Labor Force Competition Theory of Discrimination in the Labor Market." *American Economic Review* 67 (February 1977), 400–404.

Thurow, Lester C. "The Economic Progress of Minority Groups." *Challenge* 19 (March–April 1976), 20–29.

Tombari, Henry A. "Lending a Hand to the Handicapped: A Primer for Business." *SAM Advanced Management Journal* 44 (Autumn 1979), 44–51.

Van Den Haag, Ernest. "Reverse Discrimination: A Brief against It." *National Review* 29 (April 29, 1977), 492–495.

Wade, F. C. "Preferential Treatment for Blacks." *Social Theory and Practice* 4 (Spring 1978), 445–470.

Ward, Renee. "Black Films, White Profits." *Black Scholar* 7 (May 1976), 13–24.

Watson, John G., and Sam Barone. "The Self Concept, Personal Values, and Motivational Orientations of Black and White Managers." *Academy of Management Journal* 19 (March 1976), 36–48.

Wichter, Mark S. "Employment Discrimination: The Class Action from the Defendant Employer's Perspective." *Public Utilities Fortnightly* 98 (October 7, 1976), 61–62.

Willard, L. Duane. "Aesthetic Discrimination." *Business and Professional Ethics* 1 (January 1978), 6–7.

Wolkinson, Benjamin O. "Arbitration of Racial Discrimination Grievances." *Review of Black Political Economy* 8 (Fall 1977), 70–86.

Worcester, Dean A., Jr. "Discrimination in Labor Markets: Cause, Consequences, and Culpability." *Policy Studies Journal* 5 (Spring 1977), 320–325.

Multinational Corporations and Social Issues

Books

Antonides, Harry. *Multinationals and the Peaceable Kingdom.* Toronto: Clarke, Irwin, and Co., 1978.

Apter, David E., and Louis W. Goodman, eds. *Multinational Corporations and Social Change.* New York: Praeger, 1976.

Banks, Robert F., and Jack Stieber. *Multinations, Unions, and Labor Relations in Industrialized Countries.* Ithaca: New York State School of Industrial and Labor Relations, 1977.

Berkman, Harold W., and Ivan Vernon. *Contemporary Perspectives in International Business.* New York: Random House, 1979.

Brookstone, Jeffrey M. *The Multinational Businessman and Foreign Policy.* New York: Praeger Publishers, 1976.

Centre on Transnational Corporations, United Nations. *Survey of Research on Transnational Corporations.* New York: United Nations, 1978.

Craig, John G. *Multinational Co-operatives: An Alternative for World Development.* Plainview, Tex.: Prairie Books, 1976.

Crowe, Kenneth C. *America for Sale.* Garden City, N.Y.: Doubleday, 1978.

Feld, Werner J. *Multinational Enterprises and U.N. Politics.* New York: Pergamon, 1980.

Frundt, Henry J. *An Agribusiness Manual.* New York: Interfaith Center on Corporate Responsibility, 1978.

George, Susan. *How the Other Half Dies: The Real Reasons for World Hunger.* Montclair, N.J.: Allanheld, Osmun, and Co., 1977.

Gilpin, Robert. *U.S. Power and the Multinational Corporation: The Political Economy of Foreign Direct Investment.* New York: Basic Books, 1975.

Goldschmidt, Walter Rochs. *As You Sow: Three Studies in the Social Consequences of Agribusiness.* Montclair, N.J.: Allanheld, Osmun, and Co., 1978.

Goulet, Dennis. *The Uncertain Promise: Value Conflict in Technology Transfer.* New York: IDOC/North America, 1977.

Greene, James. *Assuring Ethical Conduct Abroad.* New York: Conference Board, 1976.

Hellman, Rainer. *Transnational Control of Multinational Corporations.* Trans. Marianne Grund Freidberg. New York: Praeger, 1977.

Hymer, Stephen Herbert. *The Multinational Corporation: A Radical Approach.* Cambridge, Eng.: Cambridge University Press, 1979.

International Principles and Guidelines on Social Policy for Multinational Enterprises: Their Usefulness and Feasibility. Geneva: International Labour Office, 1976.

Lappe, Frances Moore, and Joseph Collins, with Cary Flower. *Food First: Beyond the Myth of Scarcity.* Boston: Houghton Mifflin, 1977.

Ledogar, Robert J. *Hungry for Profits: U.S. Food and Drug Multinationals in Latin America.* New York: IDOC/North America, 1976.

McCurry, Dan C., and Richard Rubenstein, eds. *American Farmers and the Rise of Agribusiness: Seeds of Struggle.* New York: Arno Press, 1975.

Madsen, Axel. *Private Power: Multinational Corporations for the Survival of Our Planet.* New York: William Morrow and Company, 1980.

Morgan, Dan. *The Merchants of Grain.* New York: Viking, 1979.

Myers, Desaiz, III. *U.S. Business in South Africa: The Economic, Political and Moral Issues.* Bloomington: Indiana University Press, 1980.

Myers, Desaiz, III. *Labor Practices of U.S. Corporations in South Africa.* New York: Praeger Publishers, 1977.

Ritson, Christopher. *Agricultural Economics: Principles and Policy.* New York: St. Martin's Press, 1977.

Solomon, Lewis D. *Multinational Corporations and the Emerging World Order.* Port Washington, N.Y.: Kennikat Press, 1978.

Turner, Louis. *Oil Companies in the International System.* London: George Allen & Unwin for the Royal Institute of International Affairs, 1978.

Vernon, Raymond. *Storm over the Multinationals: The Real Issue.* Cambridge, Mass.: Harvard University Press, 1977.

Vogeler, Ingolf. *The Myth of the Farm Family: Agribusiness Dominance of U.S Agriculture.* Boulder, Colo.: Westview, 1981.

Wallace, Don, Jr. *International Regulation of Multinational Corporations.* New York: Praeger, 1976.

Wilcox, Walter William. *Social Responsibility in Farm Leadership: An Analysis of Farm Problems and Farm Leadership in Action.* Westport, Conn.: Greenwood Press, 1975.

Wortman, Sterling, and Ralph W. Cummings, Jr. *To Feed This World: The Challenge and the Strategy.* Baltimore: Johns Hopkins University Press, 1978.

Articles

Allvine, Fred C. "Thoughts on Breaking Up the Petroleum Industry: Should the Eighteen Largest Integrated Petroleum Companies Be Broken Up?" *Business Horizons* 19 (August 1976), 41–51.

Anderson, Earl V. "Code of Conduct Set for Multinational Firms." *Chemical and Engineering News* 54 (June 28, 1976), 8–9.

"Arab Blacklist: Expedient Morality." *The Economist* 261 (October 16, 1976), 56+.

Asante, Samuel K. B. "Restructuring International Mineral Agreements." *American Journal of International Law* 73 (July 1979), 335–371.

Barnet, Richard J. "Multinationals: A Dissenting View." *Saturday Review* 3 (February 2, 1976), 11+.

Barrett, M. Edgar. "Case of the Tangled Transfer Price." *Harvard Business Review* 55 (May–June 1977), 20–36+.

Blair, John M. "Seven Sisters in a Castle Built on Collusion." *Business and Society Review* 21 (Spring 1977), 36–42.

Blank, Stephen. "The International Social Responsibility of Business." *Institute of Socioeconomic Studies Journal* 4 (Winter 1979), 29–36.

Blond, David. "The Future Contribution of Multinational Corporations to World Growth—A Positive Appraisal." *Business Economics* 13 (May 1978), 80–95.

Bonaparte, T. H. "Multinational Corporations and Culture in Liberia." *American Journal of Economics and Sociology* 38 (July 1979), 237–251.

Breckenfeld, Gurney, Rawleigh W. Warner, Jr., Richard C. Longworth, and Donald Kirk. "Multinationals at Bay." *Saturday Review* 36 (January 24, 1976), 12–14+.

Castleman, Barry. "How We Export Dangerous Industries." *Business and Society Review* 27 (Fall 1978), 7–14.

Chu, J. T. "Some Thoughts on Multinational Corporations' Ethical Problems." *Business and Professional Ethics* 2 (Spring/Summer 1979), 7–8.

Ciocca, Henry G. "The Infant Formula Controversy: A Nestle View." *Journal of Contemporary Business* 7, no. 4 (1978), 37–56.

Coates, J. "Towards a Code of Conduct for Multinationals." *Personnel Management* 10 (April 1978), 41–43.

"Controlling the Multinationals." *America* 139 (November 25, 1978), 374.

Davidow, Joel. "Some Reflections on the OECD Competition Guidelines." *The Antitrust Bulletin* 22 (Summer 1977), 441–458.

"Doing Business with a Blacker Africa." *Business Week* (February 14, 1977), 64–80.

Elbinger, Lee. "Are Sullivan's Principles Folly in South Africa?" *Business and Society Review* 30 (Summer 1979), 35–40.

"Forum to Evaluate U.S. Firms' Behavior Abroad." *Commerce America* 1 (June 21, 1976), 11.

Galbraith, John Kenneth. "The Defense of the Multinational Company." *Harvard Business Review* 56 (March–April 1978), 83–93.

Gerlach, Luther P. "The Flea and the Elephant: Infant Formula Controversy." *Society* 17 (September–October 1980), 51–61.

Gladwin, Thomas N., and Ingo Walter. "Multinational Enterprise, Social Responsiveness, and Pollution Control." *Journal of International Business Studies* 7 (Fall/Winter 1976), 57–74.

Gladwin, Thomas N., and Ingo Walter. "The Shadowy Underside of International Trade." *Saturday Review* 4 (July 9, 1977), 16+.

Glascock, James Scott. "Legislating Business Morality: A Look at Efforts by Two International Organizations to Deal with Questionable Behavior by Transnational Corporations." *Vanderbilt Journal of Transnational Law* 10 (Summer 1977), 459–473.

Greene, Preston L., Jr. "The Arab Economic Boycott of Israel: The International Law Perspective." *Vanderbilt Journal of Transnational Law* 11 (Winter 1978), 77–94.

Halpern, Gerard, and Warren E. Banks. "Ethics, Leverage, and Multinational Behavior." *Business Law Review* 9 (Spring 1976), 3–10.

Harvey, Michael G., and Roger A. Kerin. "Multinational Corporations versus Organized Labor: Divergent Views on Domestic Unemployment." *California Management Review* 18 (Spring 1976), 5–13.

Harvey, Pharis J. "Multinationals in Asia: Who's Corrupting Whom?" *Christianity and Crisis* 36 (March 15, 1976), 44–49.

Heckert, Richard E. "Business Ethics in an International Setting: The Basic Values of People Differ." *Vital Speeches of the Day* 44 (May 1, 1978), 428–430.

Heymann, Philip B. "Honesty Legislated as Best Policy in Foreign Business Transactions." *New York Law Journal* 183 (February 25, 1980), 4.

"How Castle and Cooke Investigated Itself." *Business Week* (August 16, 1976), 53–54.

Iacocca, Lee A. "Multinational Investment and Global Purpose: Technological Transfer." *Vital Speeches of the Day* 43 (September 15, 1977), 720–724.

Iacocca, Lee A. "Myth of the Big, Bad Multinational." *Newsweek* 90 (September 12, 1977), 21.

Karaganov, S. "The Subversive Activities of the Multinationals." *International Affairs* (Moscow) (October 1976), 50.

Keohane, R. O. "Not Innocents Abroad: American Multinational Corporations and the United States Government." *Comparative Politics* 8 (January 1976), 307–320.

La Palombara, Joseph. "Myths of the Multinationals." *Across the Board* 13 (October 1976), 40–46.

Levy, Harold. "Civil Rights in Employment and the Multinational Corporations." *Cornell International Law Journal* 10 (December 1976), 87–115.

Levy, Phillippe. "Guidelines for the Conduct of Multinationals: How Much Use Are They?" *Prospects* (Swiss Bank Corporation) (1978), 15–16.

Lindenmuth, William E. "Divestiture and International Oil." *Journal of Energy and Development* 2 (Autumn 1976), 30–37.

McCarthy, James E. "Zimbabwe and All That: How Important Is Africa to American Business?" *Across the Board* 14 (March 1977), 54–58.

Mackie, W. A. "Multinational Corporation: A Ton of Responsibility, a Pound of Power." *Vital Speeches of the Day* 44 (June 1, 1978), 510–512.

Margulies, Leah. "Bottle Babies: Death and Business Get Their Market." *Business and Society Review* 25 (Spring 1978), 43–49.

Meier, Richard L. "Multinationals as Agents of Social Development." *Bulletin of the Atomic Scientists* 33 (November 1977), 30–35.

Miller, D. L. "PANACEA or Problem? The Proposed International Code of Conduct for Technology Transfer." *Journal of International Affairs* 33 (Spring 1979), 43–62.

Mills, David E., and Kenneth G. Elzinga. "Cartel Problems: Comment." *American Economic Review* 68 (December 1978), 938–941.

"Mobil's Unctuous Silence; Rhodesia's Endless Ordeal." *Business and Society Review* 24 (Winter 1977–78), 36.

Morgan, Edward A. "The Domestic Technology Base Company: The Dilemma of an Operating Company Which Might Be a Personal Holding Company." *Tax Law Review* 33 (Winter 1978), 233–275.

Morris, Robert. "Coca-Cola and Human Rights in Guatemala." *Interfaith Center on Corporate Responsibility* (November 1980), 3A–3D.

Moxon, Richard W., and Tugi Fagafi-nejad. "Technology Transfer and the Transnational Enterprise: the Outlook for Regulation." *Journal of Contemporary Business* 6 (Autumn 1977), 147–164.

Murphy, Betty Southard. "Multinational Corporations and Free Co-ordinated Transnational Bargaining: An Alternative to Protectionism?" *Labor Law Journal* 28 (October 1977), 619–631.

Pohlman, Randolph A., James S. Ang, and Syed I. Ali. "Policies of

Multinational Firms: A Survey." *Business Horizons* 19 (December 1976), 14–18.

Post, James E., and Edward Baer. "Demarketing Infant Formula: Consumer Products in the Developing World." *Journal of Contemporary Business* 7, no. 4 (1978), 17–35.

Reeves, Barbara. "Antitrust and International Technology Licensing: A Primer." *Cornell International Law Journal* 11 (Summer 1978), 263–274.

Rice, Victor A. "The Transnationals' Impact on Host Countries: Fact versus Fiction." *Vital Speeches of the Day* 46 (December 15, 1979), 130–133.

Rose, Sanford. "Why the Multinational Tide Is Ebbing." *Fortune* 96 (August 1977), 110–114+.

Rubin, S. J. "Developments in the Law and Institutions of International Economic Relations: Reflections Concerning the United Nations Commission on Transnational Corporations." *American Journal of International Law* 70 (January 1976), 73–91.

Schollhammer, Hans. "Ethics in an International Business Context." *Management International Review* 17 (November 19, 1977), 23–33.

Schomer, Howard. "Ethical Pressure on Transnational Corporations." *Forum for Correspondence and Contact* 9 (October 1976), 135–138.

Seidman, Ann. "Why U.S. Corporations Should Get Out of South Africa." *Issue* (Spring–Summer 1979), 37–41.

Sethi, S. Prakash, and James E. Post. "Public Consequences of Private Action: The Marketing of Infant Formula in Less Developed Countries." *California Management Review* 21 (Summer 1979), 35–48.

Sklar, Richard L. "Postimperialism: A Class Analysis of Multinational Corporate Expansion." *Comparative Politics* 9 (October 1976), 75–92.

Springer, Allen L. "Towards a Meaningful Concept of Pollution in International Law." *International and Comparative Law Quarterly* 26 (July 1977), 531–557.

Thorelli, Hans B. "Management Audit and Social Indicators: The MNC through the Glasses of the LDC." *Journal of Contemporary Business* 7 (Winter 1978), 75–91.

Ulmer, Melville J. "Multinational Corporations and Third World Capitalism." *Journal of Economic Issues* 14 (June 1980), 453–471.

Vernon, Raymond. "Storm over the Multinationals: Problems and Prospects." *Foreign Affairs* 55 (January 1977), 243–262.

Wallin, Theodore O. "The International Executive's Baggage: Cultural Values of the American Frontier." *MSU Business Topics* 24 (Spring 1976), 49–58.

Safety and Health

Books

Ashford, Nicholas A. *Crisis in the Workplace: Occupational Disease and Injury.* (A report to the Ford Foundation.) Cambridge, Mass.: MIT Press, 1976.

Bergman, Daniel M. *Death on the Job.* New York: Monthly Review Press, 1980.

Herb, Sharon. *An Introduction to Nuclear Power.* Richmond, Ind.: Friends Committee on Economic Responsibility, 1977.

Lowrance, William W. *Of Acceptable Risk: Science and the Determination of Safety.* Los Altos, Calif.: William Kaufmann, 1976.

McGillan, J. O., et al. *Consumer Product Safety Law.* Washington, D.C.: Government Institutes, 1977.

Schwing, Richard C., and Walter A. Albers, Jr., eds. *Societal Risk Assessment. How Safe Is Safe Enough?* New York: Plenum Press, 1980.

Shapo, Marshall S. *A Nation of Guinea Pigs: The Unknown Risks of Chemical Technology.* New York: Free Press, 1979.

Smith, Robert Stewart. *The Occupational Safety and Health Act: Its Goals and Its Achievements.* Washington, D.C.: American Enterprise Institute, 1976.

Articles

Acton, Jan Paul. "Measuring the Monetary Value of Lifesaving Programs." *Law and Contemporary Problems* 40 (Autumn 1976), 46–72.

Adam, Everett E., Jr. "Priority Assignment of OSHA Safety Inspectors." *Management Science* 24 (November 1978), 1642–1649.

"Alcoholism on the Job: An Interview with Joseph F. Follmann, Jr." *Association Management* 28 (November 1976), 42–44.

Ashford, Nicholas A. "Nature and Dimensions of Occupational

Health and Safety Problems." *Personnel Administrator* 22 (August 1977), 46–49.

Ashford, Nicholas A. "Regulating Occupational Health and Safety: The Real Issues." *Challenge* 19 (November–December 1976), 39–42.

Ast, David. B. "Prevention and the Power of Consumers." *American Journal of Public Health* 68 (January 1978), 15–16.

Ball, Jeff. "The Cotton Dust Standard." *Job Safety and Health* 6 (June 1978), 5–11.

Ball, Jeff. "Do-It-Yourself Safety—A Federal Agency Stresses Worker Participation." *Job Safety and Health* 5 (November 1977), 16–18.

Beal, Tita. "Safety Training That Works—and Doesn't Cost an Arm and a Leg." *Training* 14 (August 1977), 47–50.

Bell, John. "The Hair Dye Controversy." *Job Safety and Health* 6 (March 1978), 24–33.

Brown, Joan C. "Occupational Health and Safety: The Importance of Worker Participation." *Labour Gazette* 78 (April 1978), 123–128.

Califano, Joseph A., Jr. "Occupational Health and Safety: A Healthier Working Environment." *Vital Speeches of the Day* 44 (October 1, 1978), 738–741.

"Can You 'Schedule' Job Safety?" *Chemical Week* 123 (July 19, 1978), 47.

"Cancer in the Workplace." *Across the Board* 15 (July 1978), 48–52.

Capstick, Richard. "Incentive Scheme Overtakes Worker Accidents." *International Management* 33 (May 1978), 19–20+.

"Carcinogen Crackdown Proposed." *Chemical Week* 121 (October 12, 1977), 18–19.

Cole, Gordon H. "Alcoholism: Tragedy on the Job." *American Federationist* 83 (May 1976), 1–4.

Colligan, Michael J., and William Stockton. "The Mystery of Assembly-Line Hysteria." *Psychology Today* 12 (June 1978), 93–94+.

Conley, Bryan C. "The Value of Human Life in the Demand for Safety." *American Economic Review* 66 (March 1976), 45–55.

Cox, Hank. "The Right to Know about Hazards." *Job Safety and Health* 5 (December 1977), 23–25.

Curran, William J. " 'Common Sense' in Enforcement of Inspections and Regulations in Occupational Health and Safety." *American Journal of Public Health* 68 (January 1978), 73.

Curran, William J. "Occupational Safety and Health: Unconstitutional Searches." *American Journal of Public Health* 67 (July 1977), 684–685.

Etzioni, Amitai. "How Much Is a Life Worth?" *Social Policy* 9 (March 1979), 4–8.

Fallows, James. "The Cigarette Scandal." *Washington Monthly* 7 (February 1976), 4–16.

"Fear of Flying in the Face of Big Business." *New Statesman* 97 (June 8, 1979), 810.

Finnegan, Jack. "A Dangerous Business: Pesticide Formulation." *Job Safety and Health* 6 (April 1978), 20–24.

Foster, Jim. "OSHA Proposes New Approach to Setting Standards for Suspected Carcinogens." *Job Safety and Health* 5 (December 1977), 14–22.

Guzzardi, Walter, Jr. "The Mindless Pursuit of Safety." *Fortune* 99 (April 9, 1979), 54–56+.

Harris, Fred. "Burning Up People to Make Electricity." *Atlantic Monthly* 234 (July 1974), 29–36.

Hilaski, Harvey J. "Classification of Jobs by Hazards." *Job Safety and Health* 6 (December 1978), 9–10.

Hyatt, James C. "Protection for the Unborn? Work-Safety Issue Isn't As Simple As It Sounds." *Wall Street Journal* (August 2, 1977), 1+.

Kenny, T. P. "The Asbestos Situation, or Whose Safety First." *Journal of the Institute of Personnel Management* (June 1976), 46.

Komacki, Judi, Kenneth D. Barwick, and Lawrence R. Scott. "A Behavioral Approach to Occupational Safety: Pinpointing and Reinforcing Safe Performance in a Food Manufacturing Plant." *Journal of Applied Psychology* 63 (August 1978), 434–445.

Lepkowski, Will. "Toxic Substances Law: Impact on Trade Secrets." *Chemical and Engineering News* 55 (March 14, 1977), 18–19.

Long, Janice R. "OSHA Hearings on Generic Cancer Policies Begin." *Chemical and Engineering News* 56 (May 29, 1978), 15–16.

McIntyre, Kathryn J. "Workers Study Law to Learn to Foresee Product Liability Risk." *Business Insurance* 13 (June 11, 1979), 56–57.

McKee, Mary Ellen. "Health Tests Slash Firm's Work Compensation Costs." *Business Insurance* 13 (June 25, 1979), 41–42.

McKee, Mary Ellen. "Unions Demand Workers See Medical Data." *Business Insurance* 13 (June 11, 1979), 109.

Martin, Gail M. "Waste Anesthetic Gases and Vapors." *Job Safety and Health* 6 (April 1978), 4–14.

Mastromatteo, Ernesto. "Safety and Health in the Industrial Society." *Earth Law Journal* 2 (February 1976), 9–19.

Menkus, Belden. "Responsibility for Fire Risk in Modern Offices Falls Ultimately on the Shoulders of Senior Corporate Management and Their Staff." *Administrative Management* 41 (October 1980), 84+.

Miller, Ernest C. "Open to OSHA?" *Personnel* 55 (November–December 1978), 4–9.

"NIOSH Urges Generic Standard for Pesticides." *Chemical and Engineering News* 56 (December 18, 1978), 12–13.

Najarian, Thomas. "The Controversy over the Health Effects of Radiation." *Technology Review* 81 (November 1978), 74–82.

Navarro, Vicente. "The Underdevelopment of Health of Working America: Causes, Consequences, and Possible Solutions." *American Journal of Public Health* 66 (June 1976), 538–547.

Nichols, Albert L., and Richard Zeckhauser. "Government Comes to the Workplace: An Assessment of OSHA." *Public Interest* (Fall 1977), 39–69.

Nielsen, Richard P. "Should Executives Be Jailed for Consumer and Employee Health and Safety Violations?" *Journal of Consumer Affairs* 13 (Summer 1979), 128–134.

Portela-Cubria, Gloria. "Health Hazards in the Workplace: Fetal Injury and Reproductive Risk." *EEO Today* 5 (Winter 1978–79), 341–356.

Reynolds, David P., et al. "Does Business Value Human Life." *Business and Society Review* 22 (Summer 1977), 44–53.

"Risk Analysis Makes Chemical Plants Safer." *Chemical and Engineering News* 56 (October 2, 1978), 8.

Ritchey, Patrick W. "Current Developments in OSHA: Life under Barlow's." *Employee Relations Law Journal* 5 (Summer 1979), 125–128.

Ritchey, Patrick W. "Warrantless Inspection under the Occupational Safety and Health Act." *Employee Relations Law Journal* 3 (Summer 1977), 145–149.

Root, Norman, and David McCaffrey. "Providing More Information on Work Injury and Illness." *Monthly Labor Review* 101 (April 1978), 16–21.

Rosenbaum, Linda. "Does Progress Cause Cancer?" *Canadian Business Magazine* 52 (April 1979), 43–47+.

Sakabe, Hiroyuki. "Some Reflections on the Limits of Exposure to Dangerous Airborne Substances." *International Labour Review* 117 (September–October 1978), 557–568.

Settle, Russell F. "Regulating Work Hazards: What Should OSHA's Role Be?" *Challenge* 19 (November–December 1976), 37–38.

Shaw, Jane S. "Who Is Responsible for Workplace Safety?" *Business Week* (December 26, 1977), 42.

Smith, Elizabeth Bartman. "Working in Confined Spaces." *Job Safety and Health* 6 (November 1978), 4–9.

Smith, Robert Stewart. "The Impact of OSHA Inspections on Manufacturing Injury Rates." *Journal of Human Resources* 14 (Spring 1979), 145–170.

Stevenson, Robert E. "Health Risks and Equal Opportunity." *The Hastings Center Report* 10 (December 1980), 25–26.

Taylor, Bernard W., III, and K. Roscoe Davis. "Compliance with the Occupational Safety and Health Act—A Mathematical Programming Framework." *Decision Sciences* 8 (October 1977), 677–691.

Trowbridge, Alexander B. "Industry Must Convince Government of Its Concern for Health and Safety." *Food Product Development* 11 (April 1977), 14–15.

Viscusi, W. Kip. "The Impact of Occupational Safety and Health Regulation." *Bell Journal of Economics* 10 (Spring 1979), 117–140.

Wagel, William H. "OSHA: Minimizing Health Risks at DuPont." *Personnel* 54 (November–December 1977), 47–50.

Weidman, Jim. "Winning Battle to Control Workplace Asbestos." *Job Safety and Health* 6 (April 1978), 15–19.

Weinstein, Gerald L. "OSHA Issues New Arsenic Standard." *Job Safety and Health* 6 (November 1978), 15–23.

Wilson, Robert A. "Practical Loss Control Is Realistic, Thrifty." *Business Insurance* 13 (June 11, 1979), 61+.

Wirfs, Ralph M. "Fire Fighters." *Job Safety and Health* 6 (June 1978), 18–33.

Wirfs, Ralph M. "Sagebrush Safety—The Nevada Approach." *Job Safety and Health* 5 (October 1977), 15–22.

Witt, Matt. "Dangerous Substances and the U.S. Worker: Current Practice and Viewpoints." *International Labour Review* 118 (March 1979), 165–177.

Social Audit

Books

Abt, Clark. *The Social Audit for Management.* New York: American Management Association, 1977.

Biderman, Albert D., and Thomas F. Drury, eds. *Measuring Work Quality for Social Reporting.* New York: John Wiley and Sons, 1976.

Blake, David H., et al. *Social Auditing: An Action Profile.* New York: Holt, Rinehart, and Winston, 1976.

Estes, Ralph. *Corporate Social Accounting.* New York: Ronald Press, 1976.

Frankel, Maurice. *The Social Audit Pollution Handbook.* London: Macmillan Press, 1978.

John, Harold L. *Disclosure of Corporate Social Performance: Survey, Evaluation and Prospects.* New York: Praeger, 1979.

Articles

Anderson, Robert H. "Social Responsibility Accounting—How to Get Started." *Canadian Chartered Accountant* 111 (September 1978), 46–50.

Anderson, Robert H. "Social Responsibility Accounting: Measure and Reporting Performance." *Canadian Chartered Accountant* 111 (May 1978), 39–48.

Anderson, Robert H. "Social Responsibility Accounting: Time to Get Started." *CA Magazine* 110 (February 1977), 28–31.

Anderson, Robert H. "Social Responsibility Accounting: What to Measure and How." *Cost Management* (Canada) 50 (September–October 1976), 34–38.

Baker, C. Richard. "Deficit in the Social Account." *Business and Society Review* 17 (Spring 1976), 64–65.

Berg, J. L. "Social Auditing." *Armed Forces Comptroller* 21 (October 1976), 18–20.

Braiotta, Louis, Jr. "Assessing Auditor Integrity." *CPA Journal* 48 (June 1978), 82–84.

Brooks, Leonard J., Jr. "Cost-Benefit Analysis: The New Measure of Corporate Responsibility." *Canadian Chartered Accountant* 112 (October 1979), 53–57.

Brooks, Leonard J., Jr., and William R. Davis. "Some Approaches to the Corporate Social Audit." *CA Magazine* 110 (March 1977), 34–38+.

Burton, Eric James, and Manuel A. Tipgos. "Towards a Theory of Corporate Social Accounting: Comments." *Accounting Review* 52 (October 1977), 971–983.

Campbell, William L. "Regarding Corporate Social Accounting: Where Have All the Flowers Gone?" *Government Accountants' Journal* 25 (Fall 1976), 33–35.

"Can Social Accountability Be Measured?" *Chemical Week* 121 (November 16, 1977), 33.

Clement, Ronald W. "Evaluating Corporate Social Performance: Getting Started." *Arizona Business* 26 (August–September 1979), 17–21.

"Corporate Social Performance." *Management Accounting* 58 (June 1977), 69.

Dillon, Ray. "Evaluating Your Social Awareness Expenditures: A Pragmatic Approach." *Managerial Planning* 27 (May 1979), 25–28.

Engledow, Jack L. "Social Audits: Who Cares? And Who Cares about Who Cares?" *Journal of Contemporary Business* 7 (Winter 1978), 93–111.

Estes, Ralph, and Nicole Zenz. "Social Accounting in a Manufacturing Company: An Action Research Study." *Journal of Contemporary Business* 7 (Winter 1978), 33–43.

Gale, Jeffrey. "Social Decision-Oriented Measurement: Some Considerations." *Journal of Contemporary Business* 7 (Winter 1978), 55–74.

Haring, R. C., J. Tarver, and H. French. "Views on Social Responsibility of Business and Social Audit." *Arkansas Business and Economic Review* 9 (Summer 1976), 21–24.

Higgins, James M. "A Proposed Social Performance Evaluation System." *Atlanta Economic Review* 27 (May–June 1977), 4–9.

Higgins, James M. "A Social Audit of Equal Employment Opportunity Programs." *Human Resource Management* 16 (Fall 1977), 2–7.

Ingram, Robert W. "An Investigation of the Information Content of (Certain) Social Responsibility Disclosures." *Journal of Accounting Research* 16 (Autumn 1978), 270–285.

Johnston, David C-H. "Corporate Approaches to Social Accounting." *Business* 29 (July–August 1979), 45–52.

Kizilbash, A. H., et al. "Social Auditing for Marketing Managers." *Industrial Marketing Management* 8 (January 1979), 1–6.

Lessem, R. "Corporate Social Reporting in Action." *European Journal of Marketing* 4 (Spring 1979), 27–41.

McComb, Desmond. "Some Guidelines on Social Accounting in the U.S." *Accountancy* 89 (April 1978), 50–52.

Mead, Margaret. "Social Accounting and the American Dream." *Business and Society Review* 19 (Fall 1976), 5–9.

Most, Kenneth S. "Corporate Social Reporting." *Accountant* 176 (February 10, 1977), 164–167.

Murphy, Patrick E., and Eric James Burton. "Accountants Assess the Social Audit." *Business* 30 (September–October 1980), 33–40.

Nader, Ralph. "Corporate Disclosure: The Public Right to Know." *Journal of Contemporary Business* 7 (Winter 1978), 25–31.

"New Horizon of Social Measurement." *Journal of Accountancy* 143 (May 1977), 32.

Parker, Lee D. "Social Accounting—Don't Wait for It." *Accountant's Magazine* 80 (February 1976), 50–52.

Pomeranz, Felix. "Social Measurement: A Primer for Implementation." *Journal of Accounting, Auditing, and Finance* 1 (Summer 1978), 385–390.

Ramanathan, Kavasseri V. "Toward a Theory of Corporate Social Accounting." *Accounting Review* 51 (July 1976), 516–528.

Ross, Valerie. "Faith, Hope, and the Social Audit." *Canadian Business Magazine* 50 (October 1977), 59–61+.

Seidler, Lee J., and Thomas C. Taylor. "Comment on 'The Illusions of Social Accounting.' " *CPA Journal* 46 (June 1976), 6–7.

"Social Accounting: A Puff of Smoke?" *Management Review* 66 (November 1977), 4.

"Social Responsibility Disclosure Grows." *Management Accounting* 58 (May 1977), 56–57+.

Spicer, Barry H. "Investors, Corporate Social Performance, and Information Disclosure: An Empirical Study." *Accounting Review* 53 (January 1978), 94–111.

Stines, Frederic M. "Accountants' Attitudes toward Social Accounting." *Journal of Business* 16 (May 1978), 3–12.

Strawser, Robert H., Keith G. Stanga, and James J. Benjamin. "Social Reporting: Financial Community Views." *CPA Journal* 46 (February 1976), 7–10.

Strier, Franklin. "The Business Manager's Dilemma–IV. Evaluating Corporate Social Performance." *Journal of Enterprise Management* 2 (1980), 127–129.

Taylor, Thomas C. "The Illusions of Social Accounting." *CPA Journal* 46 (January 1976), 24–28.

Thomas, Arthur L. "Evaluating the Effectiveness of Social Programs." *Journal of Accountancy* 141 (June 1976), 65–71.

Tipgos, Manuel A. "A Case against the Social Audit." *Management Accounting* 58 (November 1976), 23–26.

Tipgos, Manuel A. "Reporting Corporate Performance in the Social Sphere." *Management Accounting* (August 1976), 15–18.

Van Den Bergh, Richard. "The Corporate Social Report—The Deutsche Shell Experience." *Accountancy* 87 (December 1976), 57–61.

Whistle Blowing

Books

Hayes, John P. *The Lonely Fighter.* New York: Lyle Stuart Publishers, 1978.

Nader, Ralph, et al., eds. *Whistle-Blowing—The Nader Report.* New York: Harper and Row, 1975.

Weisband, Edward, and Thomas M. Franck. *Resignation in Protest.* New York: Grossman, 1975.

Westin, Alan F., eds. *Whistle Blowing! Loyalty and Dissent in the Corporation.* New York: McGraw-Hill, 1981.

Articles

Bogen, Kenneth T. "Managing Technical Dissent in Private Industry: Societal and Corporate Strategies for Dealing with the Whistle-Blowing Professional." *Industrial and Labor Relations Forum* 13 (1979), 3–32.

Bok, Sissela. "Whistle Blowing and Professional Responsibility." *New York University Educational Quarterly* 11 (Summer 1980), 2–10.

Burnet, Arthur L. "Management's Positive Interest in Accountability through Whistleblowing." *Bureaucrat* 9 (Summer 1980), 5–10.

"Can Your Employees Blow the Whistle on Internal Wrongdoing?" *ABA Banking Journal* 72 (November 1980), 26.

Clark, Rosemary, and Frank Von Hippel. "Due Process for Dissenting Whistle Blowers." *Technology Review* 8 (June–July 1979), 48–55.

Clutterbuck, David. "Blowing the Whistle on Corporate Misconduct." *International Management* 35 (January 1980), 14–16+.

Conway, John. "Protecting the Private Sector At-will Employee Who 'Blows the Whistle': A Course of Action Based upon Determinants of Public Policy." *Wisconsin Law Review* (1977), 777–812.

"Corporate Pay-Offs: Accountants, Says Honest Abe, Should Blow the Whistle." *Barron's* 56 (April 19, 1976), 5.

Dudar, Helen. "The Price of Blowing the Whistle." *New York Times Magazine* (October 30, 1977), 41.

Ewing, David W. "Dissent in the Corporate World: When Does an Employee Have the Right to Speak Out?" *Civil Liberties Review* 15 (September–October 1978), 6–10+.

Florman, Samuel. "Moral Blueprints." *Harper's Magazine* (October 1978), 30–33.

Frome, Michael. "Blowing the Whistle." *Center Magazine* (November 11, 1978), 50–58.

Gross, Kent. "Attorneys and Their Corporate Clients: SEC Rule 2(e) and the Georgetown 'Whistle Blowing' Proposal." *Corporation Law Review* 3 (Summer 1980), 197–227.

Hacker, Andrew. "Loyalty and the Whistle Blower." *Across the Board* 15 (November 1978), 4–5+.

Hayes, John P. "The Men Who Blow the Whistle." *Saga Magazine* (May 1979), 28.

James, Gene G., "Whistle Blowing: Its Nature and Justification." *Philosophy in Context* 10 (1980), 99–117.

Kaufman, R. F. "Whistle Blowing and Full Disclosure." *Bureaukrat* 6 (Winter 1977), 35–40.

Kendall, Lynn. "A Whistle Blower Comes to Chicago." *Ethical Society* 2 (Spring 1979), 12–14.

"Laws Protect Whistle Blowers." *Bioscience* 29 (June 1979), 388.

Marks, Laurence. "Silencing the Whistleblowers." *Atlas* 25 (September 1978), 48.

Miller, Richard A. "Price-Fixing and Whistle Blowing; A Bounty for Mutiny on the Good Ship Collusion." *Anti-trust Law and Economic Review* 10 (1978), 87–96.

Raven-Hansen, Peter. "Do's and Don'ts for Whistleblowers: Planning for Trouble." *Technology Review* 82 (May 1980), 34–44.

Reeves, Richard. "The Last Angry Men." *Esquire* (March 1, 1978), 41–48.

Solomon, Lewis D., and Perry Garcia. "Protecting the Corporation Whistle Blower under Federal Anti-Retailiatin Statutes." *Journal of Corporate Law* (Winter 1980), 275–297.

Stevens, Charles W. "The Whistle Blower Chooses Hard Path, Utility Story Shows." *Wall Street Journal* (November 8, 1978), 1+.

Stewart, Leo P. " 'Whistle Blowing': Implications for Organizational Communication." *Journal of Communication* (Autumn 1980), 90–101.

"When Must a Lawyer Blow the Whistle?" *Business Week* (May 21, 1979), 117.

Women and Business

Books

Abramson, Joan. *Old Boys, New Women: The Politics of Sex Discrimination.* New York: Praeger Publishers, 1979.

Backhouse, Constance, and Leah Cohen. *The Secret Oppression: Sexual Harassment of Working Women.* Toronto: Macmillan, 1978.

Barker, D. L., and S. Allen, eds. *Dependence and Exploitation in Work and Marriage.* New York: Longman, 1976.

Blaxall, Martha, and Barbara B. Reagan, eds. *Women and the Workplace: The Implications of Occupational Segregation.* Chicago: University of Chicago Press, 1976.

Bird, Caroline. *Enterprising Women.* New York: W. W. Norton and Co., 1976.

Bird, Caroline. *The Two-Paycheck Marriage: How Women at Work Are Changing Life in America.* New York: Rawson, Wade, 1979.

Cadbury, Matheson S. *Women's Work and Wages.* New York: Gordon Press, 1976.

Center for Environmental and Consumer Justice. *Discrimination in Private Employment in Puerto Rico.* Rio Piedras: University of Puerto Rico Press, 1980.

Chiplin, Brian, and Peter J. Sloane. *Sex Discrimination in the Labour Market.* New York: Holmes and Meier Publishers, 1976.

Crawford, Jacquelyn. *Women in Middle Management: Selection Training, Advancement, Performance.* Ridgewood, N.J.: Forkner Publishing Co., 1977.

Dublin, Thomas L. *Women At Work.* New York: Columbia University Press, 1979.

Fairbank, Helen. *Women in Management and the Professions.* Princeton, N.J.: Industrial Relations Section, Princeton University, 1977.

Farley, Jennie. *Affirmative Action and the Woman Worker.* New York: American Management Association, 1979.

Farley, Lin. *Sexual Shakedown: The Sexual Harassment of Women on the Job.* New York: McGraw-Hill Book Co., 1978.

Frank, Harold H. *Women in the Organization.* Philadelphia: University of Pennsylvania, 1977.

Giraldo, Z. I. *Public Policy and the Family: Wives and Mothers in the Labor Force.* Lexington, Mass.: Lexington Books, 1980.

Harragan, Betty Lehan. *Games Mother Never Taught You.* New York: Warner Books, 1980.

Hennig, Margaret, and Anne Jardim. *The Managerial Woman.* Garden City, N.Y.: Anchor Press/Doubleday, 1977.

How Nondiscrimination and Equal Opportunity Programs Impact the Private Sector. Rye, N.Y.: Reymont, 1979.

Howe, Louise Knapp. *Pink Collar Workers: Inside the World of Women's Work.* New York: Putnam, 1977.

Jewell, Donald O., ed. *Women and Management: An Expanding Role.* Atlanta: Georgia State University Business Publications, 1977.

Kornegay, Francis A. *Equal Employment Mandate and Challenge.* New York: Vantage, 1979.

Kreps, Juanita M., ed. *Women and the American Economy: A Look to the 1980's.* New York: American Assembly/Columbia University, 1976.

Larwood, Laurie, and Marion M. Wood. *Women in Management.* Lexington, Mass.: Lexington/D. C. Heath, 1977.

Lewenhak, Shiela. *Women and Work.* New York: St. Martin's Press, 1980.

Lloyd, Cynthia B. *Sex Discrimination, and the Division of Labor.* New York: Columbia University Press, 1975.

Lloyd, Cynthia B., and others, eds. *Women in the Labor Market.* New York: Columbia University Press, 1979.

MacKinnon, Catharine A. *Sexual Harassment of Working Women: A Case of Sex Discrimination.* New Haven: Yale University Press, 1979.

McLane, Helen J. *Selecting, Developing, and Retaining Women Executives: A Corporate Strategy for the Eighties.* New York: Van Nostrand Reinhold, 1980.

Mott, Frank L. *Women, Work, and Family.* Lexington, Mass.: Lexington Books, 1978.

Newton, Derek A. *Think like a Man, Act like a Lady, Work like a Dog.* Garden City, N.Y.: Doubleday, 1979.

Palm, Septima, and Ingrid Brewer. *The Cinderella Syndrome.* Sarasota, Fla.: Septima, 1979.

Pendergrass, Virginia E., ed. *Women Winning: A Handbook for Action Against Sex Discrimination.* Chicago, Ill.: Nelson-Hall, 1979.

Peskin, Dean B. *Womaning: Overcoming Male Dominance of Executive Row.* Port Washington, N.Y.: Ashley Books, 1980.

Pettman, Barrie O. *Equal Pay for Women: Progress and Problems in Seven Countries.* Bradford, Eng.: McB Books, 1976.

Rather, Ronnie Steinberg. *Equal Employment Policy for Women.* Philadelphia: Temple University Press, 1980.

Roby, Pamela. *Where Do We Go from Here: Conditions of Women in Blue-Collar Jobs.* Cambridge, Mass.: Schenkman, 1980.

Schreiber, Carol T. *Changing Places: Men and Women in Transitional Occupations.* Cambridge, Mass.: MIT Press, 1979.

Sloane, Peter P., ed. *Women and Low Pay.* Atlantic Highlands, N.J.: Humanities, 1980.

Stead, Betty A. *Women in Management.* Englewood Cliffs, N.J.: Prentice-Hall, 1978.

Tepperman, Jean. *Not Servants, Not Machines: Office Workers Speak Out!* Boston: Beacon Press, 1976.

Wallace, Phyllis A., and Annette M. LaMond. *Women, Minorities, and Employment Discrimination.* Lexington, Mass.: Lexington Books, 1977.

Wallace, Phyllis A., ed. *Equal Employment and the AT&T Case.* Cambridge, Mass.: MIT Press, 1976.

Walsh, D. C., and R. H. Egdaht, eds. *Women, Work, and Health: Challenge to Corporate Policy.* New York: Springer-Verlag, 1980.

Welch, Mary Scott. *Networking: The Great New Way for Women to Get Ahead.* New York: Harcourt Brace Jovanovich, 1980.

Winston, Sandra. *The Entrepreneurial Woman.* New York: Newsweek, 1979.

Women in Blue-Collar Jobs. New York: Ford Foundation, 1976.

Articles

Agarwal, Naresh C., and Harish C. Jain. "Pay Discrimination against Women in Canada: Issues and Policies." *International Labour Review* 117 (March–April 1978), 169–177.

Alexander, Guvene G., and Jean E. Gutmann. "Contents and Techniques of Management Development Programs for Women." *Personnel Journal* 55 (February 1976), 76–79.

Bane, Mary Jo. "Sexual Equality (Economics Department): A Long Way to Go, in Marriage and Business." *Across the Board* 14 (March 1977), 12–24.

Biles, George E., and Holly A. Pryatel. "Myths, Management, and Women." *Personnel Journal* 57 (October 1978), 572+.

Bolton, Elizabeth B., and Luther W. Humphreys. "Training Model for Women—An Androgynous Approach." *Personnel Journal* 56 (May 1977), 230–234.

Cooney, Joan Ganz. "A Woman in the Boardroom." *Harvard Business Review* 56 (January–February 1978), 77–86.

The Corporate Woman: Doing Well in Consumer Affairs." *Business Week* (August 16, 1976), 120+.

"The Corporate Woman: How to Get Along—And Ahead—In the Office." *Business Week* (March 22, 1976), 107–108+.

"The Dilemma of Regulating Reproductive Risks." *Business Week* (August 29, 1977), 76–77+.

Eklund, Coy G. "Women in Business: What Business Must Do." *Vital Speeches of the Day* 42 (June 15, 1976), 539–542.

Enberg-Jordan, Sandra. "The Woman Manager: Opportunities and Obstacles." *AA UW Journal* 69 (April 1976), 9–12.

Erickson, Nancy S. "Pregnancy Discrimination: An Analytical Approach." *Women's Rights Law Reporter* 5 (Winter/Spring 1979), 83–105.

Ewen, Stuart. "Woman's Place in the Advertising Culture." *Business and Society Review* 27 (Fall 1978), 61–64.

Fenn, Margaret P., ed. "Women in Business: A New Look." *Journal of Contemporary Business* 5 (Winter 1976), 1–76.

Ferber, Marianne A., and Helen M. Lowry. "The Sex Differential in Earnings: A Reappraisal." *Industrial and Labor Relations Review* 29 (April 1976), 377–387.

Fonda, N. "Job Evaluation without Sex Discrimination." *Personnel Management* 11 (February 1979), 34+.

Fraiberg, Selma. "What's a Working Mother to Do? She Wants Her Job for Fulfillment or Simply Needs It for Income. But What Happens to the Kids in Her Absence—Especially the Very Young?" *Across the Board* 15 (September 1978), 14–28.

Gallas, Nesta M., ed. "Women in Public Administration: A Symposium." *Public Administration Review* 36 (July/August 1976), 347–389.

Gaylin, Jody. "His Legs Are Lovely, but Can He Type?" *Psychology Today* 9 (March 1976), 21.

Gelb, Joyce, and Marian Lief Palley. "Women and Interest Group Politics: A Case Study of the Equal Credit Opportunity Act." *American Politics Quarterly* 5 (July 1977), 331–352.

Ginsburg, Ruth Bader. "Women, Equality, and the Bakke Case." *Civil Liberties Review* 4 (November–December 1977), 8–16.

Goodman, Eileen. "Still a Long Way to Go." *Canadian Business Magazine* 50 (July 1977), 70+.

Gordon, Suzanne. "New Age Capitalist: Mixing Love and the Profit Motive." *Psychology Today* 12 (August 1978), 83–88.

Grossman, Allyson Sherman. "Women in the Labor Force: the Early Years." *Monthly Labor Review* 98 (November 1975), 3–24.

Haneburg, Ronald L. "Employee Benefit Plans—What Constitutes Sex Discrimination?" *Risk Management* 26 (January 1979), 11–15.

Hartmann, Heidi I. "Women's Work in the United States." *Current History* 70 (May 1976), 215–219+.

Herbert, Theodore T., and Edward B. Yost. "Women as Effective Managers . . . A Strategic Model for Overcoming the Barriers." *Human Resource Management* 17 (Spring 1978), 18–25.

Jacobson, C. J. "Job Problems of Women Workers." *American Federationist* 84 (February 1977), 12–16.

Jensen, Beverly. "Black and Female, Too." *Black Enterprise* 6 (July 1976), 26–29.

Kanter, Rosabeth Moss. "Tokenism: Opportunity or Trap?" *MBA* 12 (January 1978), 15–18+.

Keyserling, Mary Dublin. "The Economic Status of Women in the United States." *American Economic Review* 66 (May 1976), 205–212.

Leap, Terry L. and Edmund R. Gray. "Corporate Responsibility in Cases of Sexual Harassment." *Business Horizons* 23 (October 1980), 58–65.

LeGrande, Linda H. "Women in Labor Organizations: Their Ranks Are Increasing." *Monthly Labor Review* 101 (August 1978), 8–14.

Lyles, Jean Caffey."Women's Work: Making a Difference." *Christian Century* 94 (December 7, 1977), 1131–1132.

McGhee, Dorothy. "Workplace Hazards: No Women Need Apply." *Progressive* 41 (October 1977), 20–25.

Marcus, Gail H. "The Status of Women in the Nuclear Industry." *Bulletin of the Atomic Scientists* 32 (April 1976), 34–39.

Matteson, M. T. "Attitudes toward Women as Managers: Sex or Role-Differences?" *Psychological Reports* 39 (August 1976), 166.

Minas, Anne C. "How Reverse Discrimination Compensates Women." *Ethics* 88 (1977–78), 74–79.

Mirides, E., and A. Cote. "Women in Management: Strategies for Removing the Barriers." *Personnel Administrator* 25 (April 1980), 25–28.

Mohr, E. Sue, and Ronald G. Downey. "Are Women Peers?" *Journal of Occupational Psychology* 50 (March 1977), 53–57.

Neuse, Steven M. "Professionalism and Authority: Women in Public Service." *Public Adminstration Review* 38 (September/October 1978), 436–441.

Oaxaca, Ronald L. "Some Observations on the Economics of Women's Liberation." *Challenge* 19 (July–August 1976), 29–33).

Osborn, Richard N., and William M. Vicars. "Sex Stereotypes: An

Artifact in Leader Behavior and Subordinate Satisfaction Analysis?" *Academy of Management Journal* 19 (September 1976), 439–449.

Peterson, Robert A., and Roger A. Kerin. "The Female Role in Advertisements: Some Experimental Evidence." *Journal of Marketing* 41 (October 1977), 59–63.

Powers, Kathryn L. "Sex Segregation and the Ambivalent Directions of Sex Discrimination Law." *Wisconsin Law Review* (1979), 55–124.

Putnam, Linda, and J. Stephen Heinen. "Women in Management: The Fallacy of the Trait Approach." *MSU Business Topics* 24 (Summer 1976), 47–53.

Rankin, Deborah. "Women Accountants Are Scarcely Adding Up: Is a Gain from No Percent to One Percent 'Revolutionary Progress' or 'Insignificant Change'? " *Business and Society Review* 25 (Spring 1978), 59–61.

Reagan, Barbara B. "Report of the Committee on the Status of Women in the Economic Profession." *American Economic Review* 67 (February 1977), 460–464.

Reif, William E., John W. Newstrom, and Robert D. St. Louis, Jr. "Sex as a Discriminating Variable in Organizational Reward Decisions." *Academy of Management Journal* 19 (September 1976), 469–476.

Rosefsky, Robert S. "When Wives Work, What Factors Are to Be Weighed?" *American Druggist* 174 (July 1976), 13.

Rosen, B., and T. H. Jerdee. "On-the-Job Sex Bias: Increasing Managerial Awareness." *Personnel Administrator* 22 (January 1977), 15–18.

Ruether, Rosemary. "Working Women and the Male Workday: Toward New Solutions." *Christianity and Crisis* 37 (February 7, 1977), 3–8.

Schnepper, Jeff A. "Occupational and Sexual Segregation in the U.S.: The Underemployment of Women." *Arkansas Business and Economics Review* 10 (Summer 1977), 7–10.

Scott, Rachel. "Reproductive Hazards." *Job Safety and Health* 6 (May 1978), 7–13.

Seminario, Margaret. "Women Workers: Hazards on the Job." *American Federationist* 85 (August 1978), 18–23.

"Sexual Harassment Lands Companies in Court: Working Women

Reject Obscenities, Embraces, and Double Entendres." *Business Week* (October 1, 1979), 120+.

Seymour, William C. "Sexual Harassment: Finding a Cause of Action under Title VII." *Labor Law Journal* 30 (March 1979), 139–156.

Sher, George. "Reverse Discrimination, the Future, and the Past." *Ethics* 90 (1979–80), 81–114.

Shrank, Robert. "Two Women, Three Men on a Raft." *Harvard Business Review* 55 (May–June 1977), 100–108.

Singer, James W. "Should Equal Opportunity for Women Apply to Toxic Chemical Exposure?" *National Journal* 12 (October 18, 1980), 1753–1755.

Somers, Patricia A., and Judith Clementson-Mohr. "Sexual Extortion in the Workplace." *Personnel Administrator* 24 (April 1979), 23–28.

Taub, Nadine. "Keeping Women in Their Place: Stereotyping per se as a Form of Employment Discrimination." *Boston College Law Review* 21 (January 1980), 345–418.

Taylor, Ellen T. "Differential Treatment of Pregnancy in Employment: The Impact of General Electric Company v. Gilbert and Nashville Gas Company v. Satty." *Harvard Civil Rights-Civil Liberties Law Review* 13 (Summer 1978), 717–750.

Vaden, Richard E., and Naomi B. Lynn. "The Administrative Person: Will Women Bring a Differing Morality to Management?" *University of Michigan Business Review* 31 (March 1979), 22–25.

Veiga, John F., and John N. Yanouzas. "What Women in Management Want: The Ideal vs. the Real." *Academy of Management Journal* 19 (March 1976), 137–143.

Vick, Judy. "Sexual Harassment: Can It Be Stopped?" *Corporate Report* 10 (October 1979), 42–44.

Wall, James A., Jr., and Robert Virtue. "Women as Negotiators." *Business Horizons* 19 (April 1976), 67–68.

Wallace, Martha R. "Reflections on Women at Work." *Across the Board* 13 (November 1976), 39–42.

Warren, Mary Anne. "Secondary Sexism and Quota Hiring." *Philosophy and Public Affairs* 6 (Spring 1977), 240–261.

White, Ray S., and Stewart H. Rowberry. "Management Is a Family Affair." *Atlanta Economic Review* 27 (May–June 1977), 40–47.

White, Shelby. "The Office Pass: Women Workers Are Beginning to Speak Up about Sexual Harassment and Even File Suits. They

Charge Sexual Discrimination—but Is It That or Rather an 'Outrageous Use of Power'? " *Across the Board* 14 (April 1977), 17–20.

White, Shelby. "The Office Pass (Continued): A Case of Sexual Harassment in the Environmental Protection Agency!" *Across the Board* 15 (March 1978), 48–51.

"Women Charge Discrimination at Chase." *Banking* 68 (March 1976), 24.

Woodworth, M., and Warner Woodworth. "The Female Takeover: Threat or Opportunity." *Personnel Administrator* 24 (January 1979), 19–24+.

Theoretical and Applied Ethics

Theoretical and Applied Ethics

Codes of Conduct and Self-Regulation

Books

Adams, Randolph K. *An Analysis of Existing Ethical Guidelines and the Development of a Proposed Code of Ethics for Managers.* Springfield, Va.: NTIS, 1976.

Callis, Robert, ed. *Ethical Standards Casebook.* Washington, D.C.: American Personnel and Guidance Association, 1976.

Chatov, Robert. *An Analysis of Corporate Statements on Ethics and Behavior.* San Francisco: Roundtable, 1979.

Hammaker, Paul M., Alexander B. Horniman, and Louis T. Rader. *Standards of Conduct in Business.* Charlottesville: CSAE, The Darden School, University of Virginia, 1981.

McHugh, Joseph M. *Mass Media and Public Morality: A Problem-Law-Precept Analysis with Recommendations for Self-Regulation in the Mass Media.* New York: Vantage Press, 1976.

National Association of Realtors. *Code of Ethics and Arbitration Manual.* Chicago: National Association of Realtors, 1976.

A Study of Corporate Ethical Policy Statements. Dallas: Southern Methodist University Foundation of the Southwestern Graduate School of Banking, 1980.

Tulloch, Henry W., and W. Scott Bauman. *The Management of Business Conduct.* Charlottesville: CSAE, The Darden School, University of Virginia, 1981.

Articles

Barber, Bernard. "Control and Responsibility in the Powerful Professions." *The Hastings Center Report* 10 (February 1980), 34–36.

Barovick, Richard L. "Status Report: Code of Conduct for MNC's." *Public Relations Journal* 35 (October 1979), 30–32.

Beard, Larry H., and Philip M. J. Reckers. "Professionalism and the Spectre of Governmental Intervention." *National Public Accountant* 23 (January 1978), 12–15.

Bernstein, Henry R. "Fish Urges AAF Revive Unit for Code of Ethics." *Advertising Age* 47 (November 22, 1976), 26.

Biegler, John C. "Challenge of Self-Regulation: Reality and Perception." *Vital Speeches of the Day* 44 (October 1, 1978), 755–758.

Boeker, Paul H. "A Code for Multinationals." *Wall Street Journal* (May 28, 1976), 8.

Chance, Steven K. "Codes of Conduct for Multinational Corporations." *Business Lawyer* 33 (April 1978), 1799–1820.

Chatov, Robert. "What Corporate Ethics Statements Say." *California Management Review* 22 (Summer 1980), 20–29.

Chetkovich, Michael N. "The Accounting Profession Responds to the Challenges by Government: An Assessment amid a High Degree of Controversy and Much Meaningful Change." *Vital Speeches of the Day* 44 (July 15, 1978), 595–598.

Clowes, Allan D., and Gordon C. Fowler. "Auditing the Auditor: No Legislation with Self-Regulations." *CA Magazine* 111 (June 1978), 47–51.

"Code of Conduct." *Management Today* (February 1979), 118+.

"Code of Conduct Arises from a Workshop." *Computerworld* 12 (September 4, 1978), 12–16.

"A Code of Conduct for Multinationals." *Business Week* (April 5, 1976), 36.

"Company Codes Are Not Uncommon." *Nation's Business* 67 (October 1979), 77.

"Corporate Director's Guidebook." *Business Lawyer* 33 (April 1978), 1591–1644.

"Corruption Is Bad: Business Is Drawing Up Its Own International Rules against Bribery." *The Economist* 262 (March 19, 1977), 88–89.

Crean, John G. "Guidelines and Codes for Multinational Enterprises." *CA Magazine* 113 (March 1980), 61–64.

Cutler, Lloyd N. "The Role of the Private Law Firm." *Business Lawyer* 33 (March 1978), 1549–1564.

Davidow, Joel, and Lisa Chiles. "The United States and the Issue of the Binding or Voluntary Nature of International Codes of Conduct regarding Restrictive Business Practics." *American Journal of International Law* 72 (April 1978), 247–271.

Elliott, Robert K., and Peter D. Jacobson. "Ethics: Is Regulation the Answer?" *Issues in Bank Regulation* 4 (Autumn 1980), 27–32.

"Ethic Rules: An Empty Exercise?" *Industry Week* 189 (June 21, 1976), 7–8.

Evans, M. Stanton. "Outlawing 'Fairness.'" *National Review* 30 (September 1, 1978), 1088.

"The Financial Advertising Code of Ethics." *U.S. Investor—Eastern Banker* 87 (October 18, 1976), 5–9.

"Focus on the Community Bank: Answering Questions about Codes of Ethics." *Banking* 70 (June 1978), 8+.

Fordham, Laurence S. "There Are Substantial Limitations on Representation of Clients in Litigation Which Are Not Obvious in the Code of Professional Responsibility." *Business Lawyer* 33 (March 1978), 1193–1211.

"FTC Memo Urges Look at Media Practices in Ad Self-Regulation Area." *Advertising Age* 47 (April 12, 1976), 3+.

Gibbons, Edward F. "Making a Corporate Code of Ethics Work." *Proceedings of the First National Conference on Business Ethics*, ed. W. Michael Hoffman, Waltham, Mass., Center for Business Ethics at Bentley College (1977), 86–90.

Gillis, John G., and M. H. Earp. "Interpretations of Professional Conduct." *Financial Analysts Journal* 35 (March–April 1979), 10–12+.

Gillis, John G. "Self-Regulation of the Professions." *Financial Analysts Journal* 34 (July–August 1978), 18–19+.

"Group Lays Groundwork for Drafting of Code of Conduct for Transnationals." *UN Chronicle* 14 (February 1977), 24+.

Hanson, Walter E. "A Blueprint for Ethical Conduct." *Journal of Accountancy* 145 (June 1978), 80+.

Harris, Charles E. "Structuring a Workable Business Code of Ethics." *University of Florida Law Review* 30 (Winter 1978), 310–382.

Holt, Robert N. "A Sampling of Twenty-Five Codes of Corporate Conduct: Call for a Renascence." *Directors and Boards* 5 (Summer 1980), 7–17.

Holtzmann, Howard M. "The First Code of Ethics for Arbitrators in Commercial Disputes." *Business Lawyer* 33 (November 1977), 309–320.

Jarrett, Charles B., Jr. "Business Ethics and Codes of Conduct." *Journal of Commercial Bank Lending* 60 (February 1978), 2–13.

Kline, John M. "Entrapment or Opportunity: Structuring a Corporate Response to International Codes of Conduct." *Columbia Journal of World Business* 15 (Summer 1980), 6–13.

Korbin, Stephen J. "Comparison of Codes of Conduct for Multinational Corporations." *Journal of Business Research* 5 (December 1977), 311–323.

Kramer, Otto P. "Ethics Programs Can Help Companies Set Standards of Conduct." *Administrative Management* 38 (January 1977), 46–49.

McCue, Joseph P. "Putting Ethics to Work." *Hospital Financial Management* 32 (January 1978), 30–31.

McKean, R. N. "Some Economic Aspects of Ethical-Behavioral Codes." *Political Studies* 27 (June 1979), 251–265.

McNeese, Robert W. "1978—Year of Change in Ethics Enforcement." *Ohio CPA* 37 (Autumn 1978), 101–106.

Matlin, Gerald L. "Let's Make Ethical Codes Meaningful." *Business and Professional Ethics* 1 (Spring 1977), 7–8.

Meloon, Robert. "The Green Light on Ethics Codes—What It Means to Newspapers." *APME News* 92 (June–July 1976), 1–3.

Miller, William H. "Are Ethics Codes Just 'Window Dressing'?" *Industry Week* 207 (October 27, 1980), 37–38+.

Moeller, Clark. "Corporate Codes of Ethics: A Key to Economic Freedom." *Management Review* 69 (September 1980), 60–62.

"More CPA's Chime in on Self-Regulation." *Business Week* (June 6, 1977), 84–86.

"More Guidelines for Corporate Behavior." *Management Review* 66 (July 1977), 17.

Nash, John F., and Roger H. Hermanson. "Wanted: A Code of Ethics for Internal Accountants." *Business* 30 (November–December 1980), 12–17.

"An OECD Code of Conduct on Energy and the Environment." *OECD Observer* 83 (September–October 1976), 12–16.

"OECD Ethics Rules May Have Unexpected Benefits." *Industry Week* 190 (July 19, 1976), 22–24.

Oswald, Ruby. "Trade: Strengthening the Codes." *American Federationist* 86 (May 1979), 14–18.

Patterson, L. Ray. "Wanted: A New Code of Professional Responsibility." *American Bar Association Journal* 63 (May 1977), 639–642.

Persky, Joel. "Self Regulation of Broadcasting—Does It Exist?" *Journal of Communication* 27 (Spring 1977), 202–210.

"The Relationship between Internal Controls and Fraud, Waste, and Abuse." *Government Accountants Journal* 29 (Fall 1980), 38–56.

Rijkens, Rein. "Five Important Steps toward Self-Regulation." *Advertising Age* 50 (May 14, 1979), S–24.

Roach, Susan, and Karen Howar Brown. "Codes of Ethics—Do They Work?" *Matrix* 61 (Summer 1976), 25–29.

Rodes, Nevin J., and Peter G. Zajac. "Adopt Ethical Stance in International Marketing to Avoid Imposition of Conduct Codes." *Marketing News* 10 (June 3, 1977), 1+.

Roffe, P. "UNCTAD: Code of Conduct for the Transfer of Technology." *Journal of World Trade Law* 14 (March–April 1980), 160–172.

Rosenberg, Ernest S. "Standards and Industry Self-Regulation." *California Management Review* 19 (Fall 1976), 79–90.

Rubicam, Raymond. "Rubicam Calls for Return to Higher Code of Ethics." *Advertising Age* 41 (January 5, 1976), 30.

Sayrs, Joseph H. "Executives Need Ethics Code More Than Reporters Do, Publisher Tells AEJ." *Publishers' Auxiliary* (August 1977), 1–2.

Scheele, Hartmut. "The State of Preparations for a U.N. Code of Conduct." *Intereconomics* (November–December 1979), 273–277.

"SEC Practice Section—Self-Regulation and Public Credibility." *CPA Journal* 48 (December 1978), 8.

Shapiro, Leslie S. "Professional Responsibility: An Update." *National Public Accountant* 22 (December 1977), 8–13.

Shapiro, Samuel B. "A Time for Meaningful Codes of Ethics." *Association Management* 29 (May 1977), 34–35.

Solomon, Kenneth I., and Charles Chazan. "Wanted: A Code of Conduct for American Business." *Perspective* 4 (Fall/Winter 1978), 18–21.

"The Status of Codes of Ethics in Associations and Corporations." *Association Management* 31 (October 1979), 136–139.

Stratton, Samuel S. "New Ethics Code: What You Can and Can't Do in Dealing with Congress." *Association Management* 29 (July 1977), 32–34.

"A Stricter Code of Ethics." *Intellect* 106 (November 1977), 186.

Strother, George. "The Moral Codes of Executives: A Watergate-Inspired Look at Barnard's Theory of Executive Responsibility." *Academy of Management Review* 1 (April 1976), 13–22.

Tankersley, W. H. "Role of Business Self-Regulation in a Changing World: The Man at the Top." *Vital Speeches of the Day* 44 (December 1, 1977), 125–128.

Trowbridge, Alexander B. "Self-Reform: the Way of the Modern Corporation." *Enterprise* 4 (April 1980), 4–7.

Twomey, Sylvia M. "DPers Suffering from Lack of Conduct Code." *Computerworld* 13 (October 22, 1979), 30.

"A Voluntary Disclosure Code for the Banking Industry." *Banking Law Journal* 95 (January 1978), 4–27.

Webster, George D. "Antitrust Implications of Voluntary Standards Programs." *Association Management* 28 (January 1976), 18+.

Webster, George D. "Professional Societies Face Continuing Problems with Codes of Ethics." *Association Management* 29 (May 1977), 26+.

White, Bernard J., and B. Ruth Montgomery. "Corporate Codes of Conduct." *California Management Review* 23 (Winter 1980), 80–87.

"Who Sets Ethical Guidelines for the Association Staff?" *Association Management* 29 (February 1977), 41–43.

"World Marketing Contact Group Proposes Creed for Marketers." *Marketing News* 10 (November 5, 1976), 1.

Wyman, T. H. "Ethical Standards in Business—It's Industry's Move." *Food Product Development* 11 (June 1977), 58+*1*.

Ethics, Market Economy, and Justice

Books

Ackerman, Bruce A. *Social Justice in the Liberal State.* New Haven: Yale University Press, 1980.

Albin, Peter S. *Progress without Poverty: Socially Responsible Economic Growth.* New York: Basic Books, 1978.

Arrow, Kenneth J. *The Viability and Equity of Capitalism.* Vancouver, B.C.: Department of Economics, University of British Columbia, 1976. (E. S. Woodward Lectures in Economics, vol. 4.)

Arthur, John, and William H. Shaw. *Justice and Economic Distribution.* Englewood Cliffs, N.J.: Prentice–Hall, 1978.

The Attack on Corporate America: The Corporate Issues Sourcebook. New York: McGraw-Hill, 1978.

Bell, Daniel. *The Cultural Contradictions of Capitalism.* New York: Basic Books, 1978.

Benne, Robert. *The Ethic of Democratic Capitalism.* Philadelphia: Fortress Press, 1981.

Benson, George C. S., and Thomas S. Engeman. *Amoral America.* Stanford, Calif.: Hoover Institution Press, 1976.

Benton, Lewis, ed. *Management for the Future.* New York: McGraw-Hill, 1978.

Blumberg, Phillip I. *The Mega-Corporations in American Society: The Scope of Corporate Power.* Englewood Cliffs, N.J.: Prentice-Hall, 1975.

Bok, Sissela. *Lying: Moral Choice in Public and Private Life.* New York: Pantheon Books, 1978.

Bowie, Norman E., and Robert L. Simon. *The Individual and the Political Order.* Englewood Cliffs, N.J.: Prentice-Hall, 1977.

Brown, Lester R. *The Twenty-Ninth Day: Accommodating Human Needs and Numbers to the Earth's Resources.* New York: W. W. Norton, 1978.

Brozen, Yale, Elmer W. Johnson, and Charles W. Powers. *Can the Market Sustain An Ethic?* Chicago: University of Chicago Press, 1978.

Bruyn, Severyn T. *The Social Economy: People Transforming Modern Business.* New York: Ronald Press, 1977.

Burden, Charles, et al. *Business in Literature.* New York: Longman, 1980.

Burns, Tom R., et al., eds. *Work and Power: The Liberation of Work and the Control of Political Power.* Beverly Hills, Calif.: Sage, 1979.

Chamberlain, Neil W. *Remaking American Values: Challenge to a Business Society.* New York: Basic Books, 1977.

Clinard, Marshall B., and Peter C. Yeager. *Corporate Crime.* New York: Free Press, 1980.

Culbert, Samuel A., and John T. McDonough. *The Invisible War: Pursuing Self-Interests at Work.* New York: Wiley-Interscience, 1980.

Donagan, Alan. *The Theory of Morality.* Chicago: University of Chicago Press, 1977.

Dowd, Douglas F. *The Twisted Dream.* 2d ed. Cambridge, Mass.: Winthrop Publishers, 1977.

Edelman, Joan. *The Politics of International Economic Relations.* New York: St. Martin's Press, 1977.

Edwards, Richard C., Michael Reich, and Thomas E. Weisskopf, eds. *The Capitalist System.* 2d ed. Englewood Cliffs, N.J.: Prentice-Hall, 1978.

Eells, Richard. *The Political Crisis of the Enterprise System.* New York: Macmillan, 1980.

Einenstein, Zillah R., ed. *Capitalist Patriarchy and the Case for Socialist Feminism.* New York: Monthly Review Press, 1978.

Ethics for a Crowded World. Berkeley, Calif.: Center for Ethics and Social Policy, Graduate Theological Union, 1977.

Fried, Charles. *Right and Wrong.* Cambridge, Mass.: Harvard University Press, 1978.

Friedman, Milton, et al. *The Business System: A Bicentennial View.* Hanover, N.H.: University Press of New England, 1977.

Gabor, D., and U. Colombo, with A. King and R. Galli. *Beyond the Age of Waste: A Report to the Club of Rome.* New York: Pergamon Press, 1978.

Gaylin, Willard, et al. *Doing Good: The Limits of Benevolence.* New York: Pantheon Books, 1978.

George, Susan. *How the Other Half Dies: The Real Reasons for World Hunger.* Montclair, N.J.: Allanheld, Osmun and Co., 1977.

Glover, John Desmond. *The Revolutionary Corporations: Engines of Plenty, Engines of Growth, Engines of Change.* Homewood, Ill.: Dow Jones-Irwin, 1980.

Goldman, Alan H. *The Moral Foundations of Professional Ethics.* Totowa, N.J.: Rowman and Littlefield, 1980.

Goodpaster, Kenneth E., and Kenneth M. Sayre, eds. *Ethics and Problems of the 21st Century.* Notre Dame, Ind.: University of Notre Dame Press, 1978.

Harmon, Gilbert. *The Nature of Morality.* New York: Oxford University Press, 1977.

Harrington, Michael. *Decade of Decision.* New York: Simon and Schuster, 1980.

Harrington, Michael. *The Twilight of Capitalism.* New York: Simon and Schuster, 1976.

Heilbroner, Robert L. *An Inquiry into the Human Prospect.* (Updated and reconsidered for the 80's.) New York: W. W. Norton, 1980.

Heilbroner, Robert L. *Business Civilization in Decline.* New York: W. W. Norton, 1976.

Heller, Walter W. *The Economy: Old Myths and New Realities.* New York: W. W. Norton, 1976.

Henderson, Hazel. *Creating Alternative Futures: The End of Economics.* New York: Berkeley Publishing, 1978.

Hessen, Robert. *In Defense of the Corporation.* Stanford, Calif.: Hoover Institution Press, 1980.

Hirschman, Albert. *The Passions and the Interest.* Princeton, N.J.: Princeton University Press, 1977.

Hudson, Michael. *Global Fracture: The New International Economic Order.* New York: Harper and Row, 1977.

Jones, Donald G. *Private and Public Ethics. Tensions between Conscience and Institutional Responsibility.* Toronto: Edwin Mellen Press, 1979.

Kahn, Herman. *World Economic Development: 1979 and Beyond.* Morrow Quill, 1979.

Katona, George, and Burkhard Strumpel. *A New Economic Era.* New York: Elsevier, 1978.

Kirk, Robert. *Metadevelopment: Beyond the Bottom Line.* Lexington, Mass.: Lexington Books, 1971.

Kranzberg, Melvin, ed. *Ethics in an Age of Pervasive Technology.* Boulder, Colo.: Westview, 1980.

Kristol, Irving. *Two Cheers for Capitalism.* New York: Basic Books, 1978.

Kumar, Krishan. *Prophecy and Progress: The Sociology of Industrial and Post-Industrial Society.* New York: Penguin, 1978.

Lindblom, Charles E. *Politics and Markets: The World's Political-Economic Systems.* New York: Free Press, 1978.

Lucas, George, and Thomas W. Ogletree, eds. *Lifeboat Ethics.* New York: Harper and Row, 1976.

Lutz, Mark A., and Kenneth Lux. *The Challenge of Humanistic Economics.* Menlo Park, Calif.: Benjamin/Kummings Publishers, 1979.

Mackie, J. L. *Ethics: Inventing Right and Wrong.* New York: Penguin Books, 1977.

McManus, George J. *In Defense of Prosperity: A Common Sense Case for Capitalism.* Radnor, Pa.: Chilton, 1977.

Maguire, Daniel C. *The Moral Choice.* Garden City, N.Y.: Doubleday, 1978.

Meadows, Dennis L. *Alternatives to Growth—1: A Search for Sustainable Futures.* Cambridge, Mass.: Ballinger Publishing, 1977.

Miller, Arthur Selwyn. *The Modern Corporate State.* Westport, Conn.: Greenwood Press, 1976.

Miller, David. *Social Justice.* Oxford, Eng.: Clarendon Press, 1976.

Mishan, E. J. *The Economic Growth Debate.* London: George Allen and Unwin, 1980.

Missner, Marshall. *Ethics of the Business System.* Sherman Oaks, Calif.: Alfred Publishing Co., 1980.

Parke, John. *An American Alternative: Steps toward a More Equitable Economy.* Los Angeles: Crescent, 1976.

Reed, E. D. *Profit Makes Perfect.* New York: Vantage, 1978.

Roberts, Benjamin C., ed. *Towards Industrial Democracy.* London: Croom Helm, 1979.

Rogge, Benjamin A. *Can Capitalism Survive?* North Shadeland, Ind.: Liberty Press, 1979.

Ryn, Claes G. *Democracy and the Ethical Life.* Baton Rouge: Louisiana State University, 1978.

Sayre, Kenneth M., Ellen L. Maher, Peri E. Arnold, Kenneth E. Goodpaster, Robert E. Rodes, and James B. Stewart. *Regulation, Values, and the Public Interest.* Notre Dame, Ind.: University of Notre Dame Press, 1980.

Sennett, Richard. *Authority.* New York: Alfred A. Knopf, 1980.

Settle, Tom. *In Search of a Third Way: Is a Morally Principled Political Economy Possible?* Buffalo: McClelland, 1976.

Simpson, Kemper. *Big Business, Efficiency, and Fascism.* New York: AMS, 1979.

Singer, Marcus, ed. *Morals and Values: Readings in Theoretical and Practical Ethics.* New York: Charles Scribner's Sons, 1977.

Stanfield, J. Ron. *Economic Thought and Social Change.* Carbondale: Southern Illinois University, 1980.

Thurow, Lester C. *The Zero-Sum Society.* New York: Basic Books, 1980.

Tyler, William G., ed. *Issues and Prospects for the New International Economic Order.* Lexington, Mass.: Lexington Books, 1977.

Van den Haag, Ernest, ed. *Capitalism: Sources of Hostility.* New Rochelle, N.Y.: Epoch Books, 1979.

Ward, Benjamin. *The Ideal World of Economics.* New York: Basic Books, 1980.

Wasserstrom, Richard A. *Philosophy and Social Issues: Five Studies.* Notre Dame, Ind.: University of Notre Dame Press, 1979.

Wogaman, J. Philip. *The Great Economic Debate: An Ethical Analysis.* Philadelphia: Westminster Press, 1977.

Articles

Ahern, W. H. "Laissez-Faire vs. Equal Rights: Liberal Republicans and Limits to Reconstruction." *Phylon* 40 (March 1979), 52–65.

Amdur, Robert. "Global Distribution Justice: A Review Essay." *Journal of International Affairs* 31 (Spring–Summer 1977), 81–88.

Bakunin, Jack. "Failure of Individualism: A Disturbing New Economic Study Sees a Coming Confrontation over the Distribution of Wealth." *Christian Century* 94 (September 21, 1977), 813–815.

Balk, Walter L. "Toward a Government Productivity Ethic." *Public Administration Review* 38 (January/February 1978), 46–50.

Baumol, William J. "Smith vs. Marx on Business Morality and Social Interest." *American Economist* 20 (Fall 1976), 1–6.

Christiansen, Jens. "Marxist Perspectives on the Capitalist Macroeconomy: Marx and the Falling Rate of Profit." *American Economic Review* 66 (May 1976), 20–26.

Daly, George, and J. Fred Giertz. "Externalities, Extortion, and Efficiency." *American Economic Review* 65 (December 1975), 997–1001.

Daniels, Norman. "Merit and Meritocracy." *Philosophy and Public Affairs* 7 (Spring 1978), 206–223.

Danielsson, Christer. "Business and Politics: Toward a Theory beyond Capitalism, Plato, and Marx." *California Management Review* 21 (Spring 1979), 17–25.

DeGregori, Thomas R. "Ethics and Economic Inquiry: The Ayres-Knight Debate and the Problem of Economic Order." *American Journal of Economics and Sociology* 36 (January 1977), 41–50.

DeGregori, Thomas R. "Market Morality—Robert Nozick and the Question of Economic Justice." *American Journal of Economics and Sociology* 38 (January 1979), 17–30.

DeSchweinitz, Karl, Jr. "Ethics and Welfare in J. M. Clark's Economics." *Journal of Economic Issues* 10 (December 1976), 859–875.

DiQualtro, Arthur. "Alienation and Justice in the Market." *American Political Science Review* 72 (September 1978), 871–887.

Dougherty, Alfred F., Jr. "Concentration, Conglomeration, and Economic Democracy: A 'Concurrent Divestiture' Proposal." *Antitrust Law and Economics Review* 11, no. 1 (1979), 29–54.

Downie, R. S. "Moral Problems in a Market Economy: A Reappraisal of Adam Smith." *Dalhousie Review* 57 (Autumn 1977), 424–436.

Eckard, E. Woodrow, Jr. "The Free Market Incentive: Self-Interest vs. Greed." *Business Economics* 15 (September 1980), 32+.

Exdell, John. "Distributive Justice: Nozick on Property Rights." *Ethics* 87 (January 1977), 142–149.

Freedman, Benjamin. "A Meta-Ethics for Professional Morality." *Ethics* 89 (1978–79), 1–19.

French, Peter A. "Corporation as a Moral Person." *American Philosophical Quarterly* 16, no. 3 (1979), 207–215.

Friedman, Milton. "The Future of Capitalism: The Intellectual and the Businessman." *Vital Speeches of the Day* 43 (March 15, 1977), 333–337.

Friedman, Milton. "Nobel Lecture: Inflation and Unemployment." *Journal of Political Economy* 85 (June 1977), 451–472.

Frundt, Henry J. "Corporations and Human Economic Rights." *Interfaith Center on Corporate Responsibility Brief* (October 1979), 3A–3D.

Fry, Fred L. "A New Stage of Capitalism." *Business Horizons* 21 (April 1978), 23–25.

Gilder, George. "Moral Sources of Capitalism." *Imprimis* 9 (December 1980), 1–6.

Goldman, Alan H. "The Entitlement Theory of Distributive Justice." *Journal of Philosophy* 73 (December 1976), 823–835.

Hagaman, T. Carter. "Understanding Free Markets: Ideology or Pragmatism?" *Vital Speeches of the Day* 45 (December 1, 1978), 107–110.

Harsanyi, John C. "Bayesian Decision Theory and Utilitarian Ethics." *American Economic Review* 68 (May 1978), 223–228.

Henderson, John B. "Professional Standards for the Performance of the Government Economist." *American Economic Review* 67 (February 1977), 321–325.

Hill, Ivan. "Ethical Basis of Economic Freedom." *Vital Speeches of the Day* 42 (March 15, 1976), 345–349.

Hill, Norman C., and Gene W. Dalton. "Business and the New Egalitarianism." *Business Horizons* 20 (June 1977), 5–11.

Hirshleifer, Jack. "Competition, Cooperation, and Conflict in Economics and Biology." *American Economic Review* 68 (May 1978), 238–243.

Hundert, E. J. "Market Society and Meaning in Locke's Political Philosophy." *Journal of Historical Philosophy* 15 (January 1977), 33–44.

Husami, Ziyad I. "Marx on Distributive Justice." *Philosophy and Public Affairs* 8 (Fall 1978), 27–64.

Johannsen, O. B. "Free Market: The Arena of Individual and Social Growth." *American Journal of Economics and Sociology* 35 (July 1976), 275–276.

Kagan, Sioma. "A New International Economic Order: What Is the Price Tag?" *Business Economics* 13 (March 1978), 1–4.

Kristol, Irving. "Morality, Liberalism, and Foreign Policy." *Wall Street Journal* (November 19, 1976), 24.

Kristol, Irving. " 'When Virtue Loses All Her Loveliness'—Some Reflections on Capitalism and the 'Free Society.' " *Across the Board* 15 (June 1978), 60–66.

Krogstad, Jack L., and Jack C. Robertson. "Moral Principles for Ethical Conduct." *Management Horizons* 10 (Fall 1979), 1–7.

Kurz, Mordecai. "Economics and Ethics: Altruism, Justice, and Power: Altruism as an Outcome of Social Interaction." *American Economics Review* 68 (May 1978), 216–222.

Lambsdorff, Otto Graf. "The Social Market Economy and Its Future: The World Market and Nationalism." *Vital Speeches of the Day* 42 (April 1, 1976), 376–380.

Lutz, Christian. "Economic Liberalism: System for Tomorrow? Old-Fashioned Reflections on the Politico-Economical Order." *Prospects* (Swiss Bank Corp) (1977), 6–8.

McFarland, Dalton E. "Management, Humanism, and Society: The Case for Macromanagement Theory." *Academy of Management Review* 2 (October 1977), 613–623.

McGinn, R. E. "Workshop on the Interrelations between Science and Technology, and Ethics and Values: Reston, Virginia." *Technology and Culture* 17 (April 1976), 249–255.

McGuire, Joseph W. "Perfecting Capitalism—An Economic Dilemma." *Business Horizons* 19 (February 1976), 5–12.

Machan, Tibor R. "Capitalism's Ethical Imperative." *Humanist* 38 (July–August 1978), 14–17.

Martin, J. David. "Brotherhood and Lifeboat Ethics." *BioScience* 28 (November 1978), 718–721.

Meckling, Thomas B. "Patriotism, Capitalism and Positive Thinking." (Jay Van Andel and Richard DeVos.) *Commonweal* 107 (August 29, 1980), 459+.

Meckling, William H., and Michael C. Jensen. "Between Freedom and Democracy." *Banker* 127 (October 1977), 39–40+.

Mueller, Charles E. "Trustbusting and the Future of Capitalism: Small Could Be Beautiful." *Antitrust Law and Economics Review* 8, no.1 (1976), 47–80.

Myers, David B. "Ethics and Political Economy in Marx." *Philosophical Forum* 7 (Spring–Summer 1976), 246–259.

Norton, David. "Individualism and Productive Justice." *Ethics* 87 (January 1977), 113–125.

Novak, Michael. "An Underpraised and Undervalued System: In Defense of Democratic Capitalism." *Worldview* 20 (July–August 1977), 9–12.

Okun, Arthur M. "Capitalism and Democracy: Some Unifying Principles." *Columbia Journal of World Business* 13 (Winter 1978), 22–30.

Orr, Leonard H. "Is Capitalism the Way Out?" *Business and Society Review* 28 (Winter 1978–79), 4–27.

Pichler, Joseph A. "Is Profit without Honor? The Case for Capitalism." *National Forum* 58 (Summer 1978), 3–6.

Putnam, Robert D. "Elite Transformation in Advanced Industrial Societies: An Empirical Assessment of the Theory of Technocracy." *Comparative Policy Studies* 10 (October 1977), 383–412.

Rockefeller, Nelson A. "Human Liberties and Economic Freedom." *Vital Speeches of the Day* 42 (April 15, 1976), 386–387.

Samuels, Warren J. "The Political Economy of Adam Smith." *Nebraska Journal of Economics and Business* 15 (Summer 1976), 3–24.

Schweickart, David. "Capitalism, Contribution, and Sacrifice." *Philosophical Forum* 7 (Spring–Summer 1976), 260–276.

Silk, Leonard. "Ethics in Government: Ethics in Economics." *American Economic Review* 67 (February 1977), 316–320.

Sims, Joe. "On Faith and Free Enterprise." *Conference Board Record* 13 (May 1976), 15–19.

Sommers, Albert T. "A Collision of Ethics and Economics." *Across the Board* 15 (July 1978), 14–19.

Sommers, Albert T. "Of Markets and Ethics: The Future of the Mixed Economy." *Executive* 4 (March 1978), 10–13.

Stringfellow, William. "Justification, the Consumption Ethic, and Vocational Poverty." *Christianity and Crisis* 36 (April 12, 1976), 74–79.

Van Den Haag, Ernest. "Economics Is Not Enough—Notes on the Anticapitalist Spirit." *Public Interest* 45 (Fall 1976), 109–122.

Warren, Ben H. "Constant Values in a Changing World: Christian Faith and Economic Values." *Vital Speeches of the Day* 46 (January 1, 1980), 183–187.

Williams, Harold M. "Egalitarianism and Market Systems: The Burden of Individual Responsibility." *Vital Speeches of the Day* 45 (November 15, 1978), 91–96.

Williams, Harold M. "Free Enterprise in a Free Society." *California Management Review* 23 (Winter 1980), 29–34.

"Women and Contemporary Capitalism: Some Theoretical Questions." *Science and Society* 42 (Fall 1978), 257–381.

Religion and Business Ethics

Books

Arbruster, Wally. *It's Still Lion vs. Christian in the Corporate Arena.* St. Louis: Concordia Publishing House, 1979.

Engstrom, Ted W., and Edward R. Dayton. *The Christian Executive.* Waco, Tex.: Word Books, 1979.

Forell, George W., et al., eds. *Corporation Ethics: The Quest for Moral Authority.* Philadelphia: Fortress Press, 1980.

Fox, Marvin, ed. *Modern Jewish Ethics: Theory and Practice.* Columbus: Ohio State University Press, 1975.

Gustafson, James. *Protestant and Roman Catholic Ethics.* Chicago: University of Chicago Press, 1978.

Hayes, James L., et al. *Ethics and Corporate Responsibility.* New York: Hebrew Union College–Jewish Institute of Religion, 1980.

Herron, Orley. *A Christian Executive in a Secular World.* Nashville: Nelson, Thomas, 1979.

John, James. *Profits, Power, and Politics: An Inside Look at What Goes On behind the Velvet Curtains of Christian Business.* Irvine, Calif.: Harvest House Publishers, 1980.

Kellner, Menachem Marc, ed. *Contemporary Jewish Ethics.* New York: Sanhedrin Press, 1978.

Levine, Aaron. *Free Enterprise and Jewish Law: Aspects of Jewish Business Ethics.* New York: Ktav Publishing House, 1980.

Mieth, Dietmar, and Jacques Mieth, eds. *Christian Ethics and Economics: The North-South Conflict.* New York: Seabury, 1980.

Nelson, Martha. *The Christian Woman in the Working World.* Nashville: Broadman, 1975.

Novak, Michael, ed. *Democracy and Mediating Structures: A Theological Inquiry.* Washington, D.C.: American Enterprise Institute for Public Policy Research, 1980.

Rose, Tom. *Economics: Principles and Policy from a Christian Perspective.* Milford, Mich.: Mott Media, 1977.

Short, Mark. *The Bible in Business.* Nashville: Broadman, 1978.

Sleeman, John F. *Economic Crisis: A Christian Perspective.* Naperville, Ill.: Allenson Press, 1976.

Stanton, Peggy. *The Daniel Dilemma: Personal Morality in the Public Arena.* Albuquerque, N.M.: World Book, 1978.

Taylor, L. K., and A. S. Reid. *Can You Succeed in Business and Still Get to Heaven?* London: Associated Business Programmes, 1978.

Taylor, Hebden. *Economics, Money, and Banking: Christian Principles.* Phillipsburg, N.J.: Presbyterian and Reformed Publishing Cos., 1978.

Vogel, David. *Lobbying the Corporation.* New York: Basic Books, 1978.

Williams, Oliver F., and John W. Houck. *Full Value: Cases in Christian Business Ethics.* New York: Harper and Row, 1978.

Articles

Boland, John C. "Saints and Sinners? Church-Sponsored Critics of Private Enterprise Gain a Following?" *Barron's* 60 (May 5, 1980), 11+.

Bowman, David H. "Economics and the Paradoxical Church." *Christian Society* 66 (May–June 1976), 31–36.

Brewster, K. "Free Market . . . and Morality." *Christianity Today* 21 (October 22, 1976), 38–39.

Buchholz, Rogene A., and George E. O'Connell. "Religion and Work in America." *Business and Society* 18 (Fall 1977), 13–19.

Calian, Samuel Carnegie. "The Business of Religion." *New Review of Books and Religion* 3 (December 1978), 23–24.

Calian, Carnegie Samuel. "Theologizing in a Win/Lose Culture." *Christian Century* (October 10, 1979), 976–979.

"Catholic Nuns Rap Gen. Mills' Kidvid Ads at Company's Meeting." *Variety* 296 (October 3, 1979), 40.

"Christian Business Ethics, Incorporated." (Interview with John Houck and Oliver Williams.) *U.S. Catholic* 45 (September 1980), 18+.

Davies, C. "The Church vs. Multinationals." *Executive* 19 (October 1977), 66–68.

Davies, Mostyn D. "Sharing-In and Sharing-Out." *Theology* 80 (March 1977), 91–95.

Ditz, G. W. "The Protestant Ethic and the Market Economy." *Kyklos* 33, no. 4 (1980), 623–657.

Early, Tracy. "Sister's Job Promotes Corporate Responsibility." *National Catholic Reporter* 15 (April 13, 1979), 4.

Foegen, J. H. "Clergy as Counselors." *Personnel* 56 (July–August 1979), 70–78.

"Forming a Theology of Urban-Industrial Mission: An ICUIS Working Bibliography." *ICUIS* 2313 (February 1975), 57+.

Freedman, Benjamin. "Leviticus and DNA: A Very Old Look at a Very New Problem." *Journal of Religious Ethics* 8 (Spring 1980), 105–113.

Friedman, Hershey H. "Talmudic Business Ethics: An Historical Perspective." *Akron Business and Economic Review* 11 (Winter 1980), 45–49.

Gall, Norman. "When Capitalism and Christianity Clash." *Forbes* 126 (September 1, 1980), 100–101.

Haines, Aubrey B. "Buying Christian." *Christian Century* (September 21, 1977), 804–805.

Hammond, P. E., and K. R. Williams. "Protestant Ethic Thesis: A Social-Psychological Assessment." *Social Forces* 54 (March 1976), 579–589.

Hughey, Ann. "Hitting at Corporations on Issues." *National Catholic Reporter* 16 (November 30, 1979), 13+.

Kenkelin, Bill. "Apply Ethics from Inside, Says Sister." *National Catholic Reporter* 16 (November 23, 1979), 6+.

Kim, Hei C. "Relationship of Protestant Ethic Beliefs and Values to Achievement." *Journal of Scientific Study of Religion* 16 (September 1977), 255–262.

Kirchhoff, D. J. "Antibusiness Radicals in Clerical Garb." *Business and Society Review* 32 (Winter 1979–80), 55–58.

Kirchhoff, D. J. "Corporate Missionary: Those Who Believe in Capitalism Must Fight Back." *Barron's* 59 (February 19, 1979), 7+.

Lee, Soo Ann. "On Being a Christian Economist." *Church and Society* 66 (May–June 1976), 4–8.

McGovern, Arthur F. "Should a Christian Be a Marxist?" *Proceedings of the American Catholic Philosophical Association* 51 (1977), 220–230.

Minus, Paul M. "The Infant Formula Issue: Other Perspectives." *Christian Century* 94 (June 20, 1979), 663+.

"Mother's Milk." *America* 141 (October 27, 1979), 221.

Muir, Charlene. "Church Women United and the Nestle Boycott." *The Corporate Examiner* 7 (May 1978), 2–5.

Murray, Robert B. "A Christian's View of the Marketplace." *America* 142 (May 31, 1980), 460+.

Nickel, Herman. "The Corporation Haters." *Fortune* 101 (June 16, 1980), 126–136.

Novak, Michael. "God and Man in the Corporation." *Policy Review* 9 (Summer 1980), 32.

Ogasapian, John. "Lowell and Old St. Anne's: A Study in 19th Century Industrial-Church Relations." *History Magazine* 46 (December 1977), 381–396.

Peerman, Dean. "The Conscience of Linda Kelsey." *Christian Century* 97 (March 5, 1980), 244+.

Perham, John C. "Stockholders Attack Nuclear Power." *Dun's Review* 115 (April 1980), 91+.

Perlman, Mark. "Jews and Contributions to Economics: A Bicentennial Review." *Judaism* 25 (Summer 1976), 301–311.

Pfeffer, Leo. "Workers' Sabbath: Religious Beliefs and Employment." *Civil Liberties Review* 4 (November/December 1977), 52–56.

"Pope Paul Appeals for Universal Ethic in Ads." *Advertising Age* 47 (May 17, 1976), 4.

Razzell, P. "Protestant Ethic and the Spirit of Capitalism: A Natural Scientific Critique." *British Journal of Sociology* 28 (March 1977), 17–37.

Riesenberg, Peter. "Profit and the Church: A Gradual Accommodation." *MBA* 11 (November 1977), 46–47+.

Russell, Michael B. "A Battleground for Industrial Strife." *Sojourners* 8 (April 1979), 10–15.

Salter, Michael. "Creating an Industry to Praise the Lord." *Macleans* 92 (March 19, 1980), 45+.

Schomer, Howard. "Church Investors and Corporate Governance." *Forum for Correspondence and Contact* 9 (July 1976), 24–26.

Schomer, Howard. "The U.S. Churches: Shareholders and Prophets." *Uniapac* 10 (January 1978), 19–25.

Schomer, Howard. "Religious Perspectives on Economic Development and Structures in a New World Community." *World Conference on Religion and Peace Commission I Report*, Princeton, N.J. (August 28–September 7, 1978), 1–8.

Schomer, Howard. "The Church and the Transnational Corporation: How and Why the Churches Are Intervening in the Worldwide Business Affairs of American Corporations." *A.D.* (February 1975), 15–25.

Schomer, Howard. "Little Church and Big Business: Confrontation or Consultation?" *Forum for Correspondence and Contact* (January 1979), 50–56.

Schomer, Howard. "Church Tolls Bells for Investors' Interests." *Directorship: The Forum for the Corporate Director* 3 (September 1978), 5–6.

Sharick, John D., and James W. Malone. "Community Crisis and Corporate Responsibility: Ohio Churches Take the Lead." *The Corporate Examiner* 7 (September 1978), 1–7.

Stackhouse, Max. "Theological and Ethical Considerations for Business Decision-Making." *New Catholic World* 223 (November–December 1980), 253+.

Stott, John R. W. "Economic Equality among Nations: A Christian Concern?" *Christianity Today* 24 (May 2, 1980), 36–38.

Stringfellow, William. "Justification, the Consumption Ethic, and Vocational Poverty." *Christianity in Crisis* 80 (April 12, 1976), 74–79.

Sullivan, Patrick J. "The Churches and the Unions." *America* 140 (June 9, 1979), 473+.

Toohey, Bill. "Religious 'Davids' Tackle Corporate 'Goliaths' in Responsibility Fray." *National Catholic Reporter* 14 (February 24, 1978), 3.

Van Cise, Jerrold G. "Religion and Antitrust." *Antitrust Bulletin* 23 (Fall 1978), 455–481.

Warren, Ben H. "Constant Values in a Changing World: Christian Faith and Economic Values." *Vital Speeches of the Day* 46 (January 1, 1980), 183–186.

Waters, James A. "Of Saints, Sinners, and Socially Responsible Executives." *Business and Society Review* (Winter 1980), 67–73.

Welling, Kathryn M. "Clash of Values: A Seminar Weighs the Impact of Religion on Business." *Barron's* 59 (June 25, 1979), 9+.

Williams, Oliver F. "Christian Formation for Corporate Life." *Theology Today* 36 (October 1979), 347+.

Williamson, Clark M. "Notes on a Theology of Work." *Encounter* 37 (Summer 1976), 294–307.

Teaching and Training in Business Ethics

Books

Baum, Robert J. *Ethics and Engineering Curricula.* Hastings-on-Hudson, N.Y.: The Hastings Center, 1980.

Bowie, Norman E. *Teaching Business Ethics.* Hyde Park, N.Y.: Helvetia Press, 1979. 18 pp.

Callahan, Daniel, and Sissela Bok, eds. *Ethics Teaching in Higher Education.* New York: Plenum, 1980.

DeGeorge, Richard T. *Moral Issues in Business: An Outline of a Course in Business Ethics.* Lawrence, Kans.: The Committee on Business and the Humanities, University of Kansas, 1979.

Dill, David, et al. *Syllabi for the Teaching of Management Ethics.* New Haven: Society for Values in Higher Education, 1979.

Fleishman, Joel L., and Bruce L. Payne. *Ethical Dilemmas and the Education of Policymakers.* Hastings-on-Hudson, N.Y.: The Hastings Center, 1980.

Hall, Robert T. *Moral Education: A Handbook for Teachers.* Minneapolis: Winston Press, 1979.

Huber, C. E. *The Promise and Perils of Business Ethics: A Resource for Curriculum Development.* Washington, D.C.: Association of American Colleges, 1979.

Kelly, Michael J. *Legal Ethics and Legal Education.* Hastings-On-Hudson, N.Y.: The Hastings Center, 1980.

Ladenson, Robert F., et al., comps. *A Selected Annotated Bibliography of Professional Ethics and Social Responsibility in Engineering.* Chicago: Center for the Study of Ethics in the Professions, Illinois Institute of Technology, 1980.

Powers, Charles W., and David Vogel. *Ethics in the Education of Business Managers.* New York: Institute of Society, Ethics, and the Life Sciences: The Hastings Center, 1980.

Report of the Committee for Education in Business Ethics. (Sponsored by NEH.) Skokie, Ill.: Fel-Pro, 1980.

Warwick, Donald P. *The Teaching of Ethics and the Social Sciences.* Hastings-on-Hudson, N.Y.: The Hastings Center, 1980.

Articles

Arlow, Peter, and Thomas A. Ulrich. "Business Ethics, Social Responsibility, and Business Students: An Empirical Comparison of Clark's Study." *Akron Business and Economic Review* 11 (Fall 1980), 17–22.

Biegler, John C. "Ethics and Education: A Value Judgment." *Price Waterhouse Review* 21, no. 3 (1976), 2–3.

Bok, Derek C. "Can Ethics Be Taught?" *Change* (October 1976), 26–30.

Cooper, Robert M. "Psychopomps and Change-Agents, or Can Virtue Be Taught?" *Theology Today* 35 (October 1978), 285–291.

Donaldson, Thomas. "Ethics in the Business Schools." *National Forum* 58 (Summer 1978), 11–14.

Eger, Martin. "The Conflict in Moral Education: An Informal Case Study." *The Public Interest* 63 (Spring 1981), 62–80.

Faber, Nancy. "Arjay Miller Thinks Business Schools Should Stress Ethics, but the Bottom Line Isn't Bad: His Grads Start at $27,500." *People* 11 (June 25, 1979), 65+.

Hofstede, Geert. "Businessmen and Business School Faculty: A Comparison of Value Systems." *Journal of Management Studies* 15 (February 1978), 77–87.

"How Ethical Are You?" *Training* 14/12 (December 1977), 46–47.

Johnson, Harold L. "Adam Smith and Business Education." *AACSB Bulletin* 13 (October 1976), 1–4.

Kirk, Russell. "Ethics in the Academy." *National Review* 29 (June 24, 1977), 726.

Konrad, A. Richard. "Are Business Ethics Worth Studying?" *Business and Society Review* 27 (Fall 1978), 54–57.

Kramer, Otto P. "Ethics Program Can Help Companies Set Standards of Conduct." *Administrative Management* 38 (January 1977), 46–49.

Langholm, Odd, and Johs Lunde. "Empirical Methods for Business Ethics Research." *Review of Social Economy* 35 (October 1977), 133–142.

Larwood, Laurie, Marion M. Wood, and Sheila David Inderlied. "Training Women for Management: New Problems, New Solutions." *Academy of Management Review* 3 (July 1978), 584–93.

McMahon, Thomas F. "Will Corporate Responsibility Flunk Out of College?" *Business and Society Review* 28 (Winter 1978–79), 50–53.

"Managers 0, Students 1 in an Ethics Contest." *Management Review* 67 (June 1978), 58.

Miller, Mary Susan, and A. Edward Miller. "It's Too Late for Ethics Courses in Business Schools." *Business and Society Review* 17 (Spring 1976), 39–42.

"Morality via the Classroom." *Management Review* 67 (May 1978), 54.

Ottoson, Gerald O. "A Business Ethics Seminar for Corporate Executives." *The Lamplighter* (American Society for Training and Development), 11 (January 1980), 6–7.

Purcell, Theodore V. "Do Courses in Business Ethics Pay Off?" *California Management Review* 19 (Summer 1977), 50–58.

Rachels, James. "Can Ethics Provide Answers?" *The Hastings Center Report* 10 (June 1980), 32–40.

Rohr, John A. "Ethics for the Senior Executive Service: Suggestions for Management Training." *Administration and Society* 12 (August 1980), 203–216.

Seligmann, Jean, and Phyllis Malamud. "Game of Lying? Wall Street Journal Story on Harvard's Alleged Teaching of Unethical Business Behavior." *Newsweek* 93 (February 26, 1979), 57+.

Simon, William E. "The Great American Challenges: Education and Ethics." *Financial Executive* 45 (April 1977), 34–39.

Steiner, John F. "The Prospect of Ethical Advisors for Business Corporations." *Business and Society* 16 (Spring 1976), 5–10.

Stone, Marvin. "Let's Teach Ethics." *Conservative Digest* (April 1979), 44.

Streeter, Deborah. "Doing Ethics as a Career: Answers and Questions." *Ethics and Policy* (Summer 1979), 9.

Thomas, Kenneth W. "Toward Multi-Dimensional Values in Teaching—The Example of Conflict Behaviors." *Academy of Management Review* 2 (July 1977), 484–490.

Vaccaro, Vincent T., "Philosophers and Business and Professional Ethics." *Business and Professional Ethics* 3 (Summer/Fall 1980), 2–4.

Vidali, Joseph J., and Douglas N. Behrman. "Collegiate Education in Business Administration: How Important a Role in Student Judgments of Ethical Business Practices?" *AACSB Bulletin* 13 (Spring 1977), 7–10.

Walton, Clarence C. "To Break the Pentameter—Ethics Courses?" *AACSB Bulletin, Proceedings, Annual Meeting 1979*, 31–60.

Walton, Clarence C. "Business Ethics: The Present and the Future." *The Hastings Center Report* 10 (October 1980), 16–20.

Walzer, Michael. "Teaching Morality." *New Republic* (June 1978), 12–14.

Author Index

Author Index